hotels • restaurants • haciendas • spas • golf resorts • villas

spainchic

If your loyalty card is missing, please visit www.thechicseries.com

hotels • restaurants • haciendas • spas • golf resorts • villas

spainchic

text fiona dunlop • gary bedell • annette tan • zoë jaques • kerry o'neill

·K·U·P·E·R·A·R·D·

publisher's acknowledgements

Welcome to *Spain Chic*—number eight in the *Chic* series. So it's about time we launched our own website to support the book, www.thechicseries.com. Please take a moment to visit the site and see how it helps to support the *Chic* series.

Spain Chic is our first book in the series covering a European country; it has been a formidable task to put it together over the past 15 months. I would like to say a special thank you to Ignacio Vasallo Tome, Director of the Spanish Tourism Board in London for helping to make the book happen. To Fiona Dunlop the author; Gary 'El Giuri' Bedell, writer, photographer and networker; to Renfe for their commercial support; to Joanna Greenfield and all her fabulous colleagues at EDM Singapore; and to two ladies in Barcelona who worked around the clock: Virginia Gutierrez and Inés Turell. To all, muchas gracias.

Most of all, thank you to the many properties that you will see on the pages of this book. There are 61 properties featured from all over the country and they represent an incredible choice for the independently minded traveller looking for a different side of Spain. I hope these pages give you some inspiration to travel around this very diverse country and sample some of the food, wine, culture, scenery and—most importantly—hospitality of this vibrant, colourful land.

Nigel Bolding
editor-in-chief

executive editor
melisa teo

editors
joanna greenfield • xueyi wu

designers
annie teo • chan hui yee • felicia wong

production manager
sin kam cheong

first published in 2007 by
bolding books
enquiries : nigel.bolding@theworldsbesthotels.com
website   : www.theworldsbesthotels.com

designed and produced by
editions didier millet pte ltd
121 telok ayer street, #03-01
singapore 068590
telephone : +65 6324 9260
facsimile : +65 6324 9261
enquiries : edm@edmbooks.com.sg
website   : www.edmbooks.com

©2007 bolding books
design and layout © editions didier millet pte ltd

first published in great britain 2007 by
kuperard
59 hutton grove, london n12 8ds
telephone : +44 (0) 20 8446 2440
facsimile : +44 (0) 20 8446 2441
enquiries : sales@kuperard.co.uk
website   : www.kuperard.co.uk

Kuperard is an imprint of Bravo Ltd.

Printed in Singapore

isbn-10: 1857334167
isbn-13: 9781857334166

COVER CAPTIONS:

1–2: Sleek design of Hotel Omm.
3: Corpus Cristi Procession in Valencia.
4: A matador's colourful 'suit of light'.
5: Gaudí's surreal chimney pots.
6: The Guggenheim boat-like structure.
7: A Martin Berasatagui creation.
8: Ferran Adrià's El Bulli restaurant.
9: A fiery fiesta.
10: The bull—Spain's national icon.
11: Art installation in Barcelona.
12: Pure innovation from Ferran Adrià.
13: Quintessentially Spanish,
bullfighting is still a popular pastime.
14: The Gaudí apartments, Casa Batlló.
15: One of Estela Barcelona's art rooms.
16, 21 AND THIS PAGE: Stylish details at
Hospes hotels.
17: Traditional Spanish costume.
18: Spain's sandy beaches and blue
seas have drawn millions.
19–20: Scenic gardens at the Hacienda
de San Rafael.
PAGE 2: Gehry's Guggenheim Museum.
OPPOSITE: Calm air of Hotel Trias.
PAGE 8 AND 9: Málaga at night.

contents

spainbyregion

spainbychapter

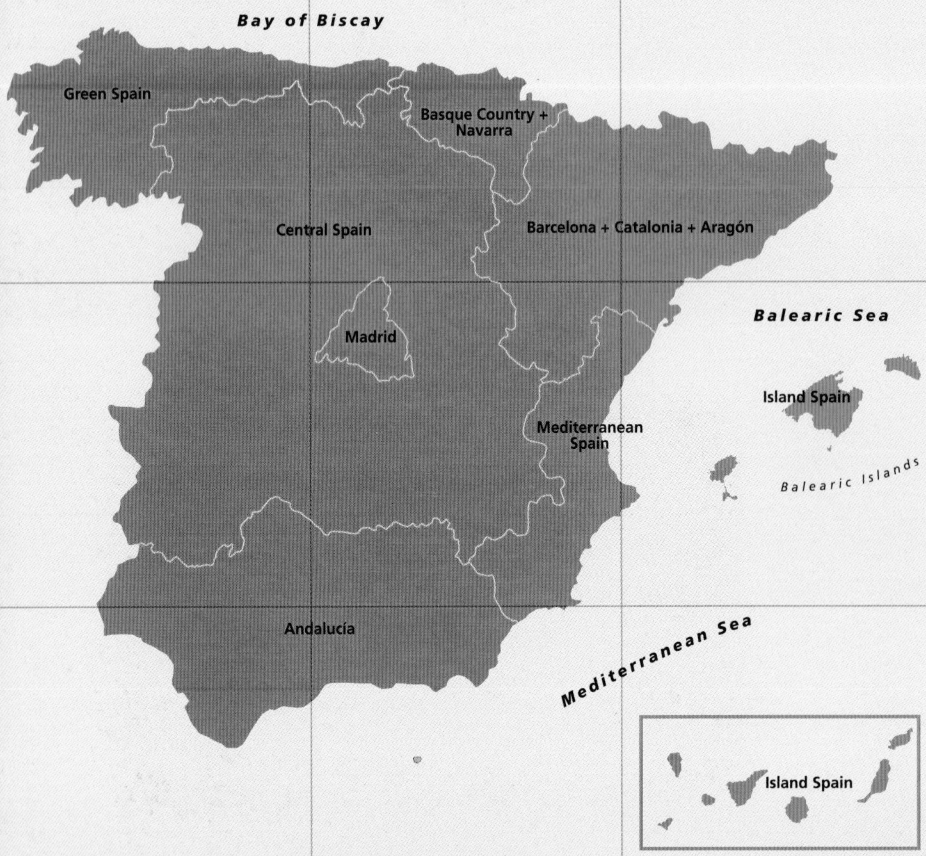

Bay of Biscay

Green Spain

Basque Country +
Navarra

Central Spain

Barcelona + Catalonia + Aragón

Madrid

Balearic Sea

Island Spain

Mediterranean
Spain

Balearic Islands

Andalucia

Mediterranean Sea

Island Spain

Galicia

**Atlantic
Ocean**

Portugal

THE CANARY ISLANDS

La Palma

Lanzarote

Tenerife

La Gomera

Fuerteventura

El Hierro

Gran Canaria

introduction

No other country in Western Europe can lay claim to such a socio-cultural turnaround in the last 20 years as Spain. Somehow, its 40 million inhabitants have wrought plenty of extraordinary and unanticipated changes, propelling their country out of a long, dark tunnel of repression into the full blaze of international attention. Now touted as being Europe's number one for innovative cuisine with design and architecture a close second, Spain offers, arguably, a palette of the most seductive and sophisticated offerings of the Mediterranean. Few can resist.

Among the many temptations that lure over 50 million annual visitors, climate plays a primordial role, as most of the peninsula and its balmy islands sizzle in lengthy, hot sultry summers, and only the far north ever sees much rain. That factor propels millions straight to the costas to be greeted by unimaginative line-ups of apartment blocks and hotels. Yet a slight shift inland opens up a very different world of unspoilt bucolic delights —including endless dramatic sierra and dozens of towns blessed with rich history and fine local cuisine. Today, you can add to these inducements a burgeoning new generation of superbly converted mansions, cortijos (farmhouses) and, in the cities, cutting-edge new architecture. These are Spain's incredibly coveted hotel destinations that are casting yet another light on this country in the throes of reinvention.

And then there is the easy-natured Hispanic temperament—that openness, warmth and lightheartedness that makes interaction such a genuine and memorable pleasure, yet which conceals a strong underlying sense of justice. The most recent and moving proof of this was the mass demonstrations which took place in March 2004 to protest against government pronouncements in the tragic wake of Al Qaeda's bomb atrocities in Madrid. Indeed, Prime Minister Aznar's political demise (his Partido Popular lost the elections just days later) was a direct result of his misleading finger-pointing at the Basques. In stepped the youthful Socialist leader, José Luis Zapatero, who could hardly believe his luck. Yet Spain is not a country to wallow in self-pity; on the contrary, attitudes are far more tilted towards carpe diem, although this may sometimes take place the next day—the mañana syndrome is slow to die.

THIS PAGE (FROM TOP): *Bullfighting, a blend of style and courage, is more ritual than competition, the suit reflects the flamboyance of a matador's skill in artistic impression and command; the garden at Port Lligat where Salvador Dalí turned a group of fisherman's houses into a home for him and his wife, Gaia.*

OPPOSITE: *The Andalucian horse is a symbol of Spain's rich history and cultural diversity. With an ancestry absorbing influences from the Iberians, Carthaginians, Romans and Moors, this exquisite breed is proud and spirited in nature—not unlike the Spanish.*

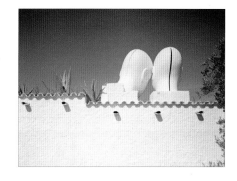

cultural mosaic

What strikes one most when travelling around this immense, sparsely populated country (second only to Russia and France in European scale stakes) is the remarkable diversity—not only of landscape but also of history and therefore of culture. More a subcontinent than a country, centralization only really came with the Bourbon monarchy of the 18th century despite 200 years of the Habsburgs and, in the south, eight centuries of Arab rule. As a result, modern Spain is a fascinating composite of regions, each with its own distinct set of cultural, economic and political characteristics—from the industrious and design-oriented Catalans to the merry, partying Andalucians, with passionate foodie Basques and firework-obsessed Valencians somewhere in between.

In many cases, loyalty to a particular town or region precedes the abstract notion of 'Spain'. This unique sense of place is greatly reinforced by a myriad of colourful local fiestas: getting pelted with ripe tomatoes in Buñol, near Valencia; coffin races in La Mancha or stylized battles between Moors and Christians in Andalucía, just to name a few. Seventeen autonomous communities represent these regional identities, with the capital of Madrid as their central guiding force—both geographically and politically. Besides the Basque country and Catalonia, Madrid is the most densely populated and industrialized part of Spain, and yet it manages fantastically to magnetize, dynamize and, somehow, control what resembles an enormous, assorted family of obstreperous children.

Encircling Madrid is the sparsely populated meseta (high plains) of Castilla, divided between La Mancha (to the south) and Castilla y León (to the north), and once the most powerful of the Iberian kingdoms. Much has changed today and, although it boasts a collection of fantastic monuments, this huge heart of the peninsula has been superseded by coastal regions of the north and east—minus Galicia, which exists happily in its far-flung Celtic corner. With the astonishing Guggenheim effect of Bilbao and the Olympics effect of Barcelona, dynamism is very much confined to the edge, a habit that is even spreading to Andalucía, that immense, arid land of sol y siesta.

Neighbouring Extremadura, sandwiched between La Mancha and Portugal, retains a wonderfully sleepy air much favoured by a roaming population of black pigs—source of some excellent jamón ibérico. Out in the deep blue Mediterranean lie the Balearics, an idyllic quartet of islands with strong links to Catalonia and Valencia. Palma de Mallorca is the town on the up here, with gentle pretensions of being the 'new Barcelona'. However, the latest coastal city to watch is Valencia itself, gunning for greatness when it plays host to the America's Cup in 2007. Finally there are the Canaries, a volcanic archipelago of seven islands tossed into the sea off the coast of Morocco, their location a reminder of much of Spain's earlier history but their culture quite other—yet again.

high colour

Flamboyance has to be the key word for Spain, whether the outrageous gastronomic inventions of Ferran Adrià, the clichéd flounces and rhythmical stamps of flamenco, the gestures of Joaquín Cortés, the high energy of Pedro Almodóvar's films, the cross-genre musical fusion of the Catalan band, Ojos de Brujo, or the audacious concrete ripples of a building by Santiago Calatrava. Discretion is certainly not part of the vocabulary, but another word might be 'fatalism'; death presents no threat, nor does experimentation. The much reviled bullfight is the perfect expression of Spanishness, as it includes pomp and ceremony, drama and tragedy, all orchestrated by the fearless furia española— the legendary rage that made Spain's historical opponents tremble in their boots.

THIS PAGE (FROM TOP): **The streets and squares of Buñol turn into a mock battlefield during Tomatina; Las Fallas—a festival of days of celebration, ending with bonfires.**

OPPOSITE (FROM LEFT): **During the summer, Córdoba's shady patios are filled with foliage and blooms—the best compete in an annual competition; Spanish winter sun lights the red hats of flamenco dancers.**

THIS PAGE (FROM TOP): Virtuoso Ferran Adrià, of El Bulli— and international—fame; a creation from another of Spain's Michelin-starred chefs, Juan Mari Arzak; Boqueira market in Barcelona.
OPPOSITE: Originally a commerical trademark, the bull silhouette has become an unoffical national symbol of Spain.

on the table

Enter the diverse gastronomic field and it is equally fearless, equally dazzling. Since the late 1990s, Iberian cuisine has been on a roll, and it looks unlikely to slow down. From Catalonia to the Basque country and from Madrid to Valencia, a revolutionary sea-change is in progress, bringing endless innovation to both techniques and flavour combinations. Dreary piles of overcooked paellas take the backseat as exquisitely conceptualized and prepared symphonies of ultra-fresh local produce find their place on the table. Spain's gourmet stakes have been raised and completely transformed by the likes of Ferran Adrià, Juan Mari Arzak, Martín Berasategui, Sergi Arola—celebrity chefs who have attained somewhat of a rock-star's status, while dozens of juniors aspire to join the rank of these luminaries. The pattern has been set.

Apart from such five-star concoctions, the rest of Spain is definitely well-advanced on the road to gastronomic self-improvement, and most large towns and cities will harbour at least a couple of serious gourmet restaurants. Like culture, traditional dishes follow a regional pattern: pulpo (octopus) in Galicia; fabada (pork and beans) in Asturias; rabo de toro (ox-tail stew) in Andalucía, or cochinillo (suckling pig) in Castilla. However, the bona-fide place to discover not only local specialities but also local accents is the ubiquitous tapas bar, that inimitable social crossroads where individuals of all generations and social strata come together for delightful fare and mingling.

Even the tapas bar, in itself, has undergone a remarkable new slate of transformations in Madrid, Barcelona and other large cities, introducing fashionable designer trappings and arty presentation to what was once a spit-and-sawdust setting. Along with cuisine comes fine wine, and Spain's oenological prowess is racing ahead parallel to the ongoing gastronomic revolution—la furia española strikes again. Neighbouring vintners over the Pyrenees gently quake. We can only wonder where this nation's creative fury will take us next.

Spain offers, arguably, a palette of the most seductive and sophisticated offerings of the Mediterranean.

Galicia

Asturias

Cantabria

Basque

Navarra

La Rioja

madrid

Castilla y León

Aragón

ortugal

Madrid

> De las Letras Hotel + Restaurante

> Hotel Urban

> Hotel Villa Magna, a Park Hyatt

> Bauzá Hotel + Restaurante

> Hotel Villa Real

Valencia

Castilla-La Mancha

Extremadura

Andalucía

Murcia

madrid

There is a distinct electric charge in the dry air of Madrid, floating down from the sierra or across the surrounding meseta. Or does it spin out of the avenues and backstreets? Nobody is immune to it, not least the thousands of northern Europeans who pour in for weekends throughout the year. So what exactly is this current? And what does Madrid offer that is so exceptional in this endlessly changing and endlessly seductive country?

Historically the capital has had a far shorter life than the rest of Spain as it was 'only' founded by the Habsburg dynasty in the 1560s. In many ways this has been an advantage, freeing it of the constricts of centuries of entrenched tradition and identity—unlike its great rival, Barcelona. Despite this relative lack of historic span, its role as the centre of government and power helped Madrid catch up fast. Architectural coherence, impressive monuments and, not least, art collections worthy of royalty, all found their place.

Since it was virtually virgin territory when Felipe II moved his court here from Toledo, the capital experienced a steady flow of migration from all over the peninsula. After tripling during the Franco era (roughly the 1940s to 1970s), the population has now stabilized at around 3 million. As a result, although proud to be Madrileño, its inhabitants are always open to change and outside influences—without losing a free and easy style that is unmistakably theirs. The result is a cosmopolitan city with a great social and generational mix as well as fabulous art, food, shopping and nightlife, all now crowned by a slew of designer hotels.

brushing with habsburg history

At the heart of this historic area lies the beautiful Plaza Mayor, a classic arcaded square watched over by an equestrian statue of Felipe III, whose reign oversaw most of the construction. More a reminder of times past than of the present, Plaza Mayor saw markets and ferias as well as bullfights and auto-da-fé (the latter—meaning 'act of faith'—during the dark days of the Inquisition when so-called heretics were tried and executed). Despite such a chequered history, its open-air cafés and obvious touristic pulling power, the

PAGE 18: Madrid's bon vivante soul is reflected in a wealth of ornate architectural detail.

THIS PAGE (FROM TOP): The Plaza Mayor, heart of Habsburg Madrid, and the Casa de la Panaderia (Bakers' Guild); Rastro flea market springs into action every Sunday morning.

OPPOSITE: The magnificent fountain of Plaza de España, where Gran Via kicks off.

square still exudes a sense of aristocratic style. Down the atmospheric backstreets is a wealth of neighbourhood bars and homely little restaurants as well as some obvious tourist traps. Here too is the central food market, Mercado de San Miguel, where produce from all over the peninsula transits before entering the kitchens of the Madrileños.

In high contrast, the Palacio Real, on the western edge of this historical zone, oozes regal opulence and decorative excess which today only comes to life on state occasions. Hardly surprisingly, King Juan Carlos and Queen Sofía choose to live in a less ostentatious environment at La Zarzuela, on the outskirts of the city, leaving these echoing salons of Italianate baroque and rococo to hordes of goggle-eyed tourists. South of the palace and its neighbouring cathedral (not the most attractive and which, incredibly, took a century to take shape between plan and completion) lies the oldest part of the city, the former morería (Muslim quarter) and medieval Madrid of pre-Habsburgian days.

from sol to soldadito

As a taster of tradition, the Los Austrias area between the Plaza Mayor and the palace is hard to beat, but for something quirkier you can't miss the inimitable Puerta del Sol that lies on the other side. Although tacky in some ways, Sol—as it's simply known— does house one of the world's strangest features to be listed for conservation: a giant Tio Pepe sign that looms above the rooftops. Take it as a symbol, because the picturesque area of winding streets leading uphill to Plaza Santa Ana is wall-to-wall bars and nightclubs, although habitués are unlikely to be drinking Tio Pepe. This area was once that of literary Madrid, reflected in streets bearing names such as Cervantes and Lope de Vega. One landmark which remains from its more illustrious days is the old-fashioned restaurant, Lhardy, where caldo (meat broth) has been served from a silver samovar since the 1830s. The interior of this upmarket pastry shop is a delight, and the upstairs restaurant one of Madrid's old classics.

THIS PAGE (FROM TOP): Like its façade, the interior of the Royal Palace drips with regal opulence; a familiar-looking Tio Pepe surveys the comings and goings of Plaza Mayor.

OPPOSITE (FROM TOP): Lhardy, Madrid's most elegant and traditional restaurant, has been an established name since 1839; the capital's street-markets are a paradise for bargain-hunters.

North of Sol, social borders blur as you can just as easily pass a cluster of ladies of the night (in blazing sunshine) as a transvestite, a businessman or a housewife going to El Corte Inglés, Spain's favourite department store. Almodóvar encapsulated this mood in his early films inspired by the socio-economic volte-face of the 1980s—la movida, a cathartic sea-change in attitude and behaviour and a reaction to the long, dour years under Franco. Sex, drugs and rock 'n roll took centre stage while Catholicism, conservatism and censorship retreated. Things may no longer be as extreme—and Almodóvar did exaggerate anyway—but the contrasts remain an intrinsic part of this neighbourhood.

This is what makes Madrid constantly seductive—an unpredictability which can be applied to virtually anything. Turn a corner beside the department store and you will find another form of institution, Casa Labra, a bar with a long history of just one specific tapa —the soldadito ('little soldier'), in reality a chunk of flaky bacalao (codfish) lightly fried in batter. Such is the capital's enthusiasm for this delicacy en route to extinction that queues form to fill takeaway bags at lunchtime. Inside, it's a battle to reach the counter but the well-honed serving system works miracles. This again is typical of Madrid and of much of Spain in general: in the midst of apparent chaos, an extraordinary order reigns.

chueca to gula gula

An updated form of this is found in the cutting-edge restaurants of Chueca; customers in search of a table leave their mobile numbers and are called the moment a table becomes available. Civilized, practical and catering for a hedonistic edge (that is, time to slip in a leisurely aperitivo at a nearby bar); that just about sums up the city. Chueca is very much where it's happening for today's cool young things and for anyone interested in design trends—although it has preserved its quirky edge.

Located just north of Sol and the imposing Gran Vía, this grid of backstreets was set into motion by Madrid's gay population and so is akin to Paris' Marais or London's Soho. During the heady days of the movida, Chueca and neighbouring Malasaña were the crossroads of artists and anyone with a creative bent. Since then, countless designer

bars and reasonably priced restaurants have cropped up, making it the 21st-century alternative to the haunts around Huertas and Plaza Santa Ana, now a bit worn at the edges. Many up and coming designers have exclusive outlets in Chueca, with fashion concentrated in and around Calle del Almirante. A few streets north is the boutique of that doyenne of individualistic audacity and colour, Agatha Ruiz de la Prada.

The central avenues of Gran Vía and Alcalá join at Plaza de España to confront a statue of Cervantes contemplating edifices of the Franco era. Gran Vía itself is an ode to the turn of the 20th century, not without architectural hints of Paris and Chicago. These come from the ornately domed Metropolis—designed by French architects in 1905— and Madrid's first skyscraper, the 14-storey Telefonica building (1929). Although native Ignacio de Cárdenas was the architect of the latter, he was assisted by an American. A highlight along Alcalá is the wonderful Circulo de Bellas Artes, an arts club whose activities are open to all. Housed in a stately 1920s building, its generous proportions, chandeliers, statues, brass, marble and leather sofas set the tone: very decadent, very visual, very Madrid. In contrast, just a few steps away is Gula Gula, a restaurant upstairs where waiters prance around in drag. As usual in Madrid, the choice is yours.

art mileage

The biggest card in Madrid's draw has to be the fabulous art collections, strung along what is now dubbed the Paseo del Arte—the 'art mile' that is in fact a segment of the impressively long Paseo de la Castellana. This north-south axis slices through the city and clearly delineates a historical divide. To the east lies the district of Salamanca, the 19th- to 20th-century grid of residential avenues where most upmarket shopping is concentrated, while to the west unfolds the older centro of Sol and Chueca.

The Golden Triangle of Spanish art collections is a stunner and continues to be the city's chief crowd-puller. The Prado, its 8,600 works ranked among the world's top six public art collections, is now gunning for even greater prominence with an ingeniously designed, but highly controversial extension. This much-needed enlargement links the back of the original neoclassical building to the cloisters of San Jerónimo church with new underground exhibition space. Until recently, curators were forced to re-hang the permanent collections to make space for temporary exhibitions, but thousands of works can now be brought out of storage to find their niche. The big hiccup was the delay—and the cost, which topped 100 million euros. The new doors are slated to open in late 2006, nearly three years behind schedule.

The concept is the work of Madrid-based Rafael Moneo, winner of the prestigious Pritzker prize 1996 and the antithesis of Spain's other architectural darling, the theatrical Santiago Calatrava. Moneo's designs are timeless and discreet, like the man himself, and function impeccably. Other outstanding examples of his work are Mérida's Museum of Roman Art, the Kursaal at San Sebastián and Palma de Mallorca's Miró Foundation. In Madrid, his other projects include the refurbishment of Atocha railway station and the initial conversion of Palacio Villahermosa into the Thyssen-Bornemisza Museum.

Back at the Prado, this is where an annual flow of 2 million visitors take in Flemish and Italian masters (which include Hieronymus Bosch's 'Garden of Earthly Delights', Brueghel, Rubens, Titian, Veronese) and, of course, the Spaniards themselves—Goya (including his exceptional 'Black Paintings'), Velázquez ('Las Meninas' takes front stage), Zurbarán, Ribera, and El Greco. The source of these art collections was the Habsburg and Bourbon kings who, over centuries, commissioned and acquired artworks with a vengeance. Their family connections ensured a solid presence of 15th- to 17th-century Flemish paintings.

For a more wide-ranging art-historical span, the next stop is across the street at 18th-century Palacio Villahermosa. Since 1992, this has been home to one the world's most impressive private art collections—only just pipped by that of Queen Elizabeth II. As the life-work of two generations of Thyssens, the 800 paintings were conceived as a survey of Western art, from early-13th-century

THIS PAGE (FROM TOP): *A slumbering sculpture in El Prado, one of the world's best classical museums; Rafael Moneo's slickly refurbished Atocha station.*

OPPOSITE: *Cervantes watches over his most famous creations, Don Quijote and the faithful Sancho Panza, in Plaza de España.*

primitives to the late-20th century. Here too there has been recent enlargement, in this case an extra wing to house acquisitions by Carmen, the merry widow of the late Baron Thyssen-Bornemisza. However, the original collection should be the priority, as this offers an unrivalled spectrum. Although not comprehensive and, in the case of late-20th-century art, very figuratively biased, each work is of exceptional quality. An added pleasure is the sunken garden area for outdoor dining in front of the new wing.

Completing this panorama of Western art is number three in the triangle, the Museo Nacional Centro de Arte Reina Sofía, which stands at the southern end of the paseo by Atocha station. Again housed in a recycled historical building, in this case 18th-century San Carlos Hospital, the Reina Sofía is a true child of the movida. When it opened in 1986 it nurtured a whole new appreciation of contemporary art, something that had been sorely lacking under the Franco regime when avant-garde artists either relied on private foundations and banks for support and exhibition space, or went abroad. Suddenly this new focal point brought performance art, video work and installations to the capital, while side streets spawned light-filled galleries with white walls. Eventually the success of the Reina Sofía was crowned by its inheritance of Picasso's world-famous 'Guernica' (1937), a graphic indictment of Franco's merciless bombing of the small Basque town.

Here too the art centre—host to the capital's most important modern art exhibitions and Madrid's equivalent of London's Tate Gallery and Paris' Pompidou Centre—quickly outgrew its premises and in 2005, after four years of construction work and 92 million euros, a new extension was unveiled. This one, a soaring triangular building designed by the maverick French architect, Jean Nouvel, gives a huge spatial boost in the form of an auditorium, a vast art library and sorely needed galleries. Not least, Nouvel has included a restaurant which boasts a menu courtesy of the country's latest gastro-star—Sergi Arola. Madrid's cultural agenda does not stop there, as a number of new projects are in the pipeline, from the long-anticipated Fundación Caja de Madrid to the Conde Duque—former army barracks—which, by 2010 or 2011, will be superbly reinvented as yet another cultural crossroads.

eating divinely

Gastronomically speaking, Madrid has tended to lag behind the Basque country and Barcelona, but even that is now changing. Many of the capital's top hotels are ensuring that their restaurants stand out on an international level, bringing a minor revolution to their kitchens. Gone are the days of staid and predictable cuisine—enter Sergi Arola. If there is anyone who has contributed single-handedly to the astounding transformation of the capital's eating habits, it is the Catalan, Arola. Formed by the gastro-god Ferran Adrià and influenced by French chefs Roger Vergé and Pierre Gagnaire, Arola moved to Madrid from Barcelona in 1997. Three years later he had transferred his restaurant,

La Broche, to the basement of the Hotel Miguel Angel and has never looked back. Another three years, and Arola was clutching Spain's most prestigious gastronomic award. So where to now, Arola? Time will tell, but anyone who has tasted his finely sliced truffle with foie gras ice-cream, his baby squid in lime marmalade, or his bacalao (salted cod) with gelée of seawater will be immune to this question—and its answer.

On a traditional level, Madrid can only really claim one homegrown dish, but that is one almighty one: the cocido. Conceived for the bitterly cold winter months when searing winds blast across the sierra, cocido is a slow-cooked stew of meat, sausage, chickpeas and vegetables, and its components are polished off separately over several courses. The broth or caldo, as mentioned before, becomes a course in its own right. And then there is tripe—cooked with chorizo and chillies to become that famous callos a la madrileña, which is often dished up in small portions in tapas bars. This brings us to the crux of the matter: it is the latter which really defines Madrid as they go hand in hand with the capital's nocturnal habits and with its easy-going, informal character. As tapas have developed in quality and quantity over the last decade, so has their mise en scène, and today even the well-heeled Salamanca district offers a choice of upmarket bars. In tandem with their fashionable designer settings, the little platters themselves are becoming increasingly sophisticated, leading some visitors to miss the good, old days.

buying brilliantly

What you go to Salamanca for, however, is less the tapas, more the clothes to sup in. For this affluent district is where the massed ranks of Madrid's designer boutiques lie in wait. The character of passers-by switches from youthful creativity on a budget to more classic, yet inimitably Madrileño, chic. From baroque slick to the minimalist, from full-on flounces to sharp tailoring, you will find the full gamut and there is no better place than Calle Serrano. But first, take a look at Spain's oldest female icon—La Dama de Baeza. This magnificent 2,500-year-old Iberian sculpture of a full-length bejewelled and finely dressed lady sits in Madrid's Archaeological Museum, right opposite where the boutique binge starts. Her head-and-shoulders 'sister', La Dama de Elche, roughly the same age, is displayed nearby.

Calle Serrano presents a lineup of homegrown designers and manufacturers such as Loewe, Pedro del Hierro, Carolina Herrera and Adolfo Domínguez, mixed with foreign classics from Yves Saint Laurent to Max Mara. Any Saturday afternoon sees a steady flow of Madrileños browsing along the tree-lined pavements in their unhurried way. Shopping here is charmingly old-fashioned in mood compared with other European capitals where congested traffic and/or people play havoc with retail therapy enjoyment. Round the corner, in Calle de Jorge Juan, is the entrance to a pedestrianized cul de sac: this tiny mecca of cutting-edge fashion includes Sybilla, Hispanic queen of style, and the precocious Alma Aguilar, alongside French labels Scooter and Robert Clergerie.

It is too easy to fulfil the mantra and shop till you drop, as the avenues lure shoppers further north and east. The coup de grace could well come in Calle Ortega y Gasset, home to Hermès and Versace, at which point it may be an idea to preserve your plastics and head for Fundación Juan March, one of Europe's most important private art foundations staging major exhibitions. And finally, no one should visit Madrid without a glimpse of the world's largest bullring, the Plaza de Toros de Las Ventas. This towering neo-Mudéjar structure lies east of Salamanca, virtually on the motorway, but that doesn't stop it packing in 23,000 spectators during the season in May to June. Like chefs, all aspiring toreadors simply have to perform in Madrid, and one could add a few more to the list.

...in the midst of apparent chaos, an extraodinary order reigns.

Bauzá Hotel + Restaurante

THIS PAGE (FROM TOP): *Bauzá's open, contemporary feel is achieved through warm lighting and simple, stylish design principles; guestrooms are characterized by a clean, elementary style and an airy brightness that creates a light, fresh atmosphere; the restaurant beckons with a long red carpet and a tasty, inventive Mediterranean menu.*

OPPOSITE: *Rooms have been specially designed and fitted out to ensure a truly homey stay for the modern jet-setter.*

Sleek, sophisticated and stunning in its modernity, Bauzá Hotel & Restaurante provides a serene oasis from the frenetic vibrancy of Madrid. With its clean lines, glass walls and impressive photography collection decorating both the rooms and restaurant, it's an ideal hotel for those drawn to contemporary design and comfort.

Located in the fashionable Salamanca quarter in downtown Madrid, the hotel is close to a host of cultural and entertainment attractions, from some of the city's best shopping—superb international brands and local designer boutiques line the streets in the vicinity—to Retiro Park and the Thyssen-Bornemisza Museum of Art.

...an ideal hotel for those drawn to contemporary design and comfort.

Retaining a true sense of modern homeliness, the rooms are light, spacious and simple. Black-and-white photographs hang on the walls, painted in unique colours ranging from slate blue to deep red. Billowing white duvets and bright cushions cover the beds, and chrome lighting adds to the overall contemporary feel. Of course, being a Habitat hotel each room comes with a plasma-screen television, playstation, CD player and accompanying CD and book menus. A separate block of seven self-catered apartments—for longer-staying guests—has similar luxuries and access to all the hotel's facilities, which include a gym, sauna and a library, complete with blazing hearth in the winter and cushioned armchairs. The ninth floor houses a spectacular suite that spans 77 m (253 ft), including a 25-m (82-ft) private teak terrace.

Bauzá Restaurant on the first floor, with Chef Ernesto Hinojal at the helm, is again ultra-modern. Long red carpets lead you into a beautiful open space where a huge window fronting onto Calle Goya provides a stunning backdrop. The Mediterranean cuisine is tasty and imaginative—starters include green fettuccini with cep sauce and tuna sashimi on a guacamole timbale; for main courses, choose from a rack of lamb with couscous and green tomato or tender venison with polenta in a pistachio-honey sauce. A tasting menu is a good way to enjoy the delicacies with a variety of starters and dishes. To complete Bauzá's inventive culinary experience, try one of their elaborate desserts.

The food is accompanied by a list of fine wines put together by wine specialist Nicolas Fernandez Trujilio and, if that's not enough, there's also a separate menu for cocktails, tea and even bottled water.

FACTS		
ROOMS	156 standard • 8 superior • 3 suites • 7 apartments	
FOOD	Bauzá Restaurante: Mediterranean/fusion	
DRINK	fine wines	
FEATURES	library • gym • sauna • bike hire • play station • CD player • weddings	
BUSINESS	conference rooms	
NEARBY	Retiro Park • Plaza Colon • Thyssen-Bornemisza Museum of Art	
CONTACT	Calle Goya 79, 28001 Madrid • telephone: +34.91.436 4546 • facsimile: +34.91.431 0943 • email: info@hotelbauza.com • website: www.hotelbauza.com	

PHOTOGRAPHS COURTESY OF HABITAT HOTELS.

De las Letras Hotel + Restaurante

THIS PAGE (FROM LEFT): Dating to the First World War, De las Letras' distinguished façade masks a quirky, cosmopolitan interior; DL's Lounge—sharply appointed in umbrageous cobalt blue and plush crimson tones—sets the scene for tapas and cocktails.

OPPOSITE: Each guest room is as distinct and enlivening as the famous inscriptions by some of history's most celebrated literati stenciled vividly across its walls.

Art. Literature. Food. Wine. And your very own private jacuzzi. De las Letras, a member of the Habitat Hotels group, has poured their love for all things literary into creating the hotel's characteristic flair. A combination of truly unique and welcoming touches with luxurious, ultra-modern rooms inside one of the city's most emblematic buildings, is what makes De las Letras such an unusual and stunning boutique hotel.

Built in 1917, the edifice is a grand sight, standing proud and dignified with three dramatic cupolas dominating the impressive exterior. Bordered by three notorious streets—Gran Via, Caballero de Gracia and Clavel—its location is perfect for exploring the surrounding theatres, cafés, cinemas and shops. Inside, the original features have been magnificently restored and the grand reception is a museum of beautiful tile mosaics and sculptures. Even the old elevator and staircase remain, fantastically re-conditioned to their sparkling, former glory.

In contrast to the majestic exterior the rooms are funky and modern, equipped with every available technological convenience—plasma television, DVD player and wireless Internet. Light and spacious with high ceilings, wide windows and wooden floors, their walls are painted in unique colours from calming ochre and burgundy to vivid orange, with stenciled inscriptions by famous writers and poets. For absolute luxury superior rooms and the duplex there are solarium terraces,

private jacuzzis and incredible views of city. If your budget won't stretch that far, the hotel offers alternative pampering in a spa area which includes a jacuzzi, Turkish hamman, sauna, massage rooms and a cardio room. If you are inspired by the wall inscriptions you can visit the hotel's library to find more works of literature and huge sofas to sink into.

As its name suggests, De las Letras places as much emphasis on its cuisine as it does on its unique accommodation, and DL's Restaurant does not disappoint. Housed in three levels, the ground floor is super-modern with dark concrete walls and metal furniture enlivened by primary colours splashed sporadically across the furnishings. Simple yet exceptionally tasty, the menu includes seasonal gazpacho with raspberries, caramelized goat's cheese with sweet apple and ox cappuccino with parmesan and shitake mushrooms for starters; and cod confit with herbs, Iberian cold meat tournado and salmon hamburger for main courses.

Next door, DL's Lounge, equally cool with stark metal fittings and shadowy blue lighting, offers delicious tapas dishes to accompany an evening of drinks; Air-Lounge—DL's rooftop summer terrace—offers stupendous views across the rooftops of Madrid and serves up copious amounts of DL's signature cocktail, the infamous and devilish red martini.

FACTS		
ROOMS	1 duplex • 6 DL's (terrace and jacuzzi) • 7 PLUS (terrace) • 15 superior • 74 basic
FOOD	DL's Restaurant
DRINK	DL's Lounge • Air-Lounge
FEATURES	spa • library • 3 banquet rooms • plasma television and DVD player in rooms
NEARBY	El Prado • Royal Palace • Reina Sofia Arts Centre • El Ritiro Park • Cibeles • Puerta del Sol
CONTACT	Gran Via 11, 28013 Madrid • telephone: +34.91.436 4546 • facsimile: +34.91.523 7981 • email: info@hoteldelasletras.com • website: www.hoteldelasletras.com

Hotel Urban

Standing eminently amid some of Madrid's most fascinating streets, Hotel Urban is in the heart of the capital's bustling cultural, political, commercial and financial hub, 5 minutes from the Prado and Thyssen-Bornemisza museums and just a stone's throw away from the lively neighbourhood of Santa Ana, where family-run restaurants and tapas bars full of authentic Spanish character line its jostling lanes.

THIS PAGE (FROM LEFT): Artefacts, deep ochre tones and plush furnishings create a distinct edge characteristic to the Hotel Urban; rich tones are softened by light through gossamer-thin drapes.

OPPOSITE: Tall and magnificent, the glass windows—stretching from ground to ceiling—give rooms the feel of a sophisticated loft.

Like its sister hotel—Villa Real—located just round the corner, Hotel Urban is owned by the Derby Hotels Collection group, creator of nine boutique hotels in Madrid, Barcelona and London. Its president, Jordi Clos Llombart, a frequent-featured personality in fashion and travel magazines, sets a high precedent for each of the group's distinctive, stunning hotels. Needless to say, Hotel Urban does not fall short of being a veritable sensation both in design and service. Named by *Condé Nast Traveller* as one of the world's top 60 hotels, Hotel Urban is a famed architectural landmark in Madrid's colourful, cosmopolitan landscape and a definitive leading luxury hotel in Spain.

The reception has the marvellous feel of a converted old warehouse, opening upward into a dramatic six-storey atrium and glassed galleria. The stark concrete floor, strong metal lines and clean, white furniture are warmed by natural sunlight which streams through the remarkable phenomenon that is the glass ceiling, while surrounding copper spotlighting softens the sharp features. The atmosphere of austere boldness is further diluted by towering sculptures and a beautiful, eclectic assortment of antiques, artefacts and paintings from Jordi Clos Llombart's own private collection.

The guestrooms are equally spectacular in décor and natural lighting, all dominated by wooden flooring in dark mahogany, lofty windows stretching from floor to ceiling, and an abundant use of dark, luxurious leather. Primitive earth-toned sculptures blend into the rich background, softening the sharp metallic lines; beds are made with the finest linen and extravagant robes lie folded in the pristine, resplendent marble bathroom. Every coveted modern luxury—flat-screen television with a full entertainment system, wireless Internet access and remarkable soundproofing throughout—has been carefully installed. A bottle of wine completes the personal welcome touch.

With sandstone walls, white furniture and large white plant jars, the roof terrace offers a more Mediterranean feel, which is heightened by magnificent views of the city across and beyond. With a cold drink in hand by the pool, it is an ideal hideaway for soaking up the Spanish sunshine and skyline sights.

Europa Decó's established reputation for incredible Mediterranean-influenced cuisine has secured its ever-increasing popularity in Madrid. Chef Joaquin de Felipe makes use of inventive seasonal recipes to create simple, yet fantastically flavoured food. For a tangy and refreshing appetizer, start with a tartare of bull tuna and Iranian caviar; alternatively, try the tasty pheasant consommé or fried partridge cannelloni with salmorejo. A diverse, mouth-watering menu of main dishes includes wild bream with croccanti noodles and belly of pork, a cauldron of lobster with mushrooms and vegetables, and a fillet of venison with mustard risotto. Worth holding out for are the absolutely sublime desserts such as the torrijas with ice-cream and chocolate. On the top floor, La Terraza del Urban is the place to enjoy breathtaking views across the city and a romantic setting for an elegant dinner.

Hotel Urban is not only at the forefront of premium luxury hospitality in Madrid; it also offers some of the most exquisite drinks and dining experiences in the city. The Glass Bar— a resplendent affair with its Moroccan crystal chandelier, famous Ghost chairs by Philippe Starck and gorgeous flooring of contrasting light and dark glass-work—is one of the most fashionable places in town for both visitors and residents alike who flock to listen to the music and indulge in the bar's outstanding cocktails, oysters and Japanese-inspired appetizers.

...an unforgettable, superlative experience in contemporary luxury.

THIS PAGE (FROM TOP): The eclectic reception exudes the fashionable air of a restored warehouse and is just one of many sensational aspects about this phenomenal work of architecture and design; La Terraza del Urban.

OPPOSITE (FROM LEFT): The Glass Bar; view of the stunning interior gazing up from the reception.

An arresting contrast to its surroundings, Hotel Urban is a prominent face in Madrid not just for its remarkable glass façade. Its innovative design and prime location within the famous Art Triangle make it a superb base for exploring the fascinating culture and history of the Spanish capital. Be it lounging in its unique contemporary interior, marvelling at the eclectic collection of artefacts from Africa, the Mediterranean and Papua New Guinea, basking in the sun by the pool on the rooftop, mingling in one of the city's most popular bars, dining at the exclusive Europa Decó or simply admiring the evening lights from the rooftop terrace, Hotel Urban offers an unforgettable, superlative experience in contemporary luxury.

FACTS	
ROOMS	4 single • 85 double • 3 junior suites • 4 suites
FOOD	Europa Decó: Mediterranean • La Terraza del Urban: Mediterranean
DRINK	Glass Bar • lounge/wine cellar
FEATURES	pool • solarium • wireless Internet • Egyptian and ancient art collection
BUSINESS	4 meeting rooms
NEARBY	Thyssen-Bornemisza Museum • Reina Sofía Art Centre • Museo del Prado • Retiro Park • Real Jardin Botanico • Puerta del Sol • Cibeles
CONTACT	Carrera de San Jerónimo 34, 28014 Madrid • telephone: +34.91.787 7770 • facsimile: +34.91.787 7799 • email: urban@derbyhotels.com • website: www.derbyhotels.com

Hotel Villa Magna, a Park Hyatt

Madrid is a vital metropolis of cultural vivacity, home to no fewer than 80 famous international art collections and museums. The world-famous Thyssen-Bornemisza, El Prado and Reina Sofía museums showcase the far-celebrated, home-grown talents of El Greco, Velázquez, Picasso, Dalí and Miró, alongside a plethora of other masterpieces. No matter how esoteric your cultural passion may be, Madrid promises to fulfil it.

Located in the city's artistic centre—also the heart of finance and premium circle of Europe's hospitality industry—is the refined realm of Hotel Villa Magna. Nearby are architectural monuments and Serrano street's exclusive boutiques; symbols of Madrid's ability to synergize its past with its present.

The capital's inspiring and ever-evolving skyline can be quietly contemplated from the comfort of cushioned rattan chairs on Villa Magna's sheltered, flower-draped terraces. For scenic views of natural beauty, repose on old wrought-iron work in the beautifully landscaped gardens that surround a number of effervescent fountains and eye-catching trellises. The hotel's advanced fitness and spa facilities offer an alternative—healthy or indulgent—way to enjoy an afternoon.

As the evening progresses, the hotel's Champagne Bar—clad in cloud-white and silver-veined marble walls and boasting a glitzy reputation in Madrid—is a glamorous venue for sipping cocktails. The omnipresence of marble throughout Villa Magna's palatial

THIS PAGE (FROM TOP): Noble interior décor and soigne furnishings reflect an air of regal bearing; suites are accompanied by exquisite dining rooms for guests' lavish entertaining; the Villa Magna is legendary for its impeccable hospitality and tasteful elegance, a quality of excellence apparent from its long guest-list of world leaders.

OPPOSITE: The hotel's restaurant— in the good hands of master chef David Millet—promises a sensational dining experience.

interior design adds to its lasting impact, the grand presidential ballroom and graceful spiral staircase being the epitome of class.

The gastronomic offerings of Hotel Villa Magna's restaurant, too, leave an indelible impression. Renowned chef David Millet's ingenious menus teem with original seafood specialities and Mediterranean influences, presented in compositions which reflect the changing seasons. Dinner may be enjoyed in the palm-lined, colonial-style dining room overlooking Castellana boulevard, where the evocative dark woods create an atmosphere of intimacy and absolute comfort. On balmy evenings the outdoor terraces beckon with their tessellated mosaic tiles that glow gently in the soft, sleepy moonlight. Madrid itself, however, is a city that never tires.

For those who do, the Villa Magna has appointed each guestroom to the highest standard, evident from the list of world leaders who frequent its presidential suites. Plush carpets underfoot, the furnishings are

crafted from gleaming, sonorous woods and warmed by spotless candelabra and lamps. Rooms are tinted with lulling tones from the delicate palette of caramel, cream, toffee and

chocolate, creating an atmospheric realm in which romantic pipe dreams are murmured, and at the same time, a calming chamber in which weighty decisions are made.

FACTS

ROOMS	junior suites • executive suites • presidential suites
FOOD	innovative Mediterranean • Cantonese
DRINK	Champagne Bar
FEATURES	Club Olympus fitness centre • sauna • steam bath • relaxation room • hair salon
BUSINESS	8 conference rooms • translation service • video-conference facilities
NEARBY	Art Triangle • Plaza Mayor • Royal Palace • Serrano street: designer boutiques
CONTACT	Paseo de la Castellana 22, 28046 Madrid • telephone: +34.91.587 1234 • facsimile: +34.91.431 2286 • email: villamagna@hyattintl.com • website: www.madrid.park.hyatt.com

PHOTOGRAPHS COURTESY OF HOTEL VILLA MAGNA, A PARK HYATT.

Hotel Villa Real

Beautifully set in an elegant, whitewashed sandstone terrace dating to the 19th century, overlooking a small plaza off the delightful tree-lined Paseo de la Castellana, Hotel Villa Real's central location makes it an ideal stay for exploring the capital of Spain. Just a few minutes walk from the celebrated Art Triangle—encompassing Museo del Prado, the Thyssen-Bornemisza Museum and Reina Sofía Art Centre—the hotel is enveloped by Madrid's most renowned museums and cultural treasures. Its situation in the very heart of the commercial district also promises exhilarating shopping trips as well as lively nightlife in Huertas.

Villa Real is one of nine unique hotels in Madrid, Barcelona and London, founded by the illustrious Derby Hotels Collection. The group and its eminent president, Jordi Clos Llombart—both are revered figures in the high-brow industries of fashion and travel—have been featured in bountiful publications ranging from *Condé Nast Traveller* and *FHM* to *The New York Times* and *La Vanguardia*. The group specializes in creating lavish and original boutique hotels which range from the time-honoured and resplendent, to the eclectic and avant-garde. A member of the first category, Hotel Villa Real has an air of orthodox elegance and modern décor that blends perfectly with the noble architecture and history of its surroundings.

Inside the bright, external walls of the hotel's traditional frontage, the atmosphere is rich with rustic tones, warm lighting, root mahogany furniture and deep leather sofas. Derby president Jordi Clos Llombart has moved numerous works of art and artefacts from his own private collection into the group's family of hotels so that an impressive assortment—which includes authentic ancient Apulian Greek vases and Roman mosaics—adorns the hallways and lounge areas.

Several of the hotel's 115 rooms feature a breathtaking balcony view of Madrid's rambling rooftops and the neighbouring parks; little surprise that the hotel has earned itself the moniker, 'The Balcony over Retiro Park'. The interior is elegant and down-to-earth, fitted with dark wooden floors, leather sofas, large beds, and a mezzanine which

divides the sleeping and lounge areas. If absolute luxury is what you are after, Villa Real's suites are quite possibly the city's ultimate choice lodgings for a short stay. Spread over two floors are a spacious, beautifully decorated bedroom and separate lounge area. Exquisite bathrooms in some of the superior rooms boast a lavish carrara marble jacuzzi. You can even order a bottle

THIS PAGE (FROM TOP): Rooms are all decorated with art pieces and even authentic artefacts, giving a warm and textured touch to the sophisticated furnishings; the richly-lit reception area leading up to the guestrooms.

OPPOSITE: Villa Real's rooms feature a mezzanine separating the lounge and sleeping spaces.

of champagne from room service and watch the sun set over Plaza de las Cortés, Retiro Park and the cloisters of Los Jerónimos from the privacy of your very own terrace.

Hotel Villa Real offers two dining areas, each with its own individual sophistication. East 47 Bar and Restaurant—named after one of Andy Warhol's studios on East 47th Street in New York—pays homage to the artist, graced with original Marilyn Monroe

pieces gazing out from stark walls. Other abstract works are arranged around the bar and restaurant, which remain otherwise minimalist in fashion. True to the memory of Warhol's era, the restaurant has a strong retro atmosphere dominated by a bar in the style of the 1960s which serves a remarkable menu of cocktails and wine. You can soak in the surroundings where the aroma of fusion cuisine mingles with the colours of Warhol's

pop art. Outside in the evening, the plaza is alive with an air of magic and the sparkling lights of the city. For dinner at East 47 you can choose from a mix of tasty, simple dishes such as tuna wrapped in pancetta, Spanish-style pizza and steak tartare.

Europa offers a more intimate, elegant dining atmosphere. Vividly decorated with original paintings by Antoni Tàpies, the restaurant is fresh and light in feel. Crisp white tablecloths and sparkling wine glasses create a classic, sophisticated setting and the subtle lighting sets the perfect mood for a romantic evening. On the streets outside, the statue of Cortéz dominating the plaza below is dramatically lit in the dark while the city behind it is dazzlingly aglow. The cuisine is invented by Chef Joaquín de Felipe and features a contemporary Mediterranean menu which includes a variety of zesty, fresh seafood dishes such as a trio of tuna and squid in sashimi, black risotto with cuttlefish, cream soup of pumpkin with scallops, small

squids with creamy rice and mild mojo and Spanish hake with clams. If diners find it too difficult to make a selection, the tasting platters come well recommended.

For those looking for a hotel to match the splendour and beauty of the city, Hotel Villa Real is the ultimate choice—a meticulous blend of traditional, opulent comfort and modern chic, it is a grand touch to any stay amid the beautiful architecture of Madrid.

THIS PAGE: View of the city streets from the terrace of Europa.

OPPOSITE (FROM TOP): Entrance to the elegant Europa restaurant; original Andy Warhol pieces in East 47 Bar and Restaurant.

FACTS

ROOMS	single • double • junior suites • suites
FOOD	East 47: fusion • Europa: Mediterranean
DRINK	cocktails • wine
FEATURES	limousine service
BUSINESS	4 meeting rooms
NEARBY	Thyssen-Bornemisza Museum • Reina Sofía Art Centre • Museo del Prado • Retiro Park • Real Jardin Botanico • Puerta del Sol • Cibeles
CONTACT	Plaza de las Cortés 10, 28014 Madrid • telephone: +34.91.420 3767 • facsimile: +34.91.420 2547 • email: villareal@derbyhotels.com • website: www.derbyhotels.com

PHOTOGRAPHS COURTESY OF DERBY HOTELS COLLECTION.

barcelona+catalonia+aragón

France

Basque

Navarra

Rioja

Castilla y León

Aragón

Huesca

La Pleta Hotel + Spa

Panticosa Resort

Catalonia

Figueres

Girona

> Hotel Trias
> Hotel La Malcontenta
> NM Suites
> Alva Park Resort + Spa
> Gran Hotel Balneario Blancafort

Barcelona

> Hotel America Barcelona
> Hotel Claris
> Hotel Condes de Barcelona
> Hotel Cram
> Hotel Gran Derby
> Hotel Granados 83
> Neri Hotel + Restaurante
> Hotel Omm
> Hotel Pulitzer
> Estela Barcelona Hotel del Arte
> Hotel RA Beach Thalasso-Spa

Tarragona

Castilla-La Mancha

Valencia

Balearic Sea

Mallorca

Menorca

Ibiza

Cabrera

barcelona + catalan spain

Famously proud, culturally dynamic and economically self-sufficient, Barcelona is a city which pulls out all the stops. It behaves like a capital, even thinks it's a capital, much to the chagrin of Madrid. Why? Because it boasts superb architectural style, sophisticated cuisine, sharp design, phenomenal shopping, world-class music and a plethora of extraodinary art. Then, periodically, it reinvents itself. A century ago this happened thanks to the Modernistas, a group of Catalan architects led by Antoni Gaudí, whose whimsical buildings reinterpreted Art Nouveau. Then again in 1992, the catalyst was the Olympic Games which bequeathed an extensive waterfront regeneration; and in 2004, Forum, a multidisciplinary arts event, brought major development north of the city beaches.

Barcelona aside, the rest of Catalonia has plenty to offer, from the cultural triangle of Girona, Figueres and Cadaqués to beautiful beaches, the Pyrenees and Tarragona's magnificent Roman monuments. Yet Barcelona dominates. Whatever the time of year or cultural agenda, it never fails to seduce, and tourism is booming. This sprawling city and its inhabitants, who simply will not bow to Madrid's hegemony, always offer something new. Proud, some say stroppy, the Catalans have always been at the forefront of Spain's commerce, as well as theatre, design and now gastronomy. Today, if there is at all one Catalan celebrity before any other, it is Ferran Adrià, maverick master of foam and of chemical precision. This polemical pioneer is the face of a culinary revolution which has helped elevate Spain to the top of Europe's cuisines.

curious cuisine

If design was the focus of the 1980s and 1990s, then cuisine is definitely Barcelona's 21st-century obsession—although the two fields are inextricably linked. Adrià is far from alone in his stellar talents, although no other chef has his outward radicalism or sense of self-promotion. Santi Santamaría at Can Fabes (who became Catalonia's first three-star Michelin chef in 1994), the Roca brothers at El Celler de Can Roca in Girona, Xavier

PAGE 44: Gaudí's surreal chimney-pots on the roof of Casa Milà (or La Pedrera) inspired endless controversy when it was built in 1910.

THIS PAGE (FROM TOP) The cornucopia of La Boqueria market; colourful street-artists who entertain along La Rambla.

OPPOSITE: The ornate ceramic fragments, sensuous concrete forms and ironwork of Casa Batlló was a redesign of a typical apartment block.

Pellicer at Abac, Ramón Freixa at El Raco d'en Freixa, Felip Planas at OT and Jean-Luc Figueras —all are brilliant Catalan chefs whose cuisines range from exquisite French-inspired techniques highlighting local produce to Adrià's one-of-a-kind form of gastro-futurism.

Today, with Adrià's star shooting through the stratospheres, his Costa Brava restaurant is accessible only to the lucky few, as reservations stack up a year ahead for the summer season. During its winter closure, far from resting on his laurels, Adrià moves his entire working team to a 'laboratory' in the middle of Barcelona. This is where they elaborate new techniques to supersede the 'airs', 'capsules' and 'foams' that made his reputation. So, watch that plate—who knows what next year's fashion will be.

catalan classics

Luckily for traditionalists, Catalan classics such as mar i montaña combinations ('sea and mountain' and, by extension, 'seafood and meat') or suquet, a divine seafood stew, still feature conspicuously on menus. As the Costa Brava is within spitting distance, many top-notch restaurants buy direct from fishermen, and seafood figures prominently. The strong Gallic influence started way back in the 9th-century heyday of Charlemagne, and was later reinforced by French monks and by Catalonia's geographic proximity to France. As a result, unlike the Castilians and Basques, the Catalans revel in aromatic herbs; fennel, bay leaf, parsley, thyme, mint and juniper berries are used abundantly. Local wines such as cava or the excellent reservas of Priorat and Penedès are stalwarts, while wild mushrooms from the Pyrenees, embutidos (a Catalan sausage) and nectar-like Siurana olive oil from the Tarragona area are just some additional specialities. Atmospheric backstreet tapas bars and homely neighbourhood restaurants nearly all serve fantastically fresh food, and no one should miss a visit to the cornucopia of La Boqueria market, even if just to visually feast on the ingredients. This is bona fide, living Barcelona at its most colourful

THIS PAGE (FROM TOP): Briefing chefs in the kitchen of El Bulli; Adrià's latest creation, Deshielo, a part-frozen pineapple dessert.
OPPOSITE (FROM TOP): A zen-like corner of the millennial Hotel Omm's stylish restaurant; the iconic spires of La Sagrada Família.

and enjoyable, and a reflection of Catalonia's tremendous agricultural and gastronomic diversity. Not least, it must be the only place in the world where the women fish-vendors look like they are in a Hollywood casting, as most are immaculately made-up platinum blondes.

eixample + a genius

La Boqueria market is located in La Rambla, Barcelona's touristy central avenue. Its wide promenading pavement, with cafés, street-artists, bird-sellers and florists, slices through the old city from Plaça de Catalunya to the revamped harbour, dividing the monumental Gothic Quarter from hip, metropolitan Raval. Inland to the west unfolds the stately 19th-century grid of Eixample, where well-heeled Catalans stroll between upmarket boutiques and Modernista marvels. This is Gaudí Land, home to some of the eccentric architect's most striking buildings. In the elegant shopping mecca of Passeig de Gràcia stands the extraordinary Casa Milà —better known as La Pedrera—completed in 1912, whose curved façade, organically-shaped balconies and intricate ironwork are only rivalled by the world-famous roof terrace. Here, a series of mosaic-clad abstract forms (in reality chimney pots) defy reference as well as offer sweeping sea and city views—wonderful on a clear day when every building seems airbrushed by the dry winds from the Pyrenees. An alternative angle on Gaudí's chimney pots is from the rooftop pool at the adjacent 21st-century Hotel Omm.

Other celebrated Gaudí buildings stand nearby, notably the glittering, mosaic-fronted Casa Batlló, as well as several by his Modernista contemporaries, Domènech i Montaner and Puig i Cadalfach. A few streets away looms the city's emblem, Gaudí's La Sagrada Família cathedral. Nobody can ignore this much-maligned and/or adulated extravaganza which, 120 years after the first stones were laid, is still in the process of being worked on. The story is a tragic one of obsession, as Gaudí's later life was entirely clouded by his efforts to obtain financing for what the art critic Robert Hughes has termed a "cash-eating monster". Steeped in increasingly wild theories of mysticism and symbolic structures,

Gaudí's ambitions escalated to such an extent that he was eventually forced to sell off his possessions and even beg from friends and strangers. It all came to an abrupt end when the disturbed and unsung genius died under the wheels of a tram. Fittingly, Gaudí is buried in the crypt of the unfinished edifice. A fresher sense of his brilliance is found at the Parc Güell on the edge of Eixample. This massive project of his youth was originally intended as a garden city, but lack of buyers prompted the far-sighted developer, Count Güell, to give full rein to the architect's fantasies. The result is a labyrinth of textured viaducts, pavilions, columns and fountains, all faced in his characteristic fragmented tile mosaic—a technique widely used by Santiago Calatrava today.

arty barcelona

However forward-looking Barcelona is, you cannot miss out on its centuries of history. In the maze of winding streets and squares of the Gothic Quarter lurk Barcelona's towering Gothic cathedral, international museums, magnificent churches, fragments of Roman wall and the beautiful Plaça del Rei which fronts a medieval palace and tower. This was the hub of power of the counts of Barcelona, whose feudal system lasted for several centuries and furthered Catalonia's maritime prowess. Across the Vía Laietana lies the arty district of La Ribera, a quaint medieval quarter where laundry still drips from overhead. This is home to the Picasso Museum, the catalyst for La Ribera's popularity in the 1980s. Interconnecting mansions display a collection with a particular emphasis on Picasso's formative years and a last burst of creative etchings made before his death. Art interest continues nearby between the stunning Barbier-Müeller museum of pre-Columbian art and dozens of idiosyncratic design and craft shops.

Within this labyrinth of narrow, shady streets is the newly hip Born district, dubbed Barcelona's Soho (after the London one) but of a very different ilk. "Rodo el mon i torna al Born" (Roam the world and come back to the Born) is a Catalan saying emphasizing the district's historic role at the heart of an expanding city, both inland and, for several

THIS PAGE (FROM LEFT): A light installation leads the way in the hip Born district; worshippers light candles at Barcelona's Gothic cathedral.

OPPOSITE (FROM TOP): The courtyard of the Picasso Museum lets visitors take a breath; quality artisan food products are constantly in demand.

centuries of imperial activity, overseas. After decades of neglect, this neighbourhood has come into its own again. Wall-to-wall consumer interest fills the streets surrounding its epicentre, the Passeig del Born—an elongated, leafy square originally used for medieval jousting. Once the centre of the fishing trade (the superb Gothic church of Santa María was actually funded by seamen), Born later became Barcelona's central marketplace; the old building is now being renovated. And, even if it has diversified into fashion designers, jewellers and design shops, the foodie origins are still present, as a plethora of gourmet foodstores, innovative tapas bars and restaurants abound. A short walk eastwards from here brings you out into the bright, breezy Barceloneta area, with its marina, post-Olympic leisure developments and city beaches.

Barcelona abounds in art interest, and the panoramic hilltop of Montjuïc offers yet another epicentre, reached most scenically by cable car from Barceloneta. Number one up here is the superb Joan Miró Foundation in its free-flowing 1970s building designed by Miró's friend, Josep Lluís Sert. Through the pine trees stands the fabulously rich Museum of Catalan Art, a treasure trove of Romanesque and Gothic art. The emblematic building, designed for the International Fair in 1929, was later renovated by Gae Aulenti, then in 2005 was again revamped to accommodate Catalan art up to the 20th century. However, its most precious asset is the Romanesque section; no other museum in the world has such an extensive collection of what was in fact Europe's first shared art movement, spread by monks and pilgrims.

At the foot of the hill, the tribute reconstruction of Mies van der Rohe's 1929 pavilion for the official reception of the International Fair is an architectural feat not to be missed; its clean forms a landmark of modernist architecture (in the European sense as opposed to Spanish Modernista, which is Art Nouveau). Close by, yet another major arts venue has taken shape at a restored factory. This is a showcase for the art collection and various related activities of the dynamic private foundation, Caixa. Another important art mecca

is MACBA (Museu d'Art Contemporani de Barcelona), where a prodigious collection of Spanish and international contemporary art is exhibited in a spanking white building designed by the American architect Richard Meier in 1995. The museum stands in the controversial, edgy and heavily fashionable district of Raval, a little south of La Rambla—an area to watch, although it veers tantalizingly between vandalism and bohemian chic. Knowing Barcelona's superb ability to reinvent, a solution to its identity will soon be found.

dalí's love-nests

Who can forget that moustache or the man? Salvador Dalí is definitely up there in Catalonia's holy trinity of creative genii—alongside the likes of Gaudí and Adrià. This native of Figueres excelled at provocation, drama and exhibitionism, all of which helped propel him to the forefront of the Surrealist movement in 1930s Paris. Dalí's image transcended nationality, as did his trademark moustache, dream-like landscapes and compulsive megalomania. Together with his adored and adoring Russian wife, Gaia, the artist later cultivated fame from his stage-set garden and house at Port Lligat, near Cadaqués, when they weren't holding court at the Hotel Meurice in Paris or the St. Regis in New York. In 1970, Gaia moved into a renovated castle, Castell de Púbol, where she gaily entertained young lovers, only admitting Dalí by written invitation.

Idiosyncratic and thoroughly absorbed with flights of fantastical grandeur right to the very end, Dalí's final years were spent devising an outrageous monument to his life and work in a converted theatre in Figueres. From the pink façade of the labyrinthine Theatre-Museum, studded with his signature model eggs and bread-rolls, to a coin-operated black Cadillac—rumoured to have belonged to Al Capone—sprayed by a fountain, the Mae

THIS PAGE: Dalí's Think Room in the converted fisherman's cottage in Port Lligat. The house became a mini stage-set, stuffed with eccentric memorabilia, the perfect backdrop for his antics.

OPPOSITE (FROM TOP): Designer comfort is taking over the Costa Brava's boutique hotels; Cadaqués maintains a delightfully cosmopolitan and arty atmosphere.

West room (her lips a red sofa, her hair yellow curtains, her eyes framed paintings and her nose a fireplace) and numerous more conventional artworks, Dalí certainly fulfilled his ambition. Curiously for someone who once declared, "I have always considered myself to be a genius", his tomb under the central stage is extremely understated.

heart of catalonia

Figueres is otherwise a pleasant though unexciting town, whereas Cadaqués has since

blossomed into a summer retreat for artists. This delightful little resort town—well-known for its seafood restaurants—curls round a picturesque bay backed by a wild headland, altogether typical of the Costa Brava's odd juxtapositions between unadulterated nature and seaside resorts. The magical coves, clear blue sea and rugged sierra spelled its fate back in the 1960s and 1970s, when this dramatic coastline was chosen for Spain's first destination for mass tourism. There are still some charming, unspoiled pockets, however, as well as the striking Greek and Roman site of Empúries.

Neighbouring Girona is, on the other hand, a town with a clear sense of place and identity. In recent years it has experienced a minor boom thanks to its strategic location (just an hour by train from Barcelona), direct international flights and intelligent planning. As a result, the colourful river frontage, Modernista buildings, cathedral and old Jewish quarter have all acquired much brighter faces. Like Barcelona, a sense of design-consciousness is high on the scale here, and there is little sense of provincialism.

Historically, Girona—like Toledo—reveals how harmoniously the three religions of Islam, Judaism and Christianity co-existed before the Reconquista as, in the older, upper part of town Arab baths, a Gothic cathedral and a rebuilt synagogue all stand within a short distance of each other. Girona's Jewish community was famed in the Middle Ages for its prestigious Cabalistic school, and the former synagogue is an important research centre and museum today. Downhill beside the banks of the Onyar river, Girona's elegant 19th-century streets are an enjoyable place to meander, shop, wine and dine.

Gourmets in the know will head for the outskirts to the highly reputed restaurant, El Celler de Can Roca, where three brothers Joan (main cuisine), Josep (wines) and Jordi (desserts) combine their talents to create a whimsical symphony of flavours and aromas. This has earned them two prized Michelin stars and a faithful following. Their menú de degustación (tasting menu) shows off fantastic imagination coupled with the flavours of Catalonia's best produce—be it sea-crab velouté with baby onions in cocoa and mint, tartare of smoked squid, or scampi with orange smoke and pumpkin foam.

roman tarragona

Catalonia's other face lies to the south, beyond the stirring monasteries of Montserrat, Poblet and Santa Creus and right in the middle of the overbuilt, unexciting Costa Daurada. Tarragona's outstanding Roman monuments are a reflection of the ancient capital being the largest and oldest Roman settlement in Iberia, described by the poet Virgil as "the most pleasant spot for resting". That was a few decades BCE, but the same epithet could be applied today, as Spain's deepest port retains a sleepy air that relates more to southern Spain than to the focused dynamism of Barcelona. The reason for coming here is obvious: a superbly located amphitheatre, massive hilltop walls, the praetorium (subsequently the residence of the Counts of Barcelona), an aqueduct and an archaeological museum. There are some fine vantage points which give a clear view of the extent of this ancient town which served as a model for provincial capitals elsewhere in the Roman empire. As a result, in 2000, Tarragona gained World Heritage status.

Wine aficionados use Tarragona as a base for heading inland into the rugged sierra surrounding Gratallops, centre of priorat production. Vineyards interspersed with wild landscapes of pine and olive trees are backed by the pinkish colours of Serra de Montsant, making a striking rural destination. In the beautiful village of Escaladei lies the historic and spiritual centre of the Priorat area, a Carthusian monastery that was responsible for introducing vine cultivation and wine-ageing techniques here in the 12th century. Proof that Catalonia, however focused it may be on the future, has deep, deep roots.

...a city which pulls out all the stops.

Alva Park Resort + Spa

THIS PAGE: *Alva Park's star spa installation, the Indian Princess Bath, is a spectacular experience in saltwater bath, chatoyant waters and underwater music.*

OPPOSITE (FROM TOP): *Luxurious settings in the Junior Suite bath; a magnificent sea view awaits behind closed curtains in the Grand Deluxe Suite.*

'World-class' is a term often used but rarely warranted. The combination of luxury and service that needs to be maintained in order for a hotel to aspire to be among the world's finest is contingent on a commitment from management and staff that can be found in only a few select properties. Yet as soon as you walk through the main entrance of the Alva Park Resort & Spa, a member of The Leading Small Hotels of the World, you get the dawning impression that this is indeed one of the best. It isn't just the superb Asian décor, exquisite antiques, original art and dramatic floral arrangements, but also the friendliness of the concierge, the discreet, efficient check-in and the sight of a housekeeper artfully arranging rose petals around a vase. Even before you set foot in the room, you know that you have arrived exactly where you should be.

The guestrooms are generous in size and overflowing with light. You enter a large bedroom complete with a Bang & Olufsen television; a small selection of music is offered in the room and an extensive catalogue of movies can be ordered from the front desk. The lighting, with several pre-programmed ambience settings, is controlled automatically from a panel beside the bed. There is a sitting room complete with a small kitchenette, complimentary coffee or tea, a minibar and a small table and comfortable chairs.

The bathroom is a dream come true, with a jacuzzi tub, marble shower, double-stone vanity and electronic blinds. Amenities are of the finest quality, including terry robes, slippers and a box of exclusive personal-care products by Molton Brown of London. A panel allows you to select the perfect lighting for makeup or a relaxing soak in the jacuzzi; a separate toilet offers convenience and privacy. There is a walk-in dressing room with ample closet space, a high-tech safe, light robes for evening use and even Panama-style courtesy hats for the pool or beach. As you will soon discover, nothing has been left to chance. The sheer curtain in the bedroom has a convenient slit that

allows you to exit onto the balcony without any fuss. The terrace has reclining lounges and expansive views of either the beach or the pool and gardens. The alarm clock projects the time discreetly onto the ceiling, ensuring that no one is molested by a luminous dial at night. It is difficult to think of anything that they may have forgotten in their efforts to make your stay absolutely perfect.

Although most people would be happy just to luxuriate in their rooms, the many dining options will prove much too tempting.

THIS PAGE (FROM TOP):
Night terrace of Lanai Lounge;
Molton Brown of London fame,
luxury spa and lifestyle boutique.

OPPOSITE (CLOCKWISE FROM TOP):
Ancient Eastern treatments and
rituals are revived at inhouse
parlour, Massages of the World;
indulge in Molton Brown's lavish
spa cabins and natural products.

Minamo is the exclusive Japanese restaurant and, with a capacity of only 12, reservations must be made well in advance. Each table stands on a wooden island in the midst of a crystal-clear pool and each course is accompanied by different lighting and sound effects, including a curtain of rain water that effectively masks conversation from other tables. A master chef from Japan prepares generous portions of fresh sushi and sashimi. The entire evening is an unforgettable sensory and culinary experience. An alternative is restaurant A Flor d'Aigua, with a contemporary menu and where guests will be treated to one of the finest breakfasts in Europe, all made-to-order. A lighter menu is available in the Lanai Lounge and Bar and guests enjoying the pool can order drinks and snacks at the Ginkgo Terrace. For those seeking adventure there is the Disaster Café, a thematic restaurant with American and regional dishes as well as the heart-racing experience of surviving a 7.8 earthquake.

The fitness room and spa will leave you breathless not just because of the exercise machines; the décor is magnificent. There are spacious changing rooms with lockers and a small centrifuge dryer to relieve guests from carrying their wet bathing suits. The spa consists of a Turkish sauna, a Nordic sauna, a snow shower and a jacuzzi. Probably the most spectacular element is the Indian Princess Bath, a heated indoor saltwater pool in the middle of an *Arabian Nights* dreamscape. The water is the perfect temperature with music piped underwater and an ever-changing kaleidoscope of colours. Pull a chord to receive a delightful tropical rain for a few moments. Altogether, an experience not to be missed.

... a private world of luxury and exquisite taste...

small children will appreciate the popular Kid's Club that offers a secure, supervised play area to keep them entertained and happy.

From the moment you arrive, you will be immersed in a private universe of luxury and exquisite taste and pampered by a devoted staff with a commitment to ensuring the finest stay possible. At the Alva Park Resort & Spa, the term 'world-class' is earned every day.

Additional spa services include Massages of the World, offering traditional methods from various cultures complemented by ancient rituals. Individual treatments include the Ayurvedic massage from India or an energizing Tibetan massage. Couples can share the Mayan massage with the Corn Ritual or the Pinda-Thai treatment with the sensual Flower Ritual. Guests can also enjoy prestigious London company Molton Brown's first continental European luxury spa and boutique branch, featuring their famous products made exclusively from flower essences, exotic plants and sea extracts.

There is a virtual golf course decorated like a private English club with a state-of-the-art simulator that allows you to play Saint Andrew's with amazing reality or to improve your drive with an instructor; all without leaving the property. Guests who come with

FACTS

ROOMS	Junior Suites • Grand Deluxe Suites
FOOD	Minamo: Japanese • A Flor d'Aigua: continental • Disaster Café: themed restaurant
DRINK	Lanai Lounge and Bar • Ginkgo Terrace
FEATURES	exercise room • spa • Indian Princess saltwater pool • Virtual Golf Course and Club • Molton Brown of London • Massages of the World
NEARBY	Fenals Beach • shopping in Lloret de Mar • bars • restaurants
CONTACT	Francesc Layret 3–5, 17310 Platja de Fenals, Lloret de Mar, Girona • telephone: +34.972.368 581 • facsimile: +34.972.364 467 • email: mail@alvapark.com • website: www.alvapark.com

PHOTOGRAPHS COURTESY OF ALVA PARK RESORT + SPA.

Hotel America Barcelona

If you are a hotel in Barcelona, you would want to be located near Paseo de Gràcia, the only street in the world where you can do serious damage with your credit card at world-class boutiques and explore one of Gaudí's architectural marvels all in the same block. Many of the best hotels are already there; the density of luxury establishments is so high that it is becoming more difficult to stand out among the crowd. Of course, what you could do is build a boutique hotel with a refreshing contemporary design, swathe it in vibrant colours, flood it with natural light, offer a full range of services only expected in the finest hotels, apply a very reasonable rate and you are certain to get noticed. This is the exact formula that has won a legion of fans for the artsy Hotel America Barcelona; a true David among the Goliaths.

This dynamo of a hotel offers up to 60 guestrooms—either standard or superior—and all of them are elegantly styled with a fresh, homey interior. The list of amenities is amazing and comprehensive, and includes satellite television, voicemail, high-speed Internet connection, minibar, digital safe, comfy robes and slippers in every room. The superior category features additional delights which include a delightful jacuzzi, digital bathroom scales, CD and DVD player, crisp complimentary daily newspapers and a stationary exercise bike on request for a workout in absolute privacy. On top of these, one of the best perks about making a reservation at the Hotel America Barcelona is the option of designing a menu of amenities à la carte, so that you can enjoy a broader range of services but pay only for those that you really use.

THIS PAGE (CLOCKWISE FROM LEFT): Quirky contemporary art and a delightful sense of imagination are welcoming hallmarks of Hotel America Barcelona; guestrooms are decorated in vibrant tones which give a modern edge and character; cocktails can be sipped to a good book in the lounge area.

OPPOSITE: Glitzy and spanking with a designer feel yet informal and budget-friendly, the hotel's amenities are offered à la carte for guests' personal tailoring.

Hotel guests have exclusive use of the pool and large jacuzzi on the roof, which offers remarkable views of busy downtown Barcelona. There is also a well-equipped gym with a full complement of exercise machines and a heavenly Finnish sauna to languish away in. Few can also resist the lure of the lobby bar for a cold aperitif or after-dinner cocktail. Several meeting rooms for business and events are available, all of them offering the very latest in audiovisual technology. In light of the hotel's superb location in the very heart of the city, they make the ideal setting for press conferences, product presentations, video-conferencing as well as private lunches or dinners. On top of this, the hotel offers a notable courtesy car service which no other four-star hotel in Barcelona does.

The Hotel America Barcelona is quite simply everything that you might desire in a hotel near the famous Paseo de Gràcia, so it is difficult to imagine why anyone would want to pay more. Now you don't have to.

FACTS

ROOMS	6 superior • 53 standard
FOOD	continental
DRINK	lobby bar
FEATURES	rooftop pool • jacuzzi • fitness centre • courtesy car
BUSINESS	meeting rooms • audiovisual technology • video-conferencing • high-speed Internet
NEARBY	boutiques • Modernista buildings • La Sagrada Família • bars • restaurants • Metro
CONTACT	195 C/ Provença, 08008 Barcelona • telephone: +34.934.876 292 • facsimile: +34.934.872 518 • email: america@hotelamericabarcelona.com • www.hotelamericabarcelona.com

PHOTOGRAPHS COURTESY OF HOTEL AMERICA BARCELONA.

Hotel Claris

The Hotel Claris—a member of the Derby Hotels Collection—is no ordinary hotel. One only has to review the list of original art and antiques that adorn the rooms and public areas to get the impression that this is indeed a very special place. Its art collection, with more than 400 exceptional pieces, would be the pride of any museum. There are 30 ancient Egyptian works, some as much as 4,000 years old; Roman sculptures from the time of Christ; mosaics from the 3rd century; 136 original etchings ordered by Napoleon in 1812; furniture from the 18th and 19th centuries; a series of etchings by Guinovart and over 100 priceless antique kilims—all of them housed in a magnificent 19th-century palace that took five years of painstaking and dedicated work by a team of expert artisans and architects to restore her to her former splendour. Undeniably, the Claris is a work of art in her own right.

The hotel offers 124 luxurious rooms—this includes 14 duplexes, 4 large duplexes, 3 suites and 18 junior suites—all featuring unique works of art in a refreshing and contemporary design that is highlighted by wooden floors and vibrant colours. Every room has been impressively soundproofed to guarantee a restful stay, and superior amenities include the convenience of three telephones, minibar, CD player, satellite television, safe deposit box, fax-modem

Undeniably, the Claris is a work of art in her own right.

connection, high-speed Internet access, complimentary shoe-cleaning service and a thoughtful welcome gift. The interior décor is energizing and so unlike most other hotels that you will find yourself constantly taking snapshots for your decorator back home.

The highly defined aesthetic extends beyond the guestrooms into every corner of the property, from the dramatic lighting of the elegant façade to the soaring heights of the grand atrium. A common theme is a striking, luminous blend of blue and white

that evokes the Mediterranean and infuses spaces with a sense of calm and relaxation. The rooftop terrace has a splendid pool and solarium with superb views over the centre of the city and a sauna and gym are available for guests to unwind after a busy day.

East 47 Restaurant and Cocktail Bar is an absolute must for any visitor to Barcelona. The bar area takes you right into the heart of Manhattan with its trendy ambience, music from the 1970s and its ever-popular Chill-out Sessions which feature tunes from East 47's

THIS PAGE: The façade is especially spectacular illuminated by night, highlighting the original rustified stone detailing and refurbished fenestration beneath the Claris' contemporary glass extension.

OPPOSITE: Stark colours, abundant lighting and original art and sculptures are a hallmark of the Derby Hotels Collection group.

a full range of services at their disposal in the hotel's business centre, which includes high-speed Internet, courtesy smart cars on stand-by and even a limousine service when the occasion demands arriving in style.

It is difficult to define greatness in a hotel; sometimes the number of stars and the degree of luxury are not the most reliable indicators. As wonderful as the Claris is to behold and to stroll past her breathtaking works of art, it would only be the Louvre with beds if it were not for the exceptional level of service, friendly staff and personal touch that have become the hallmark of this distinctive property. Yet there is something even more remarkable about the Claris. This

collection. This is cocktail heaven and the perfect transition stop before heading into the restaurant where the soft earthy colours and elegant table settings provide a subtle backdrop for an exuberant assortment of original pieces by Andy Warhol. The art almost seems to trumpet the menu, an eclectic fusion of leading-edge gastronomy featuring innovative dishes inspired by regional and international flavours. During the summer months everyone heads to La Terraza del Claris for a refreshing poolside drink while listening to music spun by the hotel's DJ. You can enjoy a romantic candlelight dinner on the terrace surrounded by the incandescent sea of downtown Barcelona, where the stars seem to have fallen from the night sky to lay twinkling stories below.

Claris Restaurant is an elegant dining room designed for breakfast meetings and private dinners. For business, the hotel has five meeting rooms of various sizes which are equipped with the latest technology and the added benefit of being located in the heart of Barcelona city's centre. The Museum and Terrace can both be booked for meetings, presentations, cocktails and social events in a truly exceptional setting. Guests also have

This is a hotel with soul.

THIS PAGE (FROM TOP): *East 47 Restaurant and Bar offers a sophisticated setting for dining; the rooftop pool is a showcase of stunning architectural design.*

OPPOSITE (FROM TOP): *Guestrooms are luxuriously furnished but have a comfortable, homely feel; each room features authentic art from a myriad of civilizations.*

is a hotel with soul. Its works of art are not here by accident; they are visible proof of the human love for all things beautiful, and the manifestation of the need to create that has been a part of all of us since we first began to paint the walls of caves. Gathering them together in a place where people come to socialize and to be reconciled is the true genius behind the Derby Claris. And all of this within streets of the great masterpieces of the Modernisme movement—sheer genius that you'll miss when you return home.

FACTS		
ROOMS	14 duplex • 4 large duplex • 18 junior suites • 3 suites	
FOOD	East 47 Restaurant and Cocktail Bar: fusion • La Terraza del Claris: modern • Claris Restaurant: exclusive breakfast and private functions	
DRINK	East 47 Restaurant and Cocktail Bar	
FEATURES	pool • sauna • solarium • fitness centre • museum-quality art collection • antique furniture • original works of art • wireless Internet • courtesy car	
BUSINESS	5 meeting rooms • limousine service	
NEARBY	Paseo de Gràcia • Modernista buildings by Gaudí • Metro • bars • restaurants	
CONTACT	Pau Claris 150, 08009 Barcelona • telephone: +34.93.487 6262 • facsimile: +34.93.215 7970 • email: claris@derbyhotels.com • website: www.derbyhotels.com	

PHOTOGRAPHS COURTESY OF DERBY HOTELS COLLECTION.

Hotel Condes de Barcelona

Housed in a landmark building of its own right, the noble Hotel Condes de Barcelona is justifiably one of the city's most popular hotels situated in the prominent district of Eixample, just opposite the far-beloved La Pedrera. Its superb location on Passeig de Gràcia places it in the heart of the city's historic, cultural, architectural, financial and business centre. Eixample—a new town to the ever-expanding Barcelona—became a fashionable living quarter for 19th-century bourgeoisie, and numerous architects were drawn to the area, commissioning exclusive homes for the city's elite. With celebrated masterpieces by Antoni Gaudí and Lluís Domènech i Montaner offering just a few of these spectacular city sights, the Eixample district makes for a truly fascinating area to wander the wide avenues.

Originally a pair of private villas, Casa J. Dauradella and Casa E. Batlló now make up one of the city's most magnificent and prestigious hotels. Opened in 1986 and with further renovation carried out in 2002, the property has maintained the authentic lineament of the majestic palaces, with their marble flooring and original columns which dominate the awe-inspiring reception area. The original high, sweeping staircase is just one of the many stately features carefully preserved to maintain the palaces' strong, dignified personalities and an overwhelming sense of their distinguished history.

Historic grandeur is mixed with modern luxury in the guestrooms which, alongside detailed cornicing and resplendent marble baths, combine smart soundproof windows and state-of-the-art technology. The newest

THIS PAGE (FROM TOP): View of the edifice's interior and wrought-iron work looking up from one of the noble marble stairways; rooms are decorated in rich tones and modern furnishings; the illuminated façade of the Condes de Barcelona, formerly a pair of private manor houses.

OPPOSITE: The grand staircase in the reception area is one of many authentic elements which have been thoughtfully restored.

rooms—with enviable views over Gaudí's La Pedrera—each boast access to a private terrace and jacuzzi. Add to that fine room service and you'll find yourself in absolutely one of the finest and most romantic settings in Barcelona for making the most of the city's spectacular panoramic landscape.

After a day spent exploring the local highlights, two outdoor pools prove to be a cool, inviting refresher. With one—a plunge pool—located on the roof, you can continue sightseeing as you look languidly out over La Predrera and the rest of the city.

Two restaurants within the hotel—under the expert direction of famous three-Michelin-star Chef Martín Berasategui—offer superb Mediterranean fare. The food is sensational and, with the charming opportunity to dine in the gentle breeze on the rooftop terrace, the sparkling views across Barcelona make a dazzling backdrop that will last long in your memory, like the tiny lights that stretch far across and beyond the city's horizon.

PHOTOGRAPHS COURTESY OF HOTEL CONDES DE BARCELONA.

FACTS

ROOMS	240
FOOD	Lasarte: Mediterranean
DRINK	pool bar • piano bar
FEATURES	2 pools • rooftop terrace • sauna • fitness centre
BUSINESS	conference centre
NEARBY	La Pedrera • Las Rambla • Eixample district
CONTACT	Passeig de Gràcia 73–75, 08008 Barcelona • telephone: +34.93.445 3222 • facsimile: +34.93.445 3223 • email: info@condesdebarcelona.com • website: www.condesdebarcelona.com

Hotel Cram

Appropriately—and indeed, prominently—nestled among the fascinating, eclectic mix of late-19th- and early-20th-century buildings in Barcelona's El Ensanche district, Hotel Cram is located in a pair of magnificent, renovated mansions dating back to 1892. The central feature is a sensational, impressive circular patio—the latest in design by Josep Riu, Paco de Paz and Beatriu Cosials of avant-garde GCA Architects, who have been instrumental in redefining luxury living in Spain.

The interior is a vivid contrast to the ostentatious frontage, made up of a mass of polished wooden floors, glass walls and steel structures all sharply defined against a stark white background. Meticulously designed right down to the elegant chandeliers, each guestroom has been carefully considered, and striking colours—inspired by Tibetan monk's robes—are strewn across the hotel in the way of paintings, furniture and accessories. Rooms are beautiful and simple, with large windows

In contrast, the bar and restaurant are dark, sexy and sultry. Luxurious suede sofas are scattered with silk and velvet cushions in rich shades of orange and brown, creating sumptuous textures in the dim light. Along the shadowed wall a gleaming red glass bar glows, ready to serve an impressive range of wine and cocktails. The restaurant next door is equally sensual with its soft lighting and dark features. Founded in 1869 and proudly donning a Michelin star since 1993, Gaig is renowned in Barcelona for its extraordinary

Catalonian fare, which includes fresh catches from the marketplace and a highly imaginative menu fusing traditional and modern.

and mirrors adding light and space. Set in a dominant theme of startling white, standard rooms may be modest in size but sport quirky and ingenious details. In ultimate studio style, a lavish bath runs alongside the bed, allowing you to enjoy a bath while watching television from the super-screen hanging from the ceiling. Large suites even include separate lounge areas with vibrant retro-style seating.

Located in the heart of Barcelona, this unique hotel is only minutes away from Paseo de Gràcia, Rambla de Catalunya and Plaza de Catalunya. Close to the historic centre and business district, smack in the middle of luxury shops and street-side cafés, and boasting a rooftop terrace and pool, Hotel Cram makes for a stylish oasis and a comfortable escape from the bustling streets below.

FACTS		
ROOMS	67	
FOOD	Gaig: Catalonian	
DRINK	Mareva	
FEATURES	rooftop terrace and pool • exhibition room	
NEARBY	Paseo de Gràcia • Rambla de Catalunya and Plaza de Catalunya	
CONTACT	Aribau 54, 08011 Barcelona • telephone: +34.93.216 7700 • facsimile: +34.93.216 7700 • email: info@hotelcram.com • website: www.hotelcram.com	

PHOTOGRAPHS COURTESY OF MARKOPA STUDIO.

Estela Barcelona Hotel del Arte

With true fiesta spirit, the small, charming town of Sitges, a former fishing village some 40 km (25 miles) southwest of Barcelona, is undoubtedly the party-town of Catalonia. Barcelonans pour in during the weekends, attracted by the string of sandy beaches and lively nightlife. For centuries artists have been drawn here, finding idyll and inspiration in the mountainous backdrop and picturesque houses lining the maze of narrow lanes that today are filled with numerous art galleries, shops, restaurants and bars.

Sharing the town's delightful vibrancy is the eccentric Hotel del Arte. The reception is ablaze with a bold and gorgeous ensemble of colours, textures, paintings, sculptures and murals. Drab it certainly is not—free artistic licence is given to the many artists who have

THIS PAGE (FROM TOP): Hotel del Arte's deceptively simple façade hides a fantastical interior which will appeal to the idiosyncratic; not one area has been left untouched in the name of Art; the guestrooms are decked in luxurious furnishings and have a funky Pop Art feel to them.

OPPOSITE: The enveloping mood of artistic imagination within the hotel is made complete by awe-inspiring vistas of the sea.

...a bold, gorgeous ensemble of colours, textures, paintings, sculptures and murals.

contributed to its fantastically unique, eclectic and brilliant atmosphere. The artistic vision began in 1993 when painter Antoni Xaus, while staying in Room 105, decided to use its walls, ceiling, doors, rugs, sheets—and even the towels—as his canvas. The hotel manager was so inspired by Xaus's creative motivation that he granted opportunities for other artists, including Josep Ma Subirachs, Josep Puigmarti, Quim Hereu, Joan Iriarfe and Marc Villalonga to explore similar revelations of the imagination. Today the Hotel del Arte is home to nine such art rooms, of which every possible surface has been affected with diverse artistic impression. Careful and innovative consideration has also been paid to overall comfort, and all rooms combine the spectacular, unconventional décor with modern technology and sumptuous en-suite bathrooms. Private sun terraces opening out over a magnificent sea view offer an equally captivating and unforgettable picture.

Painting studios and exhibition galleries encourage artists to continue visiting the hotel and are open for guests to experiment with their own creative talents. Among its regular services the dedicated hotel also offers a delightful myriad of unusual entertainment from flamenco to astonishing magic shows. Iris restaurant doubles as an art gallery with works by the likes of Tàpies, Miró and Dalí hanging on the walls. Iris offers inventive dishes unlikely to be found elsewhere in the old town, such as fillet of tunny fish served with prawns and sweet port sauce, partridge cooked with artichokes and green asparagus and roasted deer with bilberry sauce.

The whimsical world of Hotel del Arte spills into its gardens, where two beckoning pools are hemmed by sculptures. Even the car park has been converted into a stunning exhibition of murals depicting prototype cars.

FACTS

ROOMS	65
FOOD	Iris: Mediterranean
DRINK	Iris
FEATURES	2 pools • garden • painting and exhibition studios
BUSINESS	modular meeting rooms
NEARBY	beach • Sitges • Barcelona
CONTACT	Av. Port d'Aiguadolç 8, 08870 Sitges, Barcelona • telephone: +34.93.811 4545 • facsimile: +34.93.811 4546 • email: info@hotelestela.com • website: www.hotelestela.com

PHOTOGRAPHS COURTESY OF ESTELA BARCELONA HOTEL DEL ARTE.

Hotel Gran Derby

One of the most renowned and attractive aspects of any stay in a Derby hotel is the comfortable modern décor that gives guests the sensation of being at home rather than in a hotel. Every room features cosy leather sofas, rich wood panelling, colourful carpets and numerous thoughtful details that combine to make your visit—business or pleasure—all the more congenial and memorable. The objective of the group—which is, according to guest surveys, often accomplished—is for visitors to enjoy their stay so much that they will actually miss the hotel when they return home. The Gran Derby is one of the finest examples of this very successful corporate philosophy that has won fantastic reviews from tourists and business travellers alike. Like every hotel in the chain it has a distinct personality and with only 41 rooms, the Gran Derby exemplifies the charm and personal service of a boutique hotel but, at the same time, comes replete with all the

THIS PAGE (FROM TOP): Cosy, rustic furniture and subtle hues create a warm, home-like ambience much appreciated by guests; quirky details dot the rooms; each room is decorated with a comfortable blend of assorted materials and stylish furnishings.

OPPOSITE: The pool, surrounded by an interior garden, canopies and sunloungers, makes a cool spot for a quick refresher after meetings or exploring the city.

facilities of a larger establishment, not to mention a superb location in the heart of Barcelona's dynamic financial district.

One of the unique features of the Gran Derby is its 12 duplex suites, each boasting two distinct areas on separate levels which are ideal for families or extended stays. The clever flexibility of the design also allows guests to work comfortably or even hold a meeting in one area while keeping the other completely private. Each duplex suite offers views over the interior garden and pool, an oasis of calm amid the bustle of the city. The 29 junior suites maintain the advantage of a separate lounge area and come complete with a large flat-screen television and plenty of room to spread out and relax after a long day of visiting clients or taking in the sights. Every room is soundproofed and each of them provides a comprehensive array of amenities which include a safe, minibar, CD player, Wi-Fi access, high-speed Internet lines and satellite television.

The Times is a cosy, delightful coffee shop which offers breakfast at a convenient early opening time as well as light meals throughout the day. Epsom Scotch-Bar is the ideal place to meet friends for a cocktail before or after dinner and many guests take advantage of the separate salon in every room, ordering from the room service menu for the utmost in comfort, convenience and relaxation. The swimming pool and solarium are very popular in the summer months, and offer the best outdoor spaces in the property for refreshing drinks. Animal lovers will be keen to know that the Gran Derby is one of the few hotels around that invites guests to come accompanied by their dogs. Meeting rooms of various capacities complete the list of services that make the Gran Derby a winning choice for business travellers and pleasure seekers in Barcelona.

FACTS

ROOMS	29 junior suites • 12 duplex suites
FOOD	Epsom • The Times: breakfast and light meals
DRINK	Epsom Scotch-Bar
FEATURES	pool • solarium
BUSINESS	meeting rooms
NEARBY	shopping • bars • restaurants
CONTACT	Loreto 28, 08029 Barcelona • telephone: +34.93.445 2544 • facsimile: +34.93.419 6820 • email: granderby@derbyhotels.com • website: www.derbyhotels.com

PHOTOGRAPHS COURTESY OF DERBY HOTELS COLLECTION.

Gran Hotel Balneario Blancafort

For centuries, the town of La Garriga has been renowned for its sulphate-rich thermal baths. Everyone from royalty and the elite of Catalan society, to artists and modern-day celebrities, have flocked to this National Heritage Site to soak in its waters, making it an important destination for both tourists and natives alike. Situated 25 minutes away from Barcelona, one of La Garriga's main thermal centres is the Balneario Blancafort, which opened its doors in 1840. In 2002, president of Grupo VMP, Don Vincente Munoz Pomer, began an initiative to restore the property to its former glory. In 2005, Gran Hotel Balneario Blancafort was born, setting a new benchmark for thermal resorts, not only in Spain, but in all of Europe.

The Balneario Blancafort encompasses seven three-storey buildings, which house 156 beautifully appointed guestrooms. Clad in muted shades of blue and cream, the rooms boast airy balconies or terraces, some with private gardens and solariums, as well as private jacuzzis. Exquisite as these may be, these rooms are the plush support beams of the hotel's foundation—its health and beauty services.

At the hotel's 2,980 sq-m (32,000 sq-ft) Thermal Centre, guests can soak happily in the region's healing waters in treatments unique to Spain. They can also sample the Vichy showers and Asian treatments as well as a Roman thermal space, where guests may like to experience a caldarium (hot bath),

frigidarium (cold bath) and tepidarium (warm bath) in addition to other Roman treatments. 12 private rooms feature hydrotherapy tubs, a Dream Shower, ice treatments, Turkish baths and even a pediluvio (a hot footbath).

To complement this, the hotel also boasts a state-of-the-art Medical Centre managed by the best specialists in the medical aesthetics, dietetic and health industries.

Within the Medical Centre is a facility dedicated to the specialization of anti-ageing, which provides advanced anti-wrinkle treatments, facial remodelling and reconstruction, and chemical peels to fight pigmentation, scars and acne. Guests recovering from surgical procedures take advantage of the centre's safe and careful post-op care, while those seeking to quit their smoking habit or fight weight problems can put themselves in the hands of experts who will help see them through the process of achieving personal success. Naturally, an aesthetical centre is also on hand with a gym, beauty treatments, and hair-salon services, to show off the results gained at Balneario Blancafort to good effect.

Yet another attraction at Balneario Blancafort is its treasure trove of artwork by both Spanish and international artists.

THIS PAGE: Rooms are soothing with lavender and cream hues.

OPPOSITE (FROM TOP): One of Europe's most illustrious thermal resorts, Balneario Blancafort offers a spectacular range of specialist baths and treatments; they have looked after the needs of everyone, from royals and high society to stars and artists.

THIS PAGE (FROM TOP): *Lounge with cocktails and drinks at the bar; there are three restaurants serving various gourmet cuisines; languish in four exquisite indoor pools and two outdoors.*
OPPOSITE: *The refined décor reflects its founder's love for art, which bore the creation of Raspall Gallery for emerging artists.*

Carrying his passion for art and sculpture through to the hotel, Don Vincente Munoz Pomer created the Raspall Gallery, devoted to promoting the works of new artists. This in turn spurred him to create the Vicente Munoz Pomer Foundation, which complements the hotel while contributing to La Garriga's reputation as a hotbed for the arts, music and literature in Catalonia.

Indeed, a stroll around the centre of La Garriga's Raspall block will unveil a bevy of gorgeous Modernist holiday homes built by its namesake, Modernist architect Manuel Joaquim Raspall. Balneario Blancafort's staff can arrange guided Modernism tours around the area, as well as tours to nearby locations like Sitges, Terrassa, Maresme and Alt Berqueda, just to name a few.

The region's mild climate and rich natural surroundings also make for excellent conditions for the various activities that the hotel can help plan. Adrenaline junkies can visit the Circuit de Catalunya (Montmeló), located just 10 km (6 miles) from Balneario Blancafort. It is one of the world's most modern tracks and offers guests the chance to become motor-sports stars for a day with quad races, 4-by-4 circuits and other similar activities. Or get on a helicopter for a spectacular flight over the Pyrenees, the

Cadi range, Medes islands and the Olot volcanoes. Otherwise, spend the morning in a bright hot-air balloon floating 1,000 m (3,280 ft) high up in the sky with just a wicker basket between you and the heart-stopping views of the big beyond.

Golfers are spoiled for choice with a few excellent golf courses just a quick drive away. The picturesque Muntanya Golf Club is found on the northwest slope of Montseny Natural Park and is a mere 17 km (10½ miles) from Balneario Blancafort. The 12-hole, par 72 International Golf Course, Caldes, is just 12 km (7½ miles) away from La Garriga, boasting some of the best golfing conditions.

Alternatively, guests can choose simply to laze and lounge in the grand, resplendent ambience of the hotel and enjoy its six indoor and outdoor thermal pools, exquisite gourmet cuisine and impeccable service. Gran Hotel Balneario Blancafort lives by its philosophy to please the needs of each guest and honour them with the utmost personalized attention possible. With dedication like that, it's little wonder at all that the hotel is considered one of most special and impressive in the region.

FACTS		
ROOMS	28 Suites • 128 Deluxe Rooms
FOOD	Asian • gourmet Mediterranean • dietetic/Italian • bars • tisanerie
FEATURES	thermal centre • medical centre • 2 outdoor pools • 4 indoor thermal pools • esthetical centre • library • boutique • Raspall Gallery
BUSINESS	wireless Internet access • 1 auditorium (88 pax) • 1 panelled conference room • 1 break-up room • 1 exposition room (2 storeys) • team-building activities
NEARBY	golf • horse-riding • Circuit de Catalunya • Roca Village outlet shopping • Modernism excursion • helicopter rides • hot-air balloon trips • Barcelona
CONTACT	Mina, 7, 08530 La Garriga, Barcelona • telephone: +34.93.860 5600 • facsimile: +34.93.861 2390 • email: info@balnearioblancafort.com • website: www.balnearioblancafort.com

PHOTOGRAPHS COURTESY OF BALNEARIO BLANCAFORT.

Hotel Granados 83

The combination of brick and iron changed the horizons of most European cities at the dawn of the 19th century and nowhere was the impact more profound than in Barcelona, where the architectural marriage of old and new became a powerful symbol of growing industrial might and confidence in the region. While it is the Modernista wonders built during the same period by Antoni Gaudí and his contemporaries that get most of the attention from camera-toting tourists today, all one has to do is look at the magnificent public markets such as the Born, built in 1876, or the iron detailing of Francia train station, to appreciate just how much these materials changed the city. Granados 83, the newest member of the Derby Hotels Collection, incorporates blasted brick walls, iron columns, modern industrial materials, zebrawood and marble in a bold innovative design that pays homage to the city's vibrant industrial past.

The experience begins as soon as you arrive, greeted by the striking glass and brick neoclassical façade, the central colonnaded space in the entrance hall and the welcoming openness of the reception area finished with red travertine marble. The adjacent cocktail bar and library are atmospheric, comfortable spaces to enjoy a drink with friends or read a book beneath walls displaying images of fashion shows from recent years.

The heart of the hotel is the luminous courtyard, with a slender central pillar covered by a ribbing of wavy steel and supported by six walkways that serve as landing platforms for the striking pair of panoramic elevators. The courtyard also connects the two wings of the hotel, and the public hallways are lined by solid slabs of marble, their sheer whiteness peaking out between zebrawood panels that cover the doors and ceilings.

There is a total of 85 guestrooms—which include unique split-level rooms, triple rooms and suites—some of which come with their

THIS PAGE (CLOCKWISE FROM TOP): View of Granados 83's striking yellow and ochre frontage; the pool is to be found under the hotel's glass ceiling next to a solarium, gym and restaurant; bathrooms are understated yet stylish in glass and pure white.

OPPOSITE: As expected of any Derby hotel, the guestrooms are exceptionally well-designed and contemporary spaces replete with the best of amenities.

own terraces and private pools. The thematic pattern is repeated in the interior of the rooms, which boast zebrawood flooring, brick walls and solid white marble bathrooms. Much of the furniture—from the desks to headboards of beds—is built of iron plating, and raw leather on the headboards, chairs and beds add an air of elegance and warmth. Despite the ultra-modern décor, the result is relaxing and every room features the fine amenities that travellers have come to expect in Derby hotels.

The hotel is handsomely crowned by a glass ceiling on the sixth level which houses a luxurious pool and beckoning solarium, as well as La Terraza bar. There is an exquisite restaurant offering a fine menu, memorably located in the semi-underground space alongside the property's charming Japanese garden. The outdoor courtyard allows guests the pleasure of dining on terraces surrounded by brick, stone and steel beams; harsh materials that meld surprisingly to create a more human space. A Derby space.

FACTS		
	ROOMS	standard • split-level rooms • triple rooms • suites
	FOOD	courtyard restaurant
	DRINK	La Terraza
	FEATURES	art collection • Japanese garden • pool • solarium
	BUSINESS	meeting rooms (capacity of 100)
	NEARBY	Paseo de Gràcia • shopping • bars • restaurants
	CONTACT	Enric Granados 83, 08008 Barcelona • telephone: +34.93.492 9670 • facsimile: +34.93.492 9690 • email: granados83@derbyhotels.com • website: www.derbyhotels.com

PHOTOGRAPHS COURTESY OF DERBY HOTELS COLLECTION.

Hotel La Malcontenta

In the 19th century there was said to be a man nearing two metres tall, conceived by a shepherd and a mermaid on a bright moonlit night. This man, Pere el Tigre—believed to be the founder of Cala Margarida—was married to the enigmatic Malcontenta. As a mother, Malcontenta was only gentle and loving, as a wife she was beautiful and intelligent; in life, however, she was never satisfied, comparing everything she saw and felt with the mystical luminescence of the moon.

Inheriting her legendary name, Hotel La Malcontenta is regarded as the house that finally bestowed pleasure and fulfilment to the disgruntled Malcontenta. And indeed it should have, for its beauty is spectacular. Surrounded

THIS PAGE (FROM TOP): Antique wooden furniture throughout the hotel is accentuated by clean, white upholstery; a wide stone archway in the guestrooms makes for a charming passage from living area to bath and bed after a fulfilling day of exploration.

OPPOSITE: View of a tiny back path leading up to the 19th-century country manor, quietly tucked in verdant, pastoral surroundings.

by green fields, pine forests, beaches and a magnificent coastline, Hotel La Malcontenta is a stunning, homely manor house offering the best in luxury and service.

The hotel is a 30-minute drive from the medieval town of Girona; only an hour from Barcelona, it couldn't be more of a contrast to the modern capital of Catalonia. Winding cobbled lanes twist among the foothills of the mountainous background where skiing, climbing and walking are popular pastimes during the winter when it's too cold to enjoy the fine, white beaches nearby. In the town itself, boutique shops, stylish modern bars and authentic tapas restaurants line the narrow streets. Surrounding the old town are nature reserves and fascinating architectural works—12th-century bath houses, the Monastery of St. Pere de Galligants and Girona Cathedral.

Inside, the hotel's décor is refined and understated. The guestrooms feature beautiful wood and glass panelling, antique furniture, huge windows and fireplaces. Each exquisite detail is accentuated by the fresh simplicity of white sofas and beds braced with cushions. The beams, chimney stacks and various other quirks of a 200-year-old building give each room distinguishing individual traits.

The hotel's restaurant offers elegant and spacious dining with al fresco seating in the summer. Nearby, other options include a vast variety of local and international cuisines in the area of Girona, as well as the famous El Bulli, which, with three Michelin stars, is often considered the best restaurant in the world.

With an idyllic tranquil swimming pool within its grounds and the convenience of a short walk to some of Catalonia's very best beaches, Hotel La Malcontenta combines a magical setting with luxurious accommodation to satisfy even the most disenchanted.

FACTS

ROOMS	terrace suites • grand suites • bungalows with garden • Majordoma Room
FOOD	Mediterranean
DRINK	wines • cocktails
FEATURES	pool
NEARBY	Castell beach • El Bulli • Girona Cathedral • Barcelona • boutique shops • bars • restaurant
CONTACT	Paratge Torre Mirona, Platja Castell 12, 17230 Palamós, Girona • telephone: +34.972.312 330 • facsimile: +34.972.312 326 • email: reservas@lamalcontentahotel.com • website: www.lamalcontentahotel.com

PHOTOGRAPHS COURTESY OF HOTEL LA MALCONTENTA.

La Pleta Hotel + Spa

This luxury resort hotel and spa stands at 1,700 m (5,600 ft) in Baqueira-Beret, Spain's most popular ski resort, in the heart of the Pyrenees. Set in the beautiful Aran Valley, La Pleta is surrounded by ancient stone houses and Romanesque churches making up tiny villages scattered across the mountains. Outside the laidback resort town—a winter playground for the country's rich, royal and famous—the way of life is decidedly more rural and farmers continue to rear sheep, cattle and horses in the Aiguestortes National Park.

The 'después de ski' is a Spanish fiesta in Baqueira-Beret, a hub of thriving pubs, restaurants and bars. Nearby the small villages of Salardú, Arties, Unha and Montgarri—to name a few—offer traditional Aran cuisine along with the more usual haunts of an après-ski crowd.

When you're not out partying with the Spanish elite, La Pleta Hotel & Spa offers splendid relaxation and tranquillity. The guestrooms have fantastic mountain views and with under-floor heating and plasma televisions, these are not the average alpine lodgings. Built into the eaves, with beamed ceilings and cosy goose feather and down duvets, the tone is distinctly homely and comforting. The presidential suite offers the ultimate in luxury. Spread over two floors, the first includes a sumptuous lounge area with dining table, sofas, flat-screen television and DVD player. A rustic stairwell leads up to a bedroom and bathroom; an enormous bed offers uninterrupted views of the mountain range through a glass wall and, next door, the jacuzzi shares the same stunning view. For the real romanticists, you can order breakfast in bed, rose-petal baths, fresh flowers and a candlelit dinner in the privacy of your suite.

THIS PAGE (CLOCKWISE FROM RIGHT): View of the old stone architecture; the bedrooms are cosy and offer the softest goose feather and down pillows and duvets; the resort's interiors have a warm, comfortable atmosphere that is reminiscent of home.

OPPOSITE: Guests of La Pleta have exclusive use of the tranquil and luxurious spa and its ski preparation treatments, not to mention its after-ski massages.

Two restaurants serve Catalonian and international dishes, and nature lovers can enjoy walks while gathering ingredients for their dinner, such as mushrooms, berries and snails. A wide verandah around the hotel offers an ideal setting for a warming mulled wine. As the cold draws in, you can move inside and snuggle up beside the open fire.

The definitive luxury of La Pleta is the spa itself. With the lavish indulgence of a ski preparation and energy massage before you take to the slopes, as well as a herbal bath, hydrating facial or an aromatherapy massage when you return at the end of the day, you'll find a renewed lease of life in place of aching muscles.

Throughout the various seasons La Pleta organizes a diverse range of activities and sports—from fishing to rafting, dog sleighs to helicopter rides and horse riding to quad-biking—ensuring even non-skiers will not be deprived of equal opportunities for the most exhilarating and memorable experiences in this breathtaking mountain range.

FACTS		
ROOMS	67	
FOOD	Del Gel al Foc • Petita Borda	
DRINK	café • verandah	
FEATURES	spa • gym • pool • hair salon • helicopter transportation • ski rental and shop	
NEARBY	ski resort of Baqueira-Beret	
CONTACT	Ctra. de Baqueira a Beret, cota 1700, E25598 Baqueira-Lleida • telephone: +34.973.645 550 • facsimile: +34.973.645 555 • email: lapleta@rafaelhoteles.com • website: www.lapleta.com	

PHOTOGRAPHS COURTESY OF LA PLETA HOTEL + SPA.

Neri Hotel + Restaurante

Barcelona. In this city whose landscape is prone to atypical forms and appearances lies an 18th-century palace which has been remarkably transformed into an arresting, idiosyncratic sensation—the Neri Hotel and Restaurant. Its immediate attractions include its enviable location which verges on the Gothic Quarter, its feng-shui-inspired roof terrace, and a fine restaurant nestled under ancient 12th-century stone arches. Each room boasts eye-catching artworks and luxuries such as plasma televisions and bamboo-lined balconies. The interior design is an eclectic juxtaposition of classic and modern; the rough-hewn quartzite of the bathrooms, for instance, features pure, minimalistic Jacobsen fittings, and the unfinished wood of the doors conceals futuristic sensor-based lock systems.

To dwell on the hotel's physical assets, however, is to neglect the myriad elements which conspire to produce its unparalleled multi-sensory experience. Not content with furnishing guests with lavish rooms and the pinnacle of personal service, this singular hotel seeks to enrapture all the individual senses. Visually, the spectacular tonal themes range across the entire colour spectrum, from striking reds, cool silvers and deep, bruised shades of the Renaissance, to rich seams of gold and verdant jungle green. The entrancing power of music is harnessed through a specially-commissioned soundtrack which infuses the spacious, luminous public areas with its subtle notes. Mingling into this magic is an aroma designed to engender an air of sensuality through the use of essential oils and candles. Touch and taste are also enthralled and sated by iridescent, textured fabrics incorporated throughout the interior, as well as the succulent and spicy gourmet delicacies on offer in Neri's fine restaurant.

Whether you choose to make the Neri Hotel and Restaurante a base from which to explore Barcelona, or if you prefer simply to relax in the hotel's coffered library and lounge with a book and drink, one thing is certain—all your five senses will treasure their sojourn in this intricately-crafted haven. For the Neri Hotel specializes in providing amazing experiences which cannot return to guests who, fortunately, can.

FACTS		
ROOMS	7 standard • 7 deluxe • 7 junior suites • La suite	
FOOD	Neri Restaurante	
DRINK	lounge • rooftop solarium terrrace • Sant Felip Neri terrace	
FEATURES	Internet access • lounge-library • private salon	
NEARBY	Gothic Quarter • Plaza de Sant Felip Neri	
CONTACT	C/Sant Sever 5, 08002 Barcelona • telephone: +34.93.304 0655 • facsimile: +34.93.304 0337 • email: info@hotelneri.com • website: www.hotelneri.com	

PHOTOGRAPHS COURTESY OF HABITAT HOTELS.

NM Suites

In the centre of Costa Brava's rugged rocky 200-km (125-mile) coastline lies the spirited Platja d'Aro, a vivacious stretch of exquisite restaurants and bars and exclusive designer boutiques spilling out onto a long, beautiful sandy beach. Cosmopolitan with excellent service and infrastructure yet offering plenty of idyllic spots with its endless enticing coves and beaches, it is indeed an ever-buzzing hub for local weekenders and foreign visitors.

For a dose of culture, the surrounding area is riddled with historic towns. In nearby Sant Feliu de Guixols you can visit the ruins of the 10th-century Benedictine monastery. Along the coast is the medieval village of Palamós with its quaint 13th-century harbour and beautiful old quarter. Inland, Girona is nestled in the Ter Valley where, among the winding cobbled lanes, you'll find Europe's largest gothic cathedral.

Set away from the busy village of Platja d'Aro the NM Suites have their own sense of calm, surrounded by pine trees and a 100-m (330-ft) beach in front. The modern building blends in well as part of the scenery with its interesting use of metal, concrete and glass.

THIS PAGE (FROM TOP): Like its home city of Platja d'Aro, NM Suites' friendly, inviting cosmopolitan atmosphere makes its popularity; the hotel's contemporary design and architecture reflect a culture of modern and vivacious nature.

OPPOSITE (FROM LEFT): SaCova Restaurant's offerings include innovative Mediterranean fare and a signature menu for foie gras in casual modern settings; the lounge offers drinks and a cosy place for a short rest.

...the spell of pleasant living...

Each of the exclusive 15 double rooms bear the traits of fashionable designer suites, each with a separate living room and bar, a private terrace, and a spacious bedroom and attached bathroom. The contemporary minimalist décor, wooden floors, sparse white walls and funky, colourful furniture reflect perfectly the lively and exuberant character of modern-day Platja d'Aro.

The complex is an ideal place to relax; close to the beach it has a saltwater pool within its gardens and a poolside bar. With four clubs close by, the hotel can organize a day on the golf course and other activities—sailing, horse riding, cycling and hiking.

SaCova Restaurant, within the hotel, is fresh and modern with a clean, airy feel and crisp white tablecloths. Using locally-grown produce and fresh sea catches, Chef Héctor Ortega serves creative Mediterranean dishes which vary ingeniously with the seasons and are accompanied by an equally exquisite list of wines of fine Spanish ancestry.

Indeed, after a full day of taking in Costa Brava's delights, NM Suites wraps you in the spell of pleasant living with luxury relaxation, leaving little more you can ask for.

FACTS

ROOMS	15
FOOD	SaCova: Mediterranean
DRINK	Pool Bar
FEATURES	pool
NEARBY	beach • water sports • golf • horse riding • Girona • Medes islands • Palamós
CONTACT	Avinguda Onze de Setembre 70, 17250 Platja d'Aro, Baix Empordà • telephone: +34.972.825 770 • facsimile: +34.972.826 502 • email: nm-suites@nm-suites.com • website: www.nm-suites.com

PHOTOGRAPHS COURTESY OF NM SUITES.

Hotel Omm

THIS PAGE: *Guestrooms are stylishly furnished and the interior spaces designed and conceptualized in the vogue minimalist fashion of the hotel's overall architecture.*

OPPOSITE (FROM TOP): *The polished open fireplace in the lobby; Spaciomm—the hotel's health centre—is equipped with a spa, pool, hair salon and fitness area.*

Barcelona in 1990 had begun to reinvent itself. By 1992 it had transformed into the host of the Summer Olympics and, in the process, consolidated its reputation as a vital centre of avant-garde design and creativity. One of the trendiest restaurants in town was Mordisco, an innovative concept that captured the loyal tastebuds of the famous and the burgeoning artistic community. Its success soon became the foundation for a powerhouse restaurant group that has since churned out one winning model after another; and it came as little—if no—surprise when they eventually decided to apply their alchemy to a hotel venture.

Tibetan Buddhists believe repeating the mantra 'omm' will eventually lead to spiritual fulfilment and illumination. Perfecting the skill of recitation often takes years of practice, and guidance of a guru is needed to be able to pronounce it properly. Similarly, the mantra of the Tragaluz Group is 'design with soul' and the award-winning Hotel Omm is the culmination of years of getting it right.

You notice the difference as soon as you arrive—the dramatic façade by architect Juli Capella is punctuated by curved balconies that look like they have been peeled straight out of stone, and the entrance opens into a spacious interior almost free of partitions, columns, or other obstacles. The reception is set discreetly to the right so that patrons of the bar and restaurants have unfettered access to

the public areas. Large windows run along the entire wide front of the hotel, providing luminosity and a sense of reaching out into the city outside. Beckoning armchairs and sofas fill the lobby area, grouped around an open, sophisticated gas fireplace. The lighting is sensual, dim and unobtrusive, creating an ambience so warm and welcoming that at almost any hour of the day, the bar area—and this is the place to be seen or to rub elbows with actors or superstar soccer players—is packed with buzzing guests and activity.

A legion of waiting staff clad in black designer uniforms serves the crowd efficiently from the stylish bar, aptly named Moovida ('bar scene' in Spanish). It offers a light menu with extended serving hours, and a long metal table divides the area from the formal dining room that is liable to induce tears of nostalgia from friends of the original Mordisco.

THIS PAGE (FROM TOP): Moo's unique dining concept pairs tailor-made courses with the perfect wines; the lounge area is the place to brush shoulders with celebrities.

OPPOSITE (FROM LEFT): The shadowy corridors heighten the impact of entering the white guestrooms with their tall glass windows; view from the rooftop terrace.

Moo Restaurant extends all the way to the back, again without columns or divisions to obstruct the view. Large skylights and a garden of shiny metallic flowers in a sunken patio is infused with natural light during the day. Each table is artistically decorated with an original sculpture and set with unique plates designed by famous artists and personalities.

The fine cuisine—which has earned an enviable Michelin star—rests in the capable hands of Chef Joan Roca, whose well-known establishment, Celler de Can Roca in Girona, is a strong running candidate for a third star.

He has put together an innovative system of half portions that allows diners to create their own menu and sample a greater variety of dishes. Many elect to have each plate served with a different wine, meticulously selected to produce the perfect gastronomic combination. Few can resist the original desserts created with natural ingredients similar in composition to those of famous perfumes such as *Eternity* by Calvin Klein and Thierry Mugler's *Angel*.

Guestrooms are accessible by a private card-controlled elevator next to the long red reception desk. The corridors on all six levels

seem startlingly dark when you experience them for the first time; the floors and walls are lined with a soft black rubber coating that effectively muffles all sound and two strips of fluorescent lighting on the floor guide you to your room. Then the cardkey opens the door softly and your vision is filled immediately with dramatic light streaming through windows from floor to ceiling. The contrast is remarkable. The décor consists of cream colours, pine floors and a large white panelled module that divides the bedroom from the bathroom and separate toilet area but which doesn't touch the white ceiling. The result—a sense of spaciousness and depth.

The module opens to provide ample closets, space for a safe and minibar, also acting as a support for the plasma television. There are no ceiling fixtures to break the clean lines, and an electronic panel allows the guest to select the perfect lighting for every moment.

A charming terrace on the seventh level offers an outdoor pool, excellent bar service and dreamy vistas of La Pedrera. Recently, the hotel's premises expanded, locating its new swanky extension in an adjoining building on the trendy Paseo de Gràcia. The addition incorporates a 400-sq-m (4,305-sq-ft) health centre, Spaciomm, which offers a spa, pool, hair salon and gym; it also boasts 32 new suites and two shops, Corium and Jofre.

Like the horse in the Wizard of Oz, this is a hotel of a different colour and it comes as no surprise at all that it won the 2005 *Travel + Leisure Award* for Best Hotel with 75 rooms or less. Without a doubt, Hotel Omm is the epitome of modern design at the service of the guest; a winning concept.

FACTS	
ROOMS	58 double • 16 superior • 17 suites
FOOD	Moo: avant-garde • Moovida: healthy
DRINK	modern bar • rooftop terrace
FEATURES	spa • Omm Session club
BUSINESS	conference facilities
NEARBY	La Pedrera • Paseo de Gràcia • bars • restaurants
CONTACT	Rosselló 265, 08008 Barcelona • telephone: +34.934.454 000 • facsimile: +34.934.454 004 • email: reservas@hotelomm.es • website: www.hotelomm.es

PHOTOGRAPHS COURTESY OF HOTEL OMM.

Panticosa Resort

Since Roman times, people have been following the rugged valley of the Gállego river high into the Pyrenees in the ancient Kingdom of Aragón to take to the hot spring waters in a magical enclave that is known today as Panticosa. The curative properties of the thermal baths converted this privileged spot into one of the most fashionable spas in all of Europe during the late 19th century, frequented by many, from famous writers to royalty and wealthy industrialists. It wasn't an easy journey in those days and most visitors would opt for a prolonged stay during which the meditative treatments, assuasive settings, extraordinary natural beauty and invigorating mountain air became soothing balms for the stresses and ailments of urbanized life in a rapidly changing society. Fortunately, a modern road system has made the journey considerably less taxing for visitors today, and the impeccable vision and sensitivity of the reputable Nozar Group have ensured

that the charm and splendour of Panticosa Resort's halcyon days have been lovingly and tastefully maintained.

The flagship of this ambitious multiphase project—the largest integrated hospitality complex in Europe funded entirely by private investment—is undoubtedly the five-star deluxe Gran Hotel, which was first built in 1896 and reopened in June 2004 after a restoration by well-known Spanish architect, Rafael Moneo. The property has a total of 42 rooms which include 14 double rooms, 26 premium rooms and 2 junior suites. The main floor consists of the reception area, meeting rooms, a bar with an outdoor terrace, a billiard room, television lounge and library complete with a fireplace.

Virtually every guestroom offers stunning panoramic views of the mountain peaks—measuring more than 3,000 m (9,000 ft) in height—that surround the glacial plateau,

with a picturesque alpine lake that is home to the resort. The flooring of the rooms is inlaid with rich oak, while the walls, main doors and much of the furniture are cloaked in warm maple. The bathroom floors are decked in sensuous grey Macael marble and the walls are finished in polished white marble. The sensation is one of richness and luxury, complemented by pieces of vibrant contemporary art that add colour and energy. The amenities include high-speed Internet connection, flat-screen television, a

choice of divine pillows, exclusive bathroom accessories by Jo Malone of London, cosy bathrobes, slippers, a minibar and safe.

The Gran Hotel boasts its own thermal spa with a heated pool fully equipped with hydro-massage jets and a bubble bed, a sauna, a low-temperature pool, contrasting shower and comfortable poolside lounge chairs for relaxing while you sip on fresh natural juices and wait for your massage. Guests can select from a tantalizing menu of pampering treatments with everything from

full-body massage to the popular chocolate wrap. Designed especially for women are more intensive programmes which include such temptations as the 3-hour Universe of Calm or thoroughly luxurious 4-hour Dreamy Well-Being. The gentlemen have not been forgotten, with tailor-made programmes such as the tension-reducing Switch Off or 3-hour Intense Après-Ski for sporting types.

The Gran Hotel is linked by an elevated covered passageway to the elegant Casino, which first opened its doors in 1906, also restored by Rafael Moneo. The main floor features the original theatre which seats 190 and offers evenings of fine jazz and other musical and cultural events. There are also three meeting rooms with a capacity of 125

and a hair salon. The first floor houses both El Mirador restaurant with seating for 60, and a luminous sitting area with a splendid terrace for summer. The gaming hall, covered by an impressive oak dome, is located on the upper floor with its own bar and lounge replete with satellite television. Guests can try their luck at blackjack, American roulette, stud poker and a variety of slot machines, then head to El Casino restaurant offering a sumptuous dinner buffet with excellent fare in an informal setting.

With the resort located at more than 1,600 m (5,250 ft) above sea level, haute cuisine takes on a whole new meaning as the kitchen is piloted by high-flying Basque Chef Pedro Subijana, owner of acclaimed two-star Michelin restaurant Akeláre in San Sebastián.

Restaurante del Lago, attached to the main hotel, is the perfect platform for Subijana's virtuoso display of creativity, and a triumph of Moneo's architectural vision. The dining room is located in a pavilion wrapped in pine and covered by a wooden dome which floods the entire space with natural light. A terrace-like extension with floor-to-ceiling windows offers diners splendid views of the nearby lake and the mountains in the background. Subijana has a special sensitivity for seafood, and the menu offers some of the best fish recipes that you will ever sample; a miracle considering the logistics involved in transporting the day's catch up here. Not to be missed is the Gin and Tonic on a Plate.

El Mirador offers lighter fare for lunch or dinner, but with all of Subijana's originality and innovation still evident with every dish. The service in both dining rooms is superb, and enhanced by the natural friendliness of the many locals who form part of the highly professional team at the Panticosa Resort.

Every morning, guests look forward to being treated to a sumptuous breakfast buffet at El Mirador: a virtual cornucopia of tantalizing delights which include the most sensational fruit juices, local cheeses and cured meats as well a selection of fresh baked goods.

The hotel's literature includes the phrase 'touching the sky', which in Spanish can also be translated as 'touching heaven', and that is exactly what many guests will think they have found when they arrive at the Gran Hotel. At least at the Panticosa Resort, it is a sure bet.

FACTS		
ROOMS	14 double • 26 premium • 2 junior suites	
FOOD	Restaurante del Lago: haute cuisine • El Casino: dinner buffet • El Mirador: continental fusion and breakfast buffet	
DRINK	cafeteria • bar • terrace	
FEATURES	thermal spa • casino • theatre • fine art	
NEARBY	alpine skiing • cross-country skiing • ski mountaineering • snowshoeing • dog-sledding • hiking • mountain-biking • whitewater rafting • winery tours	
CONTACT	Ctra. del Balneario, km 10, 22650 Panticosa, Huesca • telephone: +34.974.487 161 • facsimile: +34.974.487 137 • email: reservas@panticosa.com • website: www.panticosa.com	

PHOTOGRAPHS COURTESY OF PANTICOSA RESORT.

Hotel Pulitzer

Capturing the exuberance of Barcelona in words is an impossible task. Its sights and sounds must be experienced first-hand, for this symphony of a city conceals a myriad of personalities which appear in different guises to every individual who seeks to know her.

At the centre of this unequivocally Mediterranean city is the Plaza de Catalunya. Simmering beneath its flagstones are great tales of maritime history, tremendous economic progress and the triumphs of Catalonian Modernisme. On ground level, this regional capital offers unrivalled cultural treasures— Gaudí's surreal imagination translates into breathtaking structural reality in the Gothic Quarter, and the Miró, Picasso and National Art Museums vie for attention. Then there are the world-renowned streets of La Rambla, teeming with markets, traditional eateries and boutiques to enthral the most ardent shopper.

Any introduction to the stylish Pulitzer must mention its superb location, within just metres of these central districts. Like its distinguished namesake prize, the boutique hotel excels consummately in all measurable criteria. The interior design is flawless, with the symmetry of lamps and frames counterbalancing the swirling geometry of plush rugs, staggering avant-garde artistry and embellishment with smooth marble, jet, onyx and ceramics.

View the city's fantastical skyline from the lofty heights of the Pulitzer's rooftop bar; descend to the library to devour the works of Gothic novelists and Catalonian historians. For business there is an intelligent meeting room replete with state-of-the-art technology. And if in the mood for a workout, a range of free gym facilities is available at an external fitness centre in adjacent Holmes Place.

THIS PAGE (CLOCKWISE FROM LEFT): The bar flaunts arresting black lines, prevalent white and red cabinets; ablaze with vermillion canopies, the rooftop terrace makes a cool retreat for drinks and city views; the Pulitzer's elegant façade.

OPPOSITE: Guestrooms are urbane and refined with tasteful modern art pieces, subtle tonal contrasts and fine white shades which filter light and partition living spaces.

Fine dining is an elegant affair at the sleek Visit restaurant, where the purity and simplicity of design allow the Spanish tapas and international delicacies to take centre stage with an accompanying menu of sublime wines. For a more casual setting, the cocktail bar offers an intimate area to relax with drinks.

Private balconies and tall, large windows admit abundant light into the Pulitzer's rooms, which are decorated with a contemporary and confident, monochromatic edge. Crisp white bedlinen offsets angular, black leather armchairs, with gossamer-thin drapes, natural light and works of modern art creating an audible contrast between these tonal extremes. The bathrooms are lavishly hewn from granite, marble and slate, and combine functionality with personalized luxuries.

As the sunset ushers in an evening of entertainment, take a moment to lounge on the bar's immaculate white leather sofas and savour a cocktail in pure Pulitzer fashion before heading out to explore the city.

PHOTOGRAPHS COURTESY OF GR HOTELES.

FACTS

ROOMS	91 standard • 5 superior
FOOD	Visit: international/Spanish
DRINK	cocktail bar
FEATURES	library • terrace • solarium • free external fitness centre
BUSINESS	intelligent meeting room • Internet access
NEARBY	La Rambla • Plaza de Catalunya
CONTACT	Bergara 8, Barcelona 08002 • telephone: +34.93.481 6767 • facsimile: +34.934 816 464 • email: info@hotelpulitzer.es • website: www.hotelpulitzer.es

Hotel RA Beach Thalasso-Spa

In 1929, King Alfonso XIII officially opened the sanatorium at El Vendrell, run by the brothers of San Juan de Dios. For more than 40 years it was a symbol of compassion, treating children with respiratory diseases until it was sold in the 1970s. It is apt today that both the building and its original vocation of care and treatment have been lovingly restored as part of the luxurious Hotel RA Beach Thalasso-Spa. The resort overlooks the beach of Sant Salvador on the famous Costa Dorada—between Sitges and Tarragona— and is only 30 minutes by car or train from Barcelona Airport. Surrounded by pristine natural beauty, it enjoys a favourable micro-climate with moderate temperatures all year round. The former hospital—incorporated into a stunning architectural development that boasts nearly 300 m (984 ft) of façade on the beach—offers 143 rooms with balconies and sea views. The exquisite contemporary décor combines luxury, comfort and all the amenities you would expect in a five-star establishment.

Hotel RA has one prime objective: to pamper and care for the body. RA Wellness Centre—with 7,000 sq-m (75,350 sq-ft) of modern installations—is wholly dedicated to achieving that goal. A key element is the high concentration of iodine in the seawater due to an bank of algae not too far away. The water is pumped into special tanks and gently heated to 34°C (93°F) in order to conserve its beneficial properties. The centre's Sea Area features a large saltwater pool with lumbar jets, microbubbles, jacuzzi, sauna, steam bath as well as a large glassed solarium. The Thalassotherapy Centre provides treatment with seawater and other marine products, jet showers, Vichy showers, mud and algae therapies as well as hydro-massages. In the dry area, guests will find a full complement of treatments from massages and aromatherapy to reflexotherapy and shiatsu. La Prairie's renowned spa product range offers sensual indulgences for the face and body and there are also fitness, aesthetic and medical centres staffed by experienced professionals. A Tissanarie serves teas and infusions while guests contemplate the zen garden waterfall.

Neit Gastronomic offers signature cuisine by Chef Xavier Pellicer in a cozy and intimate space. A lighter menu with tapas and a great selection of wines is available at La Vinya del Penedès and the Pool Grill serves burgers and barbeque dishes in the summer. Blau Marí Buffet is famous for its impressive breakfast buffet which is included in the room price, and there is also a café, Salon de Mar, which sports large comfortable armchairs and sofas accompanied by sea views and a terrace. The sanatorium's former chapel, transformed into a piano bar, is the perfect place to enjoy a cocktail before dinner.

At Hotel RA Beach Thalossa-Spa, guests are wrapped in absolute luxury and delight, impeccably pampered and expertly cared for from the moment they arrive.

PHOTOGRAPHS COURTESY OF HOTEL RA BEACH THALASSO-SPA.

FACTS		
ROOMS	double • suites • duplex junior suites • 1 presidential suite	
FOOD	Neit Gastronomic: signature cuisine • La Vinya del Penedès: tapas • Pool Grill: barbeque • Salon de Mar: café • Blau Marí Buffet: buffet	
DRINK	Piano Bar • Beach Club	
FEATURES	RA Wellness • Medical Centre • Thalassotherapy • Beauty and Aesthetics Centre • 63 treatment cabins (2 exclusive for La Prairie) • Fitness Area • nautical activities	
NEARBY	Pau Casals Museum • Poblet and Santes Creus monasteries • Roman ruins • Sitges • Port Aventura theme park • Barcelona • winery tours • sailing • golf • tennis	
CONTACT	Avinguda Sanatori, 1, 43880 El Vendrell, Tarragona • telephone: 34.977.694 200 • facsimile: +34.977.694 302 • email: hotelra@grupoamrey.com • website: www.hotelra.com	

Hotel Trias

Contrary to an unjustly tainted image as a common and prosaic tourist destination that came about some years ago, Costa Brava's coastline encompasses dramatic rocky cliffs tumbling into gorgeous clear waters, isolated coves with alluring sandy beaches, verdant sub-tropical landscapes and a fascinating 200-km (120-mile) stretch of old picturesque towns. One such historic town is Palamós, a charming and spirited 13th-century fishing port that lies just one hour north of the Catalonian capital of Barcelona.

Here you can lose hours wandering the narrow lanes and the bustling working port hemmed in by boisterous local restaurants serving the day's catch. Just a few minutes walk from the town's enchanting old quarter, the grand Hotel Trias occupies a prominent seafront position, looking directly out across the crystal blue bay of Palamós and the fine sandy beach of Platja Gran.

Opened in 1900, Hotel Trias defies its age. An immaculate refurbishment in 2005 has rendered the interior design wonderfully clean and modern. The original arches and floor-to-ceiling windows remain in place, but new rough, sanded wooden floors, stark contemporary furniture and eclectic sculptures scattered around the hotel all work to create a superlative in design sophistication that is synchronous with the present day.

The reception and lobby are dominated by svelte black and white stripes which mark billowing muslin curtains, wooden beds, and even rugs and cushions. The rooms are bright and airy with white walls, curtains, furniture and bed linen. With many offering terraces

THIS PAGE (CLOCKWISE FROM LEFT): The sun terrace and pool are the perfect spots for a cool drink; rooms sport thin muslin curtain strips for a contemporary edge and uniquely framed beds create a 'reinvented poster bed' effect; Palamós is a quaint 13th-century fishing town well-visited for its working port and restaurants.

OPPOSITE: Floor-to-ceiling windows bathe the interior in light, giving it a light and fresh atmosphere.

looking out across the Mediterranean and all with luxurious bathrooms, their fresh and peaceful ambience has an instant calming effect. For an unforgettable night of absolute luxury, ask for Ava Gardner's suite or David Niven's room on the seventh floor.

Be it with a book, golf club or cocktail in hand, there are plenty of activities to pass the day. The beach is opposite and there are a pool and sun terrace within the property, not to mention a wide range of sports—including golf, sailing, hiking and horse riding—as well as the leisurely option of exploring the medieval villages nearby.

Serving exquisite Mediterranean and international cuisine, the hotel's restaurant is well-decorated and lovely with a simple, stylish interior and an outdoor terrace for the summer. Nearby within the town, a dazzling variety of smart international restaurants and vibrant local eateries alongside numerous bars and shops ensure the opportunity of a new experience every night.

PHOTOGRAPHS COURTESY OF HOTEL TRIAS.

FACTS		
ROOMS	83	
FOOD	Mediterranean	
DRINK	Ruark • pool bar	
FEATURES	pool • sun terrace • day-trips • Internet access • Wi-Fi access	
NEARBY	beaches • Dalí museum • Peratallada medieval village • La Bisbal ceramics • Girona • Barcelona	
CONTACT	Passeig del Mar s/n, 17230 Palamós, Girona • telephone: +34.972.601 800 • facsimile: +34.972.601 819 • email: infotrias@hoteltrias.com • website: www.hoteltrias.com	

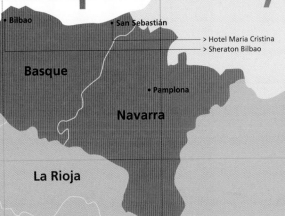

basquecountry+navarra

France

Bay of Biscay

sturias

Cantabria

• Bilbao   • San Sebastián

> Hotel Maria Cristina
> Sheraton Bilbao

Basque

• Pamplona

Navarra

La Rioja

Castilla y León

Catalonia

Aragón

Madrid

Balearic Sea

Castilla-La Mancha

Valencia

xtremadura

basque country

Tucked in a corner of the Bay of Biscay, from where it rolls inland
across pastoral hills and craggy peaks, is the Basque country, País
Vasco or, in the local lingo, Euskadi. It may look small on the map
but, proportionally, this region pulls its punches more than any other.
Economically, it has long been at the fore of Spain and in cuisine,
despite Catalonia knocking hard at the door, it is difficult to beat.
Proof of this—the region boasts the world's highest concentration of gourmet restaurants
per capita. And these talents are now being joined by an impelling third element—culture.

Look at the Spanish property price table and you will find San Sebastián (Donostia,
in Basque) at number one, Bilbao at number four and Vitoria, the Basque capital which
has tripled in population since the 1980s, at number five. The health of their economy is
clear. What is unfortunate is that the Basque image has been so coloured by the brutal
extremism of the ETA (an acronym meaning 'Euskadi' and 'freedom'), a movement that
developed under Franco's heavy-handed repression. Picasso's seminal work 'Guernica'
(1937) portrayed the obliteration of the small Basque town of Gernika. Not everyone
realizes that after the three-hour bombing raid by a German squadron on Franco's orders,
Bilbao and Durango became the next targets in a concerted nationalist attempt to
annihilate Basque wealth and industry. The Basques had reason to rebel.

blasts of independence

Although autonomy was granted by Adolfo Suárez's new democratic government in
1979, this was not deemed enough and, with an unrealistic aim of uniting with their
French Basque neighbours as an independent state, the ETA continued to make head-
line news. Its fatal bomb attacks and assassinations galvanized the rest of Spain into
massive demonstrations of outrage, while successive governments made sporadic arrests
and negotiations stopped and started. Today, at last, it seems the worst is over and signs
are that this thorn in Spain's side has been considerably blunted, if not quite removed.

*PAGE 102: Inside Frank O. Gehry's
extraordinary Guggenheim
Museum, which set the
standard for a new Bilbao.*

*THIS PAGE: The legendary and
spectacularly sited hermitage of
San Juan de Gaztelugatxe is
filled with votive offerings from
Biscay's sailors—its bell warns
of approaching storms.*

*OPPOSITE: The Bosque de Oma
near Gernika, where Basque
artist Agustín Ibarrola painted
pine-tree trunks with signs,
symbols and images to suggest
magical forest-dwellers.*

Putting aside this violent wing, the Basques are an individualistic and proud people, known for their business acumen which, historically, gave rise to a strong industrial base and a string of banks. Today that rather colourless identity is fading, replaced by a more creative one of refined cuisine and intelligent urban development. This is not forgetting Spain's foremost 20th-century sculptor, Eduardo Chillida (1924–2002), a native of San Sebastián. Yet nothing will change the introspective identity of the Basques, nor their incomprehensible language peppered with 'k's, 'z's and 'x's. Predating Indo-European languages, its only links are with Central Asian languages and the Berber language of North Africa's pre-Arab inhabitants. Studies in fields as diverse as blood-groups and morphology have eventually produced one common theory: the Basques have been in these valleys since the Stone Age and they could well be directly descended from Cro-Magnon man. It's true they are certainly different.

the basque soul

Pintxos (the Basque form of tapas) are the big year-round attraction in San Sebastián, a seductive resort and fishing port boasting the architectural style of its late-19th-century heyday, an Art Déco quarter (Gros) and a web of medieval streets offering wall-to-wall tapas bars. A hundred kilometres (62 miles) or so west along a coastline that alternates between windswept cliffs, small-scale resorts and pockets of light industry is the other urban face of the Basques, Bilbao. This former dark, hardworking industrial hub has been transformed, in less than a decade, into a leading cultural pole. The catalyst? Undoubtedly the incredible impact of the Guggenheim Museum.

Inland, the third city, Vitoria (or Gasteiz in Basque), home to the Basque parliament and an attractive medieval hilltop quarter, finds it difficult to shake off a sleepy provincial air. Pamplona, although officially part of Navarra, is equally Basque in character in the food stakes and language, and of course proud host to one of Spain's most high-profile annual events—the running of the bulls of San Fermín. Hemingway still has a lot to answer for. One aspect shared as much by the lush countryside as the towns is the persistent

sirimiri (drizzle) and rain that characterizes the climate. Most public venues in Bilbao incorporate umbrella stands with individual locks—a sign of the regularity of downpours. The only time you can be reasonably sure of clear skies and sunshine is during the summer months, from June to early September.

Anyone intent on penetrating the true Basque soul should head into the green valleys dotted with cows and caserios (stone farmhouses with steeply pitched roofs), monasteries and shrines. The small rural towns are where the traditions of dance, bizarre sports such as harriekta (stone-lifting) and pelota (a ball and bat game), costumed parades, as well as improvised poetry by bertsolaris, are strongest. The most spectacular route through the hills is the 'mountain motorway' which swings and dips from Navarra down to the Bay of Biscay. However, the hinterland further west is the real heartland.

Here you may come across the little-known Oñati, home to the Basque university of Sancti Spiritu (founded in 1540), besides other impressive historic sights. Up in the hills nearby, an unusual sanctuary dedicated to the local patron saint, Arantzazu, is a recent collaboration between local architects and sculptors Eduardo Chillida, Lucio Muñoz and Jorge Oteiza. The overall patron saint of the Basques is Ignatius de Loyola, founder of the Jesuit order, and his rural birthplace near Azpeitia has today become a burgeoning pilgrimage complex centred on the tower-house in which he was born in 1491.

bilbao

Few foreigners used to visit Bilbao (Bilbo, in Basque), although Shakespeare unconsciously alluded to it when writing about a bilbo, or a sharp knife, one of the spin-offs of its steel industry. Once the centre of Spain's prosperous shipbuilding and iron and steel industries, like Hamburg and Glasgow, Bilbao's fortunes plunged, and by the 1980s the city had reached a low ebb. The sea-change came in 1997 when Frank O. Gehry's architectural icon, the Guggenheim Museum, opened its doors. Since then, this sprawling city—home to half the population (1.5 million) of Euskadi—has experienced a cultural renaissance fuelled by a stream of visitors who flow through the striking airport—a Calatrava design.

Cutting-edge hotels, state-of-the-art transport, public sculptures and internationally-renowned architects (think the likes of Frank Gehry, Cesar Pelli, Santiago Calatrava, Arata Isozaki, Pedro Arrupe, Ricardo Legorreta, Sir Norman Foster and, still working on the drawing board, Zaha Hadid) have all been drawn into the dynamic Bilbao net. Like a chrysalis, the previously inward-looking Basque country seems to be breaking open to the world.

Abandoibarra, the riverside district dominated by the Guggenheim's curved titanium planes, continues to undergo massive redevelopment overseen by Pelli. Phoenix-like, this area has emerged from the greasy old shipyards to become Bilbao's cultural epicentre. A congress centre (the Euskalduna, its metallic façade the work of ex-shipbuilding welders), funky boutique hotels, the phenomenal Sheraton by Legorreta, Pelli's tower, Arrupe's foot-bridge and Calatrava's Zubi-Zuri bridge now join existing venerables like the Bellas Artes museum (recently extended to better accommodate its superb collection of treasures by Zurbarán, Ribera, El Greco, Gauguin and Chillida) and the lovely Iturrizar gardens. From this 21st-century skyline, Sir Norman Foster's gleaming metro whizzes silently to the beach and to the Old Town—the latter also served by a new riverside tramway.

Here, overlooked by hills, an atmospheric web of pedestrianized streets boasts an incredible architectural diversity, from the neoclassical Plaza Nueva (incidentally, also a great foodie destination) to a Gothic cathedral and a baroque stock exchange. Most backstreets harbour a tapas bar or two, while down by the river looms a massive food-market building and the Arriaga theatre, an 1890s classic.

This enclave is a complete contrast to its neighbour across the river, Bilbao's 'extension', where an elegant 19th-century grid of avenues all converge on the old Carlton Hotel. This is where Bilbao's best shopping is located, mostly concentrated along the Golden Mile of Gran Vía. Apart from international and Castillian signatures, homegrown Basque designers such as Angela Arregui, Inarkadia and Mercedes de Miguel have outlets here.

The city's future development is slated to appear west of here in an area named Zorrozaure. Zaha Hadid's master-plan envisages the construction of 5,000 new homes and a host of commercial facilities on an island in the river which is currently a decaying industrial peninsula. With completion estimated at ten years' time, it is proof that Bilbao's authorities are not resting on their laurels.

THIS PAGE (FROM TOP): Legorreta's new Sheraton Bilbao was inspired by the late Spanish sculptor Eduardo Chillida; Sir Norman Foster's metro integrates architectural and engineering features in a sleek and innovative form.

OPPOSITE (FROM TOP): Sculptural, reflective and mesmeric, the deconstructed lines of the Guggenheim Museum have turned Bilbao's fortunes; Martín Berasategui's restaurant at the Guggenheim.

seaside san sebastián

Over in San Sebastián, the change in mood is palpable. This far more outgoing town sweeps majestically around a hill-backed bay that was once only used by fishermen and navigators—the Basques have produced some great maritime explorers, from Sebastián Elcano to the dreaded Lope de Aguirre, made famous by Werner Herzog's film. From languid beaches to the September film festival and pintxos to txokos (gastronomic clubs), San Sebastián has a clearly self-indulgent bent.

The city initially developed under the mid-19th-century impetus of Queen Isabel II, who was advised by her doctor to spend her summers in this relatively cool, breezy climate. Her presence, and those of imitators, kick-started expansion and the modest town soon became a burgeoning, fashionable resort stretching round the Bahía de la Concha and eventually west along the Río Urumea.

At its centre, not far from the illustrious, historic Maria Cristina Hotel, rise the translucent geometric forms of the Kursaal, the award-winning congress hall by Rafael Moneo and host of the film festival since 1999. On the river's eastern side is the up-market residential area of Gros, its smart Art Déco buildings and some select pintxo bars. To the west unfurls the scenic horseshoe bay overlooked by the headland of Monte Urgull, where the atmospheric old quarter below opens onto the fishing harbour. These streets, also a bar-crawlers' paradise, harbour too the heavy baroque façade of Santa María and, in the neighbouring museum, a series of murals by Catalan artist José Maria Sert (1876–1945) depicting the province's history. There are few other monuments apart from a plethora of Chillida sculptures; his impressive museum and its 12-hectare (30-acre) sculpture garden are just outside town at Hernani. Compensation comes in the beautiful natural site and, above all, at the table.

kings of the kitchen

No other city in Spain, even France, offers such a Michelin-starred gastronomic galaxy, nor such a density of bar counters piled high with plates of mountainous pintxos. Though most pintxos look better than they taste (they are often on a great slab of bread), in some cases borders become distinctly blurred. This is when some select tapas bars emulate the inventive cuisine of top chefs; inversely, the dishes at these restaurants shrink in size and multiply in number. Yet the status of Juan Mari Arzak, or of Pedro Subijana or Martín Berasategui cannot be disputed: these are the three kings of Basque cuisine.

Berasategui, trained by Alain Ducasse in Monaco, likes to claim that 95 per cent of his raw ingredients are from his native region. True or not, his dishes are consistently exciting, innovative and visually stunning. They can be sampled not only at his welcoming, almost homely restaurant in Lasarte, just outside San Sebastián, but also in the Kursaal

THIS PAGE (FROM TOP): Santa María's baroque exuberance watches over the pintxos bars of San Sebastián in the shadow of Monte Urgull; celebrity chef extraordinaire Juan Mari Arzak.

OPPOSITE (CLOCKWISE FROM TOP): Award-winning superstar chef Martín Berasategui heads restaurants at the Kursaal, the Guggenheim as well as his own; Pedro Subijana's spectacular clifftop restaurant, Akeláre; a Berasategui composition.

and at Bilbao's Guggenheim where he collaborates with Joseán Martínez Alija, one of his disciples. You might sample squid soup with squid-ink ravioli, wild sea-bass with a seaweed cream and sliced raw ginger, or a dessert such as a rich pistachio cream with coffee glaze. Or, go for lamb chops with a 'cake' of foie gras, bacon and mushrooms in a sauce of walnuts and orange. The contrasts in flavour and texture seem infinite.

There is only one place to go for Pedro Subijana's concoctions, and that is Akeláre. His superbly designed restaurant sits dramatically on the clifftop of Igueldo, its sea views competing with exquisitely prepared seasonal dishes. Choose from oysters with artichokes and parsley juice, foie gras with walnut soup, sea-bass with goose barnacles, olive pearls and arrugala or Subijana's memorable milk-fed lamb cooked in two stages; first sous-vide (in a sealed bag) then roasted at a fierce temperature until the skin is crackling. The dessert could be a poetic-sounding 'sudden curdled milk with red fruits and petals' or nuts, lemon and cinnamon in crispy 'equilibrium'. Subijana himself, is a genial, moustachioed figure who toils with love over his creations.

This overwhelming passion for food is shared with the French Basques across the Pyrenees. It was they who accelerated the influence of Gallic nouvelle cuisine back in the 1970s which, in turn, led to the mushrooming of nueva cocina. The chef responsible for this was Juan Mari Arzak, the doyen of Basque cuisine who gained his coveted third Michelin star in 1989. Now in his 60s, he runs the elegant family restaurant with his daughter Elena, the fourth generation of this family to embrace the fine art of gastronomy. Constantly experimenting, they develop their creations from a flavour 'bank' containing over 1,600 products and ingredients. Here is a man so obsessed that he will even admit to being inspired by traffic lights—leading to a dessert in three colours. What appears on your plate could even be an 'ugly tortilla'—a kind of crêpe stuffed with chocolate and mango with a delicate strip of lettuce sauce on the side. Indescribable, but unforgettable.

txokos

Despite the accolades awarded to their chefs, the general population is slow to adapt to new trends—unlike their rivals, the Catalans. One reason for this conservatism could be the ongoing popularity of txokos, the basis of all Basque gastro-obsession. Developed in the late-19th century in San Sebastián, these male-only clubs worship food, but are also a retreat for henpecked husbands to play cards, chat and share the preparation of classic Basque meals. Recent 'alternative' txokos are devoted to a single product: it could be potatoes from Álava or kidney beans from Tolosa. In the Basque country, you cannot miss venerable specialities such as zurrukutuna (salt cod with garlic and peppers), porrusala (leek and potato stew), piperrada (peppers and eggs) and bacalao (salt cod) with pil pil—a sauce of olive oil, garlic and parsley. With the Atlantic at their feet and their fleets scooping up spiny lobsters, clams, squid, sea-bass, red and grey mullet, anchovies, tuna, hake, monkfish and many others, seafood is always prominent on menus. Some Basques even maintain that the fish caught in the Bay of Biscay has an inimitable muscular texture due to the strong currents encountered—in contrast with the placid Mediterranean waters. Take that with a pinch of Basque salt?

THIS PAGE (FROM TOP): Pintxo style is to pile 'em high; Basque wines include the addictively refreshing txakoli, a slightly bubbly white wine, as well as Rioja Alavesa which is separated from the 'other' Rioja by the Ebro river.

OPPOSITE: Siete Calles in Bilbao with glassed-in balconies that are typical of northern Spain.

gulp

On the alcohol front, the Basques again have their favoured specialities, notably cider, which is theatrically poured from great height for extra bubbles and zest. Nine million litres (2.3 million gallons) of this local tipple are downed annually in San Sebastián alone. A close rival is the refreshing, slightly petillant txakoli (white wine from Guetaria or Vizcaya, two Basque provinces) which, due to limited production, is rarely exported. One wine that does travel beyond its frontiers is Rioja Alavesa, which is produced in southern Euskadi on the borders of La Rioja province. Navarra, too, is coming up with increasingly sophisticated and acclaimed red wines. All in all there is no danger of deprivation on any level in the Basque country—if you can take the gentle drizzle.

Like a chrysalis, the previously inward-looking Basque country seems to be breaking open to the world.

Hotel Maria Cristina

Without doubt the pulse of the Basque region, the magnificent city of San Sebastián has been a fashionable destination since the pre-war era, and a trip to this historic and cultural metropolis deserves to be enjoyed with a taste of extravagance. To really live like royalty, the only choice is the stately, resplendent Hotel Maria Cristina.

Opened in 1912, generations of world-famous and prestigious guests have passed through these noble doors, the first being its namesake, Queen Maria Cristina herself, who came here to visit this majestic building christened in her honour. In following years, Don Alfonso XIII, the Queen of Bulgaria, the King of Egypt, Japan's Crown Prince Akihito and a successive host of dukes, marquises and presidents have, too, become a part of its long and fascinating history. Even the edifice's old walls tell a story; bullet holes from the 1936 Civil war can still be seen in the legendary façade.

THIS PAGE (FROM TOP): Gourmet Basque fare is served in the palatial Easo Restaurant; the elegant interior décor; the hotel's waterfront façade keeps an intriguing history.

OPPOSITE (FROM LEFT): The junior suites on the top floor each boast a bright terrace with sunloungers and sea views; the hotel's central location in San Sebastián's Old Quarter makes its many terraces ideal spots for soaking in the city.

Every last detail of the Maria Cristina exudes opulence—from the palatial, ornate corridors and marble columns to its elegant vintage furniture and impressive gargantuan chandeliers. The guestrooms are, in the style of local tradition, luxuriously decorated with heavy, pleated curtains and lush, intricately embroidered rugs which complement the hotel's regal ambience. Across the top floor, junior suites each feature a private terrace from which its privileged guests can enjoy spectacular views out to sea.

Located next to the Urumea river and only metres from the sea, Maria Cristina is surrounded by promenades and gardens. A short walk will take you to the Old Quarter and its centre, La Plaza de la Constitución, the city's former bullring. Here you can wander the lively streets filled with shops and bars, museums and churches, ending up among the traders in the busy fishing port, and then onto the beaches of Playa de la Concha and Playa de Ondarreta.

The hotel offers two very different dining experiences. Easo Restaurant, set in a grand dining room with high ceilings and marble columns, serves traditional Basque cuisine and, in the summer, guests can dine on the terrace overlooking the hotel's central plaza. Café Saigon offers an inventive Vietnamese menu in a more relaxed setting. After dinner, the Gritti Bar and Lounge, having over the years served drinks to a long line of royalty, is an exquisite place to add a final touch of grandeur to the end of your day.

FACTS		
ROOMS	136	
FOOD	Easo • Café Saigon	
DRINK	Gritti Bar and Lounge	
FEATURES	babysitting	
BUSINESS	business centre	
NEARBY	beach • fishing port • Old Quarter • Guggenheim Museum • shopping • bars • restaurants	
CONTACT	Calle Oquendo 1, E-20004 San Sebastián • telephone: +34.943.437 600 • facsimile: +34.943.437 676 • email: hmc@westin.com • wesbite: www.westin.com	

PHOTOGRAPHS COURTESY OF HOTEL MARIA CRISTINA.

Sheraton Bilbao

THIS PAGE (FROM TOP): *In a city whose architectural landscape has been shaped by some of the world's most famous virtuosos— the likes of Norman Foster and Frank Gehry—the Sheraton Bilbao by Ricardo Legorreta is a true landmark in its own right; gracing the hotel's stark walls are contemporary works by renowned native artists.*

OPPOSITE: *The edifice and its interiors reflect a supreme blend of space, colour and light, using thick walls and tones to enclose areas, creating absolute privacy.*

Bilbao has developed over seven centuries. The city is now emerging confidently from its formerly industrial chrysalis, and its impressive new wings welcome the discerning visitors of today. Situated in the middle of the gorgeous Cantabrican coast and within easy reach of mountains, harbours, La Rioja's vineyards and international airports, Bilbao is certainly taking full advantage of its ample assets.

The city's rejuvenation was spearheaded by the spectacular Guggenheim Museum, a Frank Gehry creation. His adventurous, future-facing aesthetic emphasizes the art inherent within architecture itself, and parallels Bilbao's contemporary cultural growth.

This 'New Bilbao' gravitates around the central Abandoibarra area, with the arresting Sheraton Bilbao located in its hub. Designed by Ricardo Legorreta, the property includes among its prestigious neighbours, world-class facilities such as Euskalduna Congress Centre, Bilbao Exhibition Centre, and the home of the Basque Opera. Culture exists not merely in its vicinity, but echoes throughout the building itself, with a collection of contemporary art bursting with works by Francisco Amat, Jorge Castillo, Antonio Clavet and Manolo Valdés.

Like an adept party host, the Sheraton Bilbao seamlessly adapts itself to each guest's unique needs. Business travellers may avail themselves of its smart meeting room facilities and beds designed to encourage deep sleep. Relaxation seekers may prefer to unwind in the Wellness Centre overlooking the Nervión river which features an advanced gym, a pool, sauna and meditative massage options.

Expansive views of the city seep into the bright rooms through large windows. Suites are furnished in materials and colourways to reflect regional themes—with flashes of colour interrupting neutral furnishings and honeyed wood—while maintaining an almost Eastern simplicity and symmetry. Facilities include plasma television and climate control for sultry summer evenings, with suites also boasting hydro-massage baths into whose warming waters you can slip into on cooler nights.

Back at ground level, soak in Bilbao's thriving street scene with a stroll through the lively Doña Casilda Park. Explore the Museum of Fine Arts housed within, before retreating to the clean, angular lines of Sheraton Bilbao's Café Chillida. Alternatively, after a satisfying shop at Siete Calles (Seven Streets), indulge in a gastronomic feast in Aizian Restaurant. The soft cream furnishings and elegant, gleaming wood interior nurture the perfect ambience for feasting on locally and internationally inspired dishes prepared by leading chefs.

With such an enjoyable experience available within the Sheraton Bilbao itself, it might slip your mind until check-out that you haven't actually discovered the city proper. As the Spaniards say, there's always mañana.

FACTS		
ROOMS	190 rooms • 20 suites • 1 presidential suite	
FOOD	Aizian	
DRINK	Café Chillida	
FEATURES	Wellness Centre: pool, sauna and hydro-massage baths	
BUSINESS	meeting rooms	
NEARBY	Santander • San Sebastián	
CONTACT	Calle Lehendakari Leizaola 29, Bilbao 48001 • telephone: +34.94.428 0000 • facsimile: +34.94.428 0001 • email: bilbao@sheraton.com • website: www.sheraton.com	

PHOTOGRAPHS COURTESY OF SHERATON BILBAO.

Bay of Biscay

greenspain

Atlantic Ocean

A Coruña •

Santiago de Compostela •

Galicia

• Oviedo

Asturias

Santander •

Cantabria

Basque

Vigo •

• Ourense

> Pazo do Castro
> AC Palacio del Carmen
> Pazo los Escudos Hotel + Resort

La Rioja

Castilla y León

Portugal

Madrid

Extremadura

Castilla-La Mancha

green spain

A great swathe of verdant hills, craggy granite peaks and indented coastline stretches across northern Spain from the Basque country to the Atlantic coast. Three provinces form the line-up: Cantabria, Asturias and Galicia. All of them are pastoral in nature and deep in history—from the prehistoric cave paintings of Altamira to that pilgrims' epiphany, the cathedral at Santiago de Compostela. Not least, the towering Picos de Europa which crown the Cordillera Cantábrica create a daunting barrier from the rest of Spain. Apart from acting as a magnet for rain-clouds—hence the epithet 'green'—they gave the northern belt a very ^different history to the rest of Spain. It was the only region untouched by the Moors and, to this day, Asturias prides itself on being the place where the Reconquista—and the eventual unification of Spain—began.

Throughout, Asturias and Cantabria are wonderful examples of Romanesque and even pre-Romanesque (notably in Asturia's capital Oviedo) architecture—be they remote hermitages, monasteries or cathedrals. Today, despite improved road and rail networks, the northwest still feels geographically isolated and somewhat of a time warp—dreamy sensations that, together with its mists and menhirs, greatly aid de-stressing. The true beauty of these provinces lies on the vast periphery beyond their cities; any meander along the tortuous roads breathing in stunning, lush landscapes brings endless discoveries.

galician mists + mellow fruitfulness

Galicia is, without a doubt, the most tantalizing part of the north as, apart from feeling out on a geographical limb, its inhabitants speak Gallego, a language that is a minor variant of Portuguese and, like the Basque and Catalan tongues, incomprehensible to Castilian-speakers. Yet again, this is one in the eye to central government and another good reason for Spain's autonomous regions. The ancient Celtic culture, too, sets this region firmly apart, and bagpipes are just one of the unexpected sounds that penetrate the air—along with pealing church bells and the raucous cries of seagulls, for the coast

PAGE 118: Galicia's damp climate nurtures bountiful farmland and verdant hills.

THIS PAGE (FROM TOP): A remote chapel at Los Arcos, on the way to Santiago de Compostela; a Celtic bagpiper.

OPPOSITE: Agustín Ibarrola's 'Cubes of Memory' line the harbour of Llanes in Asturias.

is never far. Galicia is, in fact, far more closely related to northern Portugal, with which it shares not merely a language but also a love of young white wines (such as refreshing albariño), an expansive national park, Miño river, and a coastline blessed with glorious sunsets over the Atlantic. Whatever Galicia's fidelities, it leaves an indelible impression.

Like the rest of Spain, the northern cities are not standing still, and A Coruña, notably, is forging ahead. Visually striking for its swathes of elegant, glassed-in balconies overlooking the sea, it harbours, as well, a surprisingly atmospheric and much older heart tucked away in the backstreets. Its most iconic landmark stands on a headland to be spotted from afar: the Torre de Hércules, a 1790s lighthouse that replaced a Roman version, allegedly making it the world's oldest. Close by is the minimalist structure of Domus, the truly innovative Museum of Mankind ingeniously designed by the Japanese architect, Arata Isozaki.

A Coruña—and Galicia in general—is at the forefront of much of Spain's recent fashion boom. Zara was just one of the labels born here, along with Adolfo Domínguez, Roberto Verino and Purificación García. All have developed over the last 30 years out of an existing and highly prolific textile industry. Galicia's neighbour Asturias specializes more in the heavy industries of iron and coal—although its verdant hillsides and ruminating cows are the source of much of Spain's dairy products.

piscean prowess

Wherever you are, Galicia spells fish and more fish, boasting Europe's most important fishing fleet—almost half Spain's total. As an indication, a mind-boggling 133 million kg (293 million lb) of fresh seafood—from cephalopods (that includes octopus and squid, the local passion) to crustaceans and regular fish, were caught in 2002.

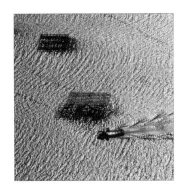

Seafood is, of course, the mainstay of northern cuisine, and you are unlikely to find fresher. Vieira (scallop) is a Galician delicacy that seems plumper and tastier than coquilles Saint-Jacques or scallops anywhere else, and is eaten raw with a squirt of lemon or baked in a coat of breadcrumbs and spices. Next in line is pulpo (octopus), traditionally beaten, boiled in a large pan then cut with scissors into bite-size pieces. Seasoned with paprika,

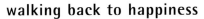

salt and virgin olive oil, it is usually served with potatoes. Favourites such as calamares (squid), navajas (razor clams), percebes (goose barnacles), almejas (mussels), langosta (lobster) and langostinos (large prawns) are other marine delicacies that Galicians revel in.

Meat is by no means forgotten, in particular during the long winters. Veal and pork win over lamb in the form of peasant-style stews in which they may join root vegetables and haricot beans. In contrast, Cantabrians have more of a penchant for beef, and are known for delicious cheeses as well as the famous morcilla de Liébana—black pudding from the Picos de Europa mountains.

walking back to happiness

If one image remains imprinted on the retina after any time spent in this region, it is the very humble scallop shell. It is everywhere—on your plate, on pilgrims' staffs, and on roadside signs pointing the way to Europe's greatest pilgrimage site and Spain's westernmost city, Santiago de Compostela. In the Middle Ages, the Camino de Santiago (Way of St. James) was a major communication link between people from all over Europe and for centuries nurtured rich cultural, artistic and trade exchanges. In many ways it was a proto-European

THIS PAGE (FROM TOP): *Superb 12th-century sculptures of the apostles by Master Mateo adorn Santiago's Romanesque portals; the long, straight pilgrim's road to Santiago de Compostela.*
OPPOSITE: *The cathedral towering over the Praza do Obradoiro.*

Union, as it led Scandinavians and Germans to cross paths with French, Italian, English, Irish and, of course, Spanish pilgrims. At its peak, in the 11th and 12th centuries, over half a million people are said to have converged annually on Santiago. As a result, the main route (from France through Roncesvalles in the Pyrenees then to Pamplona, Burgos, León, Astorga then Santiago) stimulated an extensive infrastructure, bringing bridges, churches, monasteries and hostels to Galicia and northern Castilla.

The number of pilgrims subsequently slumped, but in recent years there has been an unexpected revival, with participants soaring from 2,500 in 1986 to 75,000 in 2003. In the Holy Year (every five years), numbers leap further, the last one (in 2004) doubling the number of plucky souls walking or cycling—even with a few on horseback—along the 800-km (497-mile) route to the promised city. It is a fascinating phenomenon which, even if not due to a Catholic renaissance, reflects a true desire for simple pleasures and shared hardships. Many people embark on the route at a moment of crisis or a crossroads in their life; it seems that a month spent musing on the calming landscapes of northern Spain solves most human dilemmas.

end of the road

In Santiago de Compostela itself, the magnificent cathedral towers over an entrancing old town peopled by staff-clutching pilgrims, nuns, promenading families and shoals of tourists. Monasteries and churches—all rich in ecclesiastical treasures—crop up every corner and there is little which postdates the 18th century. The narrow streets become particularly entrancing at night, when tapas bars dish up plate after plate of pulpo.

The exception to the historical rule is Galicia's Centre of Contemporary Art standing next to the Museum of the Galician People—housed in a 14th-century convent whose Gothic chapel is today the Pantheon of Famous Galicians—which was built in 1993 to a minimalist design by Portugal's leading architect, Álvaro Siza. On a far more ambitious scale, the Galician City of Culture is taking shape at Monte Gaiás, a tiny hill just outside town. This is not without controversy and, inevitably, spiralling costs (the final budget of over 400 million euros more than triples the original estimate). Designed by the American architect, Peter Eisenman, the ingenious 70-hectare (173-acre) complex of arts, museum and research facilities replicates Santiago's layout with buildings clad in local stone carved into the undulating terrain.

Back in the real town, the cathedral rises between four plazas, its ornate towers, carved doorways and façade an incredible mixture of periods. First erected in the 11th to 13th centuries in Romanesque style, it later acquired a baroque façade to front the original and magnificent Pórtico de la Gloria. This was carved by Master Mateo in 1188. Its attraction has been immense as, over the centuries, so many pilgrims have bent down to touch the central pillar that the stone has actually worn away. Mateo's eloquent sculptures of religious figures are echoed by his depiction of biblical scenes on the south portal, the Puerta de las Platerías. Inside the cathedral, those lucky enough to witness a major mass will see the immense botafumeiro (incense burner) in action, swinging in front of the altar as frankincense clouds the air.

Across the square stands arguably the finest of all the pilgrims' hostels, Parador Hostal dos Reis Católicos, today one of Spain's most sought-after paradors. Dating from 1499 when it was commissioned by King Ferdinand and Queen Isabela, it boasts an exquisitely carved doorway, a vast lobby, four superb courtyards and a Gothic chapel. Even if not enjoying one of its four-poster beds, it is a perfect place for a drink or dinner.

to the lighthouse

Back in medieval times, many pilgrims would resume their long and tortuous trudge to reach Cape Finisterre, Spain's westernmost point. Today, its headland lighthouse which overlooks thundering waves is visited more for symbolic than spiritual value. To the south, the entire coastline is one of beautiful rías (inlets) alternating with largely unspoilt, white, sandy beaches, all of which end at

the Celtic-Roman settlement of Santa Tecla. For the moment, domestic tourism has the upper hand along this coast and, out of season, it has a potent, somewhat melancholic ambience. Inland along the Miño river looms the immense fortified cathedral of Tui while across on the opposite bank unfolds Portugal, land of porto and vinho verde. A typical sight along this route (also shared with Portugal) is the hórreo, a raised stone grain-store with a pitched roof—an unusual structure that vies with dolmens and menhirs.

cantabrian stars

The other great highlights of northern Spain are to be found in Cantabria, east of cider-quaffing Asturias. Resistant to the slow southward march of the Reconquista, Asturias may keep a low profile, but the quality of its cuisine is soaring. Fabada (a rich stew of beans and sausages) is no longer alone, and Asturian chefs like Pedro Moran, Sergio Rama and Nacho Manzano are hitting the headlines. On top of this, the region recently invested 4 million euros in a museum devoted entirely to the Jurassic period. Designed to resemble a dinosaur's footprint, it's located near beaches where dinosaurs left tracks.

Further east, swinging round a large bay is Santander, the genial Cantabrian capital and queen of a beautiful stretch of coast. Both port and resort, it has plenty of old world romance and a charming variety between stevedores, trendy shoppers, shady bodegas and stylish pavement cafes. Apart from such contrasts, Santander is the perfect launch pad for Santillana del Mar and a cluster of caves rich in prehistoric paintings. World-famous Altamira (stumbled upon in 1879 by one Marcelino Sanz de Sautuola and his daughter María, it is around 15,000 years old and dubbed the 'Sistine Chapel of Quaternary Art') is closed to visitors for conservation reasons, but lesser ones such as Puente Viesgo and Covalanas are open. Santillana del Mar itself is a picture postcard, UNESCO-World-Heritage-listed village due to its harmonious, 1,200-year old architecture lining a maze of delightfully atmospheric cobbled-stone streets from the Romanesque masterpiece, La Colegiata. High-season popularity does reduce the impact but, this being Green Spain, it is a toss-up between weather and crowds.

...it seems that a month spent musing on the calming landscapes of northern Spain solves most human dilemmas.

AC Palacio del Carmen

Located in Spain's northwesterly reaches, the old city of Santiago de Compostela has been immortalized as the capital of Galicia and as the ultimate destination in legendary medieval pilgrimage, the Way of St. James. Today, the city's monuments generate much cultural fascination, its renowned university attracts talent of the highest calibre and its inspirational skyline exists in a league of its own. The cathedral's delicate spires creep skyward like manmade stalagmites, and the wide, golden-hued Obradoiro Square is a stunning showcase of the region's historical development. Here, one will marvel at the early-built chapels, the Gothic and Baroque creations, and the intriguing examples of Románico Compostelano—an architectural style unique to the city.

The AC Palacio del Carmen lies metres away from this romantic flagstoned square in the heart of Santiago de Compostela. It is next to impossible to find a description for this property—whether verbal or written—that would exclude the word 'splendid'; nor would such compliments be mere hyperbole. The 18th-century building was originally the Convent las Oblatas, and its genuine charm shines effortlessly through today. The AC Hotels group recently welcomed Palacio del Carmen into its stable of stylishly designed and sensitively refurbished properties, and has respectfully retained and enhanced the convent's architectural originality.

Guestrooms are comfortable and come replete with every modern convenience. The endearing, irregular colouring on the walls flows through tones of cream and ochre to terracotta, and the rich, chocolatey depths of the burnished woods provide a pleasing contrast against the crisp brightness of the bedlinen. The requirements of the discerning

THIS PAGE (CLOCKWISE FROM TOP RIGHT):
The bright, inviting whitewashed façade of Palacio del Carmen; the hotel's restaurant Saraiba serves Galician cuisine fused with haute international flavours; much of the former 18th-century convent's architecture and interior have been kept, complemented by the perfect modern touch.

OPPOSITE: All rooms are warmly coloured and richly atmospheric.

business traveller are equally well-attended to. Meetings and conferences may be held either in the informal setting of equipped rooms featuring exposed stone walls and wooden-beamed ceilings or in larger, more stately surroundings where arched ceilings and commanding, authentic frescoes preside.

The hotel's candlelit restaurant pays homage to the region's cultural history and culinary excellence by using products and ingredients which are predominantly sourced from local markets. Its masterful chefs commingle traditional Galician cuisine with the finest contemporary flavours from all around the world. The wine cellar—tantalizingly visible behind a wrought-iron screen—boasts a selection of wines with distinguished Spanish ancestries. Sample some of Galicia's world-renowned seafood, such as the fish pie Empanada Gállega, before treating yourself to a much sought-after vintage as the sun melts into dusk beyond the hotel's immaculate gardens.

Galicia is far-famed as the 'land of a thousand rivers'. Whether the Palacio del Carmen is your base from which to explore the region's fishing villages and coastlines, or if immersing yourself in the indoor pool is as much activity as you can muster, one thing is certain—it is difficult to refrain from using the word 'splendid' at the Palacio del Carmen.

FACTS		
ROOMS	74	
FOOD	traditional Galician haute cuisine	
DRINK	bar	
FEATURES	indoor pool • fitness centre	
BUSINESS	5 conference rooms • translation and secretarial services • equipment hire • Internet	
NEARBY	city centre • Santiago de Compostela Airport	
CONTACT	Calle Oblatas s/n, 15703 Santiago de Compostela, A Coruña • telephone: +34.981.552 444 • facsimile: +34.981.552 445 • email: pcarmen@ac-hotels.com • website: www.ac-hotels.com	

PHOTOGRAPHS COURTESY OF AC HOTELS.

Pazo do Castro

The tiny village of O Castro in eastern Galicia is located on a hill with splendid views of the valley keeping River Sil. Of strategic importance since Roman times when a major road was built through the valley connecting Braganza in Portugal with Astorga, O Castro was the administrative capital of the region in the Middle Ages and the seat of important noble families for almost 900 years. They first lived in a fortified castle, then in a magnificent country estate constructed in the 17th century, now converted into a resplendent country hotel.

Continuously inhabited by descendants of those families until well into the 20th century, Pazo do Castro has suffered few alterations and offers the visitor a privileged glimpse into the rural lifestyle of the Spanish nobility.

The experience begins with the very first glimpse of the palace's magnificent façade, with its elegant stone porticos and wrought-iron balconies. It is easy to imagine the days when the entire family of the Marquises of Esteva de las Delicias, Grandees of Spain, would line up before the main entrance to greet their guests as they arrived by carriage

THIS PAGE (FROM TOP): The portico keeping the grand entrance; each named after an honoured member of the Marquis' family, the guestrooms have all been beautifully conserved and fitted with the best of modern luxuries; the patio is an ideal quiet corner for soaking in the estate's history.

OPPOSITE: A treasure trove of centuries-old priceless tomes is housed in the library and guests are permitted to pore over them.

from the train station. The memory of the former occupants is a constant presence as you wander through the common areas filled with old photographs and paintings of an illustrious lineage that boasted connections with many of Europe's royal houses. In tribute, each of the 30 rooms bears the name of a distinguished member of the family.

Every effort has been made to conserve historic authenticity without compromising modern comforts. The guestrooms are all decorated with period antiques, yet offer air-conditioning, satellite television, generously-sized bathrooms (some with jacuzzi), a safe and minibar. The elegant corner suite is the culmination of the extravagance and taste that form the hallmarks of the establishment. Guests are invited to use the luminous salons and drawing rooms, all virtually unchanged over time. The library is of special interest, and visitors may request the key to view its valuable collection containing volumes dating to the 16th century. The private chapel has a

lovely baroque altarpiece and, until recently, housed relics of Saint Francisco Blanco who died a martyr in Japan in 1597.

The former kitchen, with its massive fireplace, is the perfect place for a cocktail before dinner, and the restaurant—by far the best in the region—offers traditional Galician cuisine with a contemporary touch.

Guests will appreciate the contemporary spa facilities complete with a Finnish sauna, large jacuzzi, Turkish steam bath, heated pool and aromatherapy.

The unique combination of history, luxury and tranquillity makes Pazo do Castro a destination worthy of a detour and a voyage of discovery to a different place and time.

FACTS		
ROOMS	22 double • 1 suite • 5 matrimonial rooms • 2 apartments (4 beds each)	
FOOD	personalized menu • traditional Galician	
DRINK	outdoor patio • bar	
FEATURES	spa • tennis • golf • historical architecture • antiques • Carriage Museum	
BUSINESS	meeting rooms • Wi-Fi zone	
NEARBY	Roman goldmines of Las Medulas • Monastery of Las Ermitas • Ribera Sacra • Way of St. James • winery tours	
CONTACT	32318 O Barco de Valdeorras, Ourense, Galicia • telephone: +34.988.347 423 • facsimile: +34.988.347 482 • email: info@pazodocastro.com • website: www.pazodocastro.com	

PHOTOGRAPHS COURTESY OF PAZO DO CASTRO.

Pazo los Escudos Hotel + Resort

Seated magnificently along the picturesque waterfront of Vigo, modern metropolis and one of Spain's most important historic ports, Pazo los Escudos Hotel & Resort is the city's first and finest luxury five-star hotel. Nestled amid an idyll of scenic beaches and misty mountain views, the hotel is a distinguished amalgamation of noble tradition and urbane indulgence where guests are surrounded by a degree of opulence and attention to detail that can only result from the 'no expenses spared' philosophy in the style of Conrad Hilton.

This is a hotel of uncommon lavishness and superb taste, located on a former private estate with beautiful views of the estuary of Vigo. Its 54 guestrooms are divided between two buildings—one modern and the other a restored 18th-century pazo (a seigniorial house). The name of the property derives from the magnificent collection of 94 coats of arms carved in stone that dot the grounds, which will delight any student of medieval heraldry.

Many of the rooms have balconies with wonderful views of the estuary, always filled with sailing and fishing boats. In the distance you can even make out the platforms for cultivating the wonderful mussels for which the area is justifiably famed. Apart from sunsets of incomparable beauty, every room features a minibar, Wi-Fi and Internet access, a Bang & Olufsen television, bathrobes and slippers, feather pillows and duvets, Bvlgari

...a hotel of uncommon lavishness and superb taste...

accessories, and a large bathroom decked in gorgeous travertine marble. Guests will also appreciate the sumptuous breakfast buffet.

The Pazo's common areas are nothing less than palatial, and guests have private access to the impeccably appointed salon on the main floor, complete with a business centre and views over the gardens and the sea. Noble woods complement the stone walls decorated with fine tapestries, antiques and original works of art. Nothing has been left to chance, and the friendly staff at the guest services desk are always at hand to look after your every request. A stunning grand staircase leads up to the guestrooms or down to Alcabre Restaurant, which offers traditional Galician dishes with a modern flair in an elegant setting. Café Medusa offers a lighter menu and Bar Los Escudos in the main building is the ideal place for cocktails or to sample the hotel's famous homemade bakes with coffee (the chocolate brownies are sinfully delicious).

Hotels such as Pazo los Escudos don't come around very often, but when they do, they are not to be missed. Just like a three-star restaurant in the Michelin Guide, Pazo los Escudos Hotel & Resort is worth a detour from just about anywhere.

FACTS		
ROOMS	premium • superior • privilege suites • Grand Suite • Royal Suite	
FOOD	Alcabre • Café Medusa	
DRINK	Bar Los Escudos	
FEATURES	beach • Wi-Fi access • Bvlgari accessories	
BUSINESS	meeting facilities	
NEARBY	Museum of the Sea • Isla Cíes Natural Park • golf • private yacht charter • deep-sea fishing • sailing • winery tours • shopping	
CONTACT	Avda. Atlántida 106, 36208 Vigo, Pontevedra • telephone: +34.986.820 820 • facsimile: +34.986.820 801 • email: reservas@pazolosescudos.com • website: www.pazolosescudos.com	

PHOTOGRAPHS COURTESY OF PAZO LOS ESCUDOS HOTEL + RESORT.

central spain

Rugged, dry, scorching in summer and bone-chilling in winter, central Spain is, superficially at least, not the most hospitable of regions. But this is where, by casting your imagination, you might hear Moorish and Christian armies thundering across plains, where Catholicism and conservatism run deep, and where castles are two a penny. Castilla's two great rivers, Ebro and Duero, were the frontlines between Catholic Spain and Muslim Al-Andalus for centuries, and this has left a permanent mark on the territory. To the south unfolds the flatter and less inspiring La Mancha with, on its western flank, the unassuming but fascinating province of Extremadura. Other than well-conceived town centres and the odd outstanding new building, any sense of New Spain is overtaken by an intriguing depth of history.

The heart of Castilian Spain beats in tandem with the wings of storks, the optimism of cathedrals and the sails of La Mancha's windmills. It takes time to know, but it is easy to be hooked, so great is the choice. From Salamanca to Segovia, Zaragoza to Toledo, Mérida to Valladolid and Cáceres in nearby Extremadura, each city cradles monumental line-ups, while smaller places may display Mudéjar and even Roman remains. In La Rioja, a more lighthearted province biting into Castilla's northern perimeter, modern developments are creating a novel allure (whether bodegas designed by Calatrava and Gehry, hip tapas bars or castles transformed into museums) and most town centres have been intelligently revamped for traffic. Yet traditions run deep, and Castilla's classic image of silent cloisters, austerity, dark wooden interiors and menus in pseudo-Gothic script, is hard to uproot.

old castilian morsels

In northern Castilla, crenellated castles stud the horizon, waves of alternating hot and cold blast across the high plateau, and suckling pigs, spicy chorizo, cecina (cured beef), jamón, morcilla and tender lamb pile on your plate. Food resoundingly equals meat here, giving vegetarians a particularly hard time. Pork is a prime product as absolutely nothing from the animal is wasted, not even the bristles, which become nailbrushes, or the ears, which are devoured with relish. Fortunately, pulses and grains also figure prominently, and offer

PAGE 134: Once a royal residence, the Alcázar sits resplendently over Segovia.

THIS PAGE (FROM TOP): Vines dominate much of northern Castilla and La Rioja. Here, tempranillo grapes are cultivated to make Pedrosa's Ribera del Duero wine; the ubiquitous stork.

OPPOSITE: The UNESCO World Heritage site of Cáceres with its blend of Roman, Islamic, Northern Gothic and Italian Renaissance architecture.

endless variants; lentils from La Armuña, chickpeas from Zamora or judíones (big beans) from La Granja, just to name a few. La Rioja, on the other hand, plays the valuable role of northern Spain's market garden, with field after fertile field of succulent red peppers, artichokes, asparagus and aubergines. Wine-buffs enter a kind of dreamy Arcadia, as the region is responsible for producing some of Spain's best wines—from Ribera del Duero to up-and-coming Bierzo and Toro and, of course, Rioja's lauded reservas.

Salamanca stands out due to its prestigious university (founded in 1218) and youthful population which endows it with a livelier, more cosmopolitan edge than other Castilian towns. A wealth of striking architecture ranges from the much-photographed House of Shells to the university buildings themselves, as well as two massive adjoining cathedrals—the older one being a superlative example of the Romanesque and the 'new' one of the Renaissance. The city's greatest urban feature is the arcaded Plaza Mayor, one of Europe's most beautiful squares. Its elegant 1720s architecture incorporates distinguished busts of Spanish kings, Christopher Columbus, El Cid and Cervantes who, every evening, look down upon an impromptu stage-set of musicians, students swishing around in traditional capes, street artists and burgeoning outdoor cafés. It could be a cliché, but somehow it never is. Apart from this majesty, Salamanca's student population means that it is not short of cyber cafés or rowdy tapas bars.

little pigs, big cathedrals

Any Spanish gourmet goes to Segovia for only one reason: suckling pig. Even King Juan Carlos and his late mother have frequented restaurants here just to sample this speciality. Little snouts poke over many a restaurant or butcher's counter and they are now slated to acquire DOC status (Denominación de Origen Controllada). Food aside, this entrancing town, crowning a high outcrop, boasts a dramatic Roman aqueduct and the curious turreted Alcázar which, like a mirage, overlooks the plains below. Its whimsical Bavarian style was in fact courtesy of the owner, the Habsburg King Felipe II.

Cathedral enthusiasts should not miss either Burgos or León, as both cities lie in the shadow of imposing Gothic edifices. The cathedral of Burgos ranks third in size after Sevilla and Toledo, and represents a five-century labour of love by brilliant craftsmen, although the predominant style is Flamboyant Gothic. León's 13th- to14th-century masterpiece overpowers through a hundred or so stained-glass windows, and the town itself makes for a friendly, relaxing stopover. Both cathedrals, situated along the long road to Santiago de Compostela, have drawn millions of pilgrims. Between Burgos and Zaragoza stretches the breathtaking Sierra de la Demanda, rich in monasteries, Romanesque sights and game, and, on its Riojan flank, home to the region's most innovative chef, Francis Paniego. This youthful award-winner shares a restaurant in Ezcaray with his mother, Marisa Sánchez, so offering a choice between nueva cocina and more traditional cuisine. The choice is yours.

land without bread

Bordering La Mancha and nudging the perimeter of Portugal, Extremadura is Spain's least prosperous region—a sparsely populated, rural province out on a limb. Back in the 15th and 16th centuries, its extreme climate and harsh conditions drove many a desperate man to set off as conquistadores; Hernán Cortés and the ruthless Francisco Pizarro were the most (in)famous, colonizing Mexico and Peru respectively. In a different vein entirely, the region's hardships inspired Luís Buñuel's first film in 1932, a surrealistic documentary by the name, *Land without Bread*—the title says it all.

Today, Extremadura is the source of some of Spain's finest jamón ibérico, a result of acorn-fed pigs snuffling in shaded groves of cork-oaks. The latter is the region's other great money-earner, or was, until plastic corks entered the wine sector. Fertile valleys nurture cherry and olive groves, while trout, game, sausages, garlic and cheese are other delights. Despite such produce, Extremadura is not known for sophisticated cuisine and only one chef stands out. This is Toño Pérez of the Michelin-starred restaurant, Atrio, in Cáceres. Sobriety is the keyword here, whether in the interior décor or monastic tone of the dishes.

THIS PAGE (FROM TOP): Agricultural plains in Burgos, where Catholicism and agriculture are inextricably linked; beech-forests in the sierra are perfect for autumnal walks.

OPPOSITE (FROM LEFT): Meseta's rolling farmland is studded with wildflowers in spring; a black Iberian pig spells excellent jamón iberico—one of 39 million hams cured annually.

THIS PAGE: *Stilt dancers in Anguiano spin around the streets every June 22 in honour of Mary Magdalene.*

OPPOSITE (FROM TOP): *The 2000-year-old Roman theatre at Mérida is Spain's best preserved; an ornate, and typically Spanish, tile at Mérida.*

Mérida, the capital, Cáceres and, to a lesser extent, Trujillo and Guadalupe, are the urban highlights, each with a distinctive flavour. To the south, nudging Andalucía, a trio of charming border towns (Olivenza, Jerez de los Caballeros and Zafra) display Manueline —15th-century Portuguese—style dating from Portuguese incursions. Another spin-off of those warring days was the network of fortresses, many of which were erected by the crusading Knights Templar in the late Middle Ages. Altogether it is hard to avoid the weight of history here, as signs of the modern world are rare.

roman mérida

Mérida is the great exception, thanks to its groundbreaking Museum of Roman Art designed by Rafael Moneo. Although over 20 years old, the lofty brick design is timeless and subtly echoes the forms of the Roman capital of Lusitania, from 25 BCE. Few Spanish museums compare in quality of exhibits and setting, and only Tarragona in Catalonia rivals Mérida's monuments of this era. The most impressive survivor of these is the colonnaded theatre, closely followed by the amphitheatre (once used for gladiator fights, chariot races and, when flooded, for mock sea-battles), the Temple of Diana, two aqueducts and a bridge spanning the Guadiana river. In July and August, Mérida hosts a summer drama festival in the magnificent Roman Theatre, so combining a rare sense of past and present.

cáceres + trujillo: stork cities

Beak-rattling storks are everywhere in northern Extremadura, and in spring and summer they sit contentedly on gigantic nests atop any vaguely vertical, lofty structure. This is the Extremaduran heartland, a land that, out of season, can feel dark and inhospitable but, once spring arrives, is pure delight. Cáceres perfectly encapsulates 16th-century Spain; a Renaissance town overlaying an earlier Moorish structure visible in the old walls and watchtowers. The immaculately preserved old quarter (a UNESCO World Heritage site) is almost pristine and heavy with a dramatic air, but the few bars and restaurants nestled amid the grandiose emblazoned mansions in recent years have lightened the atmosphere.

Next door, Trujillo is more of a charmer, similar in Renaissance style but smaller and more animated. An instant attraction is the majestic central square where an equestrian statue of the dreaded Pizarro lords it triumphantly. Opposite is a mansion now inhabited by an order of Hieronymite nuns; pull the bell chain and a nun opens up, attempts to sell you cakes, then points you to a rarely-seen structure, a 'flying' staircase. Life is quaint here. However the most evocative aspect of this town is the walled, upper part, crowned by a castle, scenically sited churches and Pizarro's childhood home. A bonus is the exuberant vegetation—cacti, palms, magnolia, olive and orange trees—and, of course, the storks.

arty extremadura

Despite being off the radar in many ways, in the 1980s to 1990s Extremadura did lure one major foreign artist (and an art movement in his wake). Just a few kilometres west of Cáceres in a haunting, boulder-strewn landscape (protected as the Monumento Nacional de los Barruecos), the German artist Wolf Vostell (1932–98) converted a sheep-shearing complex into a museum. The result is the Museo Vostell, a startling pocket of provocative and eccentric 1960s works and installations by the Fluxus movement, which include MIG fuselages, Cadillacs, old TV sets and a wall of motorbikes conceived by Dalí. Concrete sculptures even rub shoulders with sheep and fishermen beside the adjoining lake.

Further east towards Toledo, the town of Guadalupe is overshadowed by a massive 14th-century Franciscan monastery, home to a major Hispanic symbol. Busloads of pilgrims descend daily on the huge plaza to pay homage to a black-faced statue of the Virgin of Guadalupe who sits serenely in a revolving shrine above the church altar. This venerated 12th-century image is the patron of 'all Spains', the very essence of Catholic Spanishness.

el greco's toledo

Over the hills in La Mancha, Toledo has a much higher profile. A mesmerizing town rich in Spanish history and culture, it is capital of Castilla-La Mancha, not the most compelling of regions. Mainly flat and drab, this region—not surprisingly—drove Don Quijote to mad hallucination in Cervantes' seminal allegorical novel. Windmills aside (which became Don Quijote's 'giants'), La Mancha is renowned for manchego, a delectable sheep's cheese.

Toledo itself is not a great gastronomic destination as its proximity to Madrid makes it a classic day-trip destination—and thus something of a quick-fix food town. Its attractions are best experienced overnight; the town comes into its own at dusk when shadowy alleys, high stone walls and deserted streets impart a poignant sense of a long, illustrious past.

Leaving an indelible mark was the painter, El Greco, who chose to live and work here until his death in 1614. His works can be seen in the cathedral museum—a masterpiece of Gothic spires crowning a construction spanning 250 years. Inside—carved alabaster seats, polychrome altarpieces and an extraordinary baroque folly, the Transparente. Gold and silver displayed in the Treasury illustrate the might of the church in 16th-century Spain.

El Greco reappears in Casa de El Greco, a bit of a misnomer, as he never actually lived here. Yet it reflects the style of residence he would have inhabited and houses an impressive collection of his work. His magnum opus, 'The Burial of the Count of Orgaz', is uphill from here, in the church of Santo Tomé. This western part of Toledo is also home to two former synagogues, all that remain of a flourishing community that vanished in 1494 when Jews were expelled from Spain. The Sephardic Museum in 14th-century Sinagoga del Tránsito has some illuminating exhibits about this culture and the Sephardic diaspora.

THIS PAGE (FROM TOP): A statue of Queen Isabel I, or Isabel la Catolica, in Castilla-La Mancha; a bridge too far brings you to Toledo, the former spiritual capital of Spain where the painter El Greco once lived.

OPPOSITE: La Mancha's numerous windmills reminded Cervantes' tormented character, Don Quijote, of menacing giants.

...it is hard to avoid the weight of history here, as signs of the modern world are rare.

AC Palacio de San Esteban

A UNESCO World Heritage site, the old city of Salamanca is a historic university town where troves of magnificent cathedrals and various masterpieces of architecture—legacies which gained the town its cultural accolade—exist alongside several densely visited markets, trendy bars and nightspots. Located northwest of the Spanish capital near the Portuguese border, Salamanca is home to what has often been described as the finest square in Spain, the 18th-century Plaza Mayor. This elegant Baroque square has acquired a rather modest title as the 'living room' of the Salamantinos—despite the astonishing grandeur of its impressive galleries and medallion-encrusted arcades—a name emblematic of the city's reputation for keeping a quaint, down-to-earth village atmosphere in spite of its elevated city status.

Here in Salamanca, the AC Hotels group has continued with its truly visionary theme of creating exceptional properties converted from historic buildings situated in the heart of distinctive cities, each carefully selected for its unique, deep-rooted sense of history and artistic offerings. Palacio de San Esteban is one such enchanting transformation of the group's numerous Selection hotels. Formerly a

THIS PAGE (FROM TOP): Views of the old city of Salamanca can be enjoyed from every window; the rooms are cosy and retain much of the original interior; the AC Hotels group is renowned for seeking out historic buildings in important heritage cities and converting them into memorable, exceptional hospitality properties.

OPPOSITE: The library and reading room, comfortably furnished in earthy tones and warm lighting.

convent, the entrance to the building is a walk via a mosaic courtyard with miniature guiding lights underfoot. Modernization has kept intact the convent's old world charm, with luxurious suites leading out onto private balconies from which views of ancient roofs and cathedrals may be admired. Fortunate guests may even catch a glimpse of storks nesting in the golden-ochre towers nearby.

Palacio de San Esteban's spacious lobby looks up through the open-plan centre of the building to the exposed woodwork of the floors above. Choose a book from the hotel's library walls and read in the comfort of the sofas, in warm tones of deep cherry, chocolate and coffee. All bedrooms offer enticing cushioned beds, beautiful window ledges hewn from stone, as well as unusual pieces of furniture designed to give each room its own character.

The hotel's culinary pièce de résistance is El Monje Restaurant, housed beneath the old cavernous, domed ceilings of the former convent's kitchens. Supported by the original stone masonry, exposed timbers and smooth archways, the restaurant has an elegant air, with polished wooden floors and tables laid resplendently with rich cream linen. These elements conspire to create a beckoning, intimate ambience in which to enjoy all the traditional and modern dishes created by El Monje's highly inspired and capable chefs.

Before taking a slow stroll through the town's arteries radiating from Plaza Mayor, pop upstairs to your room to freshen up. The colourful bathrooms are an effortless blend of features both old and contemporary—frosted glass washbasins, sumptuous white robes and gleaming steel fixtures are set against rustic, mosaic-tile walls. Relax and let the bath fill with oil-scented water as the Salamancan light and views of the town's honey-coloured buildings fill the room. A refreshing glass of leche helada, a local vanilla and almond-flavoured speciality, makes for a delightful start to exploring the old city.

FACTS		
ROOMS	51	
FOOD	El Monje: traditional	
DRINK	bar	
FEATURES	fitness centre	
BUSINESS	business centre • translation and secretarial services • equipment hire • Internet	
NEARBY	city centre • Valladolid Airport	
CONTACT	C/ Arroyo de Santo Domingo 3, 37001 Salamanca • telephone: +34.923.262 296 • facsimile: +34.923.268 872 • email: psanesteban@ac-hotels.com • website: www.ac-hotels.com	

PHOTOGRAPHS COURTESY OF AC HOTELS.

Pago del Vicario Hotel + Winery

THIS PAGE (FROM TOP): *View of the property's extraordinary semi-circular edifice which houses a portion of the rooms and suites; the expansive outdoor pool; glass panels allow most of the interiors to bathe in natural light.*

OPPOSITE (FROM LEFT): *Guestrooms sport rich colours, contemporary décor and luxurious amenities; the innovative design of the restaurant incorporates a long glass wall offering views of the winery's Ageing Room below.*

Many experts feel that wine tourism is the way of the future in Spain, and one of the properties at the forefront of this new trend is the Pago del Vicario Hotel & Winery near Ciudad Real. Driving through these gentle rolling hills along the Guadiana river just a few years ago, you would not have noticed the ordered rows of grapevines or the avant-garde architecture. There was nothing here, and that is precisely what makes this venture so unique. There existed only a vision to make fine wines and a commitment to develop a fully-integrated and multi-sensorial project that would allow everyone to experience wine-

making and to savour the finished result in an elegant, luxurious ambience. Pago del Vicario has succeeded admirably on both counts.

The lavish guestrooms are divided into two zones. The first—located in an innovative semi-circular building—offers ten large double rooms and a spacious suite. The design is cutting-edge minimalism, and one would be forgiven for thinking that they have stepped into a chic urban hotel in Madrid. Panoramic windows provide expansive views over the garden and dramatic red-soiled topography of the region. Each of the beds is oriented toward the window, framing the vista as a

singular piece of art. Each room offers Internet, plasma television and superior amenities. A complimentary breakfast is served in the small cafeteria situated close to reception. The lower floor is reserved only for guests, and houses a comfortable reading room, television area and Internet zone. A second wing, built into the side of a hill and covered with a verdant carpet of grass, has an additional 13 double rooms, all of them overlooking the tree-lined banks of Guadiana river. The outdoor pool ingeniously incorporates remnants of a former hacienda and is surrounded by acres of

gardens. A poolside bar and cosy patio with splendid views make this the perfect spot for a romantic cocktail on a summer's evening.

The hotel's restaurant, located in the same building as the winery, has a wall of glass that converts the dining area into a privileged balcony overlooking the Ageing Room, which is filled with casks of wine. The cuisine is proudly rooted in the tradition of Castilla-La Mancha, but prepared with modern flourishes. Each course is accompanied by a different wine from the impressive range produced on the estate, and expert staff are always at hand to suggest the ideal combination.

Guests are encouraged to sign up for a guided tour of the winery, which includes a tasting, or to stroll through the vast vineyards. Few will be able to resist the temptation to stop at the wine store for a case to take home, and every sip is guaranteed to bring back memories of the tranquillity and the smell of the rich soil. Every bottle will bring you back to Pago del Vicario and entice you to return.

FACTS		
ROOMS	23 double • 1 suite	
FOOD	contemporary regional cuisine	
DRINK	wine store • cafeteria • pool bar	
FEATURES	reading room • television area • Internet • winery tours	
BUSINESS	meeting facilities (capacity of 450) • Wi-Fi access • high-speed Internet	
NEARBY	Cabañeros National Park • Las Tablas de Daimiel (migratory bird sanctuary) • historic city of Almagro • shopping • bars • restaurants • Madrid • Seville	
CONTACT	Carretera Ciudad Real, Porzuna, km 16, 13080 Ciudad Real • telephone: +34.926.666 027 • facsimile: +34.926.666 029 • email: reservas@pagodelvicario.com • website: www.pagodelvicario.com	

PHOTOGRAPHS COURTESY OF PAGO DEL VICARIO HOTEL + WINERY.

Navarra

La Rioja

Catalonia

Castilla y León

mediterraneanspain

Aragón

Balearic Sea

Madrid

Castilla-La Mancha

Valencia

> Hospes Palau de la Mar
> Hotel Neptuno

Ibiza

> Hospes Amérigo

Formentera

• Alicante

Murcia

Andalucía

Mediterranean Sea

mediterranean spain

In the last few years, Spain's third largest city, Valencia, land of oranges and paella, has been grabbing the headlines and this attention looks set to continue. In 2007, this urban dynamo will host the America's Cup, and expects to attract over a million people. As such, it is consciously competing with Bilbao as the face of the future. Yet until only a few years ago, Valencia was mainly known as a rather derelict addendum to Costa Blanca and that legendary high-rise haunt of the not-so-glitterati—Benidorm. Equally low in profile but also gunning for more visible status is the neighbouring province of Murcia, where resort hotels and golf courses have mushroomed around La Manga. The shared Mediterranean coastline, from Costa del Azahar to Costa Blanca and Costa Cálida, has always been favoured by expatriates for its virtual year-round sunshine, sandy beaches and invitingly calm waters. Misguided planning has resulted in major urban blots and lengthy traffic jams, but just a few kilometres inland it feels as if time has stood still.

eating in the levante

'The land where the east wind blows', the Levante (Spain's eastern seaboard) is where historical influences, naturally enough, landed from across the Mediterranean. Fertile soil and temperate climes helped create the huerta—the vegetable garden of Spain south of Valencia, developed by the Moors who laid rice-fields and an irrigation network around the Albufera lagoon. All this still exists today, 500 years after the last Moors were thrown out on Madrid's orders, although the lagoon is visibly shrinking. Before the Moors even, the Romans left a taste for fish preserved in salt or brine and this technique has endured.

Today's reflection of this bountiful past is found at Valencia's central market, a soaring iron and glass-roofed structure recently restored and extended. Here finds a cornucopia of local produce and far more. Seafood is abundant and fresh. Rice—be it grains of bomba, granza or secreti—sold in huge sacks remains a mainstay of local cuisine, not in the form of soggy tourist paella but refined, inventive and multifarious. Some specialized restaurants clock up 70 different rice dishes—suddenly Italian risotto is relegated to the shadows.

PAGE 148: A classic beach scene at Benidorm, the epitome of Spain's pioneering resorts.

THIS PAGE (FROM TOP): Costa Blanca's white beaches stretch from Valencia to south of Alicante; cornucopian produce offered at Valencia's central market.

OPPOSITE: A shadowy picador looms over Valencia's bullring during the frenetic July Fair.

Gastronomy-wise, Valencia is coming up with the goods, although, for the moment at least, there are no Michelin-style celebrities. Instead there is a tantalizing choice of voguish restaurants and tapas bars serving sensational local and fusion fare with modern accents. Many chefs hail from afar, deserting cities such as Bilbao and Barcelona, even London, for Valencia's balmier climes and more relaxed pace. This is the place to sample clochinas (local mussels), escalibada (roasted vegetables doused in olive oil) and, of course, paella.

past glories

Marketing is in Valencia's blood as this was a much-respected region of traders. After the Moors bowed to Aragón in 1238, Valencia blossomed into a walled town with towering gateways (two of which survive) and, together with Barcelona, became the mercantile hub of a powerful Mediterranean kingdom which encompassed Naples and Sicily. The Italian Renaissance proved heavily influential on the city's architecture. A symbol of this heyday is the Lonja (Silk Exchange), built to cater for the booming silk trade (yet another Moorish innovation). Curving rib-vaults and twisted, rope-like columns embellish a soaring interior, just about rivalled by Valencia's various other historic highlights—the strangely asymmetrical cathedral and its octagonal bell-tower, the incredible baroque façade of the Museum of Ceramics and the stunning art collection of the Bellas Artes. Every one of these is proof that Valencia was a highly sophisticated city well before contemporary developments. However, as the location for the Republican troops' last stand during the Civil War, it suffered from decades of neglect under Franco; its rebirth is all the more significant.

explosive city

Valencia's other symbolic feature is its embroidered shawls. These originated with refugee Genoese weavers who churned out damask, brocade, taffeta and shantung silks. Today, dyeing and weaving techniques continue to survive, and Francis Montesinos, Valencia's answer to Jean-Paul Gaultier, flaunts it brilliantly and with absolutely no reserve. Traditional costumes hit the streets during Las Fallas, an exuberant annual fireworks and bonfire festival.

THIS PAGE (FROM TOP): A staircase at the back of the exquisite Lonja, built as the Silk Exchange during the city's 15th-century heyday; elaborate crenellations edge the edifice's main façade.

OPPOSITE (FROM LEFT): Parading giant mannequins in Valencia's famed Corpus Christi celebrations; this is the birthplace of the paella.

Even if you miss the delirious week (March 12–19), you are quite likely to encounter minor versions at any time of the year. Machine-gun-like explosions and sulphurous smoke clouds often greet a newly-married couple outside church. Detonations (to the extent that major displays have been moved to the riverbed to preserve the window panes of the old centre), noise and fire are a Valencian addition and pyrotechnics, another of their exports.

new cultural landmarks

A huge part of Valencia's renaissance is due to its ambitious cultural agenda. Countless contemporary structures have now joined the magnificent relics of Valencia's golden age— the 13th to 15th centuries. First came the IVAM which, when it opened in the early 1980s, was Spain's first museum of modern art and, as follows, a groundbreaking institution. A major extension by Japanese architects Kazuyo Sejima and Ryue Nishizawa will cover the entire block in a second 'skin' and vastly increase exhibition space.

Then came Sir Norman Foster's oval-shaped Congress Centre in 1998, and finally, the project to beat them all (and to empty municipal coffers), Santiago Calatrava's City of Arts and Sciences. Some say visionary, some say megalomaniac, but his masterwork leaves no one cold. Erected in the dried-up riverbed of the Turia that bisects the city, the massive concrete, steel and glass structures stand defiantly between pools of white mosaic and lush gardens. Calatrava himself is a native of the city who came to fame as an engineer when he built a controversial bridge for Seville's Expo '92. Ambitious, sculptural in form but not always practical, the City of Arts and Sciences took nine years to complete and cost an estimated 400 million euros. The mind-boggling complex offers L'Hemisfèric (an enormous eye-shaped planetarium and IMAX theatre), a science museum, a massive opera house shaped like a helmet and said to be Europe's largest, a gigantic 8-hectare (20-acre) oceanarium—in this case the work of Mexican architect Félix Candela—and endless promenades. Prestige is the goal here, with scale a close second; never mind the cost.

The city has commissioned British architect David Chipperfield and b720 Architects from Barcelona to design the centrepiece of the America's Cup in the re-organized port area of Valencia. With such high-profile precedents to live up to, it is unlikely to be an unassuming design. Valencia's other globally oriented arts undertaking is the Biennial of Contemporary Art, an international event that brings the city alive with installations, exhibitions and performing arts events.

escaping the hordes

Even if there remain one or two beautiful pockets along this coastline, from the majestic sweep of Sagunto's Roman amphitheatre to Alicante with its palm-lined avenues, engaging old quarter and hilltop castle, it is the hinterland that wins. Guadalest, for example, up a twisting road through the sierra behind Calpe, is an extraordinary sight. Granite pinnacles topped by towers and a ruined castle rise above undulating valleys of olive and almond trees—a mass of pink and white blossoms in February. South of Alicante, at Elche, lies a corner of Africa—Europe's largest palm grove, thought to have been originally planted by the Phoenicians, and today's source of all those fronds clutched throughout southern Spain every Palm Sunday. The history of this vast grove is echoed by the area's most important find, Dama de Elche, a superb Iberian sculpture now in Madrid's archaeological museum.

THIS PAGE: Valencia's profile will rise further with the America's Cup in 2007. Meanwhile, there is no shortage of yacht charters and delightful sailing holidays.

OPPOSITE (FROM TOP): Resembling a giant futuristic beetle, Santiago Calatrava's opera house is part of the City of Arts and Sciences built in Valencia's old riverbed; lace mantillas (shawls) and vivid silk dresses come into their own during the city's many festivals.

murcia + the mar menor

South of Alicante's tourist belt, the less-trodden province of Murcia offers its own huerta and a similarly serious emphasis on food, not least on the region's 35 and more varieties of tomatoes. Murcianos are very different from their more joyful neighbours; business-like in character, they demand high-quality cuisine and, as a result, their city is home to some excellent venues, from old-fashioned restaurants to buzzy tapas bars. The father of Murcian cuisine was Raimundo González, who brought local produce and dishes into the spotlight at his renowned restaurant, Rincón de Pepe, in the 1960s and 1970s. His torch is now carried by a French-born chef, Hervé Medina, while another of his 'descendants', Miguel González Molina, minds with great dedication Restaurante Raimundo González in the sumptuous setting of the city's former casino.

Beyond gastronomic diversions and Murcia's wedding cake of a cathedral where styles range from the Gothic to Churrigueresque baroque, the province's main interest is an immense saltwater lagoon, the Mar Menor. It is an obvious magnet for wildlife and, every autumn, the northern end turns a pale pink from thousands of flamingos en route to warmer climes. However, it is not just birds and bees, but also sun-loving humans, who head to La Manga, a narrow spit of land lined with beaches on either side. Development is rampant; often high-rises and sports head the list of priorities.

Things look distinctly drier around the town of Lorca, which marks the starting line of a limestone and chalk desert which extends into the provinces of Almería and Granada. The coastal highway actually misses out on Lorca completely by tunnelling through the hill crowned by the ruined Moorish castle, so preserving Lorca and its attractive centre of baroque mansions. The town's main claim to fame comes at Easter, as the sensational Semana Santa processions are among Spain's finest, and most colourful and traditional. Hooded penitents belong to one of two major brotherhoods (the whites and the blues) who, year after year, maintain a healthy rivalry. Their magnificent embroidered costumes are exhibited in their respective church-museums. However much this region tilts towards the future, silk never leaves the agenda.

THIS PAGE (FROM LEFT): Every Semana Santa (Easter week) Spain comes to a stop, above all in Andalucía, where a procession of hooded penitents take over the streets; Lorca and nearby Caravaca have especially strong traditions.

OPPOSITE: The marshlands of Mar Menor see flocks of migratory birds arriving at summer's end, from herons to flamingos.

...virtual year-round sunshine, sandy beaches and invitingly calm waters.

Hospes Amérigo

In 1858, Queen Isabella II inaugurated the new railway line from the capital Madrid to the Mediterranean city of Alicante. It was the first direct link from the nation's capital to a port, and launched an era of unprecedented growth and prosperity for the small regional centre. One of the promoters of the railroad was a local businessman named José Gabriel Amérigo, who also participated in many of the other initiatives that were to change the face of Alicante in a matter of decades. One of his most important projects was the redevelopment of a substantial parcel of land that had, until recently, been the church and convent of Santo Domingo. In collaboration with a prominent builder, Vicente Pérez Pérez, he converted the tract into a large apartment building that also incorporated a commercial passage through

its centre—a new innovation that first began to appear in Europe in the mid-19th century. These were spaces that mixed the public with the private; places to pass through on the way to work or a spot to while away over coffee with friends, and the passage soon became a dynamic microcosm of a rapidly changing urban lifestyle, filled with dazzling energy and commercial vitality. The Amérigo Passage, as it became known, represented a whole new concept of city dwelling. It stands today as a symbol of the vision and entrepreneurial spirit that helped to forge a modern, vibrant Spain and as a fitting addition to the Hospes chain.

The stunning Hospes Amérigo is the combination of a meticulous restoration with loving reverence for the original architecture and a minimalist interior design that imbues the property with the peace and tranquillity of its previous incarnations. One of the most impressive elements is the passageway that

reaches almost three storeys high and serves as a luminous central heartland. The designers were able to restore some of the convent's original stone walls, which can still be seen on each floor. The pointed arch windows in the reception area, restaurant, meeting rooms and suites add an air of elegance. There is a total of 80 guestrooms—including two junior suites and one full suite—all equipped with plasma television, free Internet access, high-capacity safe, Egyptian cotton sheets, natural essence bath amenities, terry bathrobes, slippers and minibar. To ensure a full and restful sleep, guests can select the perfect fit for their beds from the hotel's sumptuous pillow menu. The profusion of wood, earthy tones, avant-garde furniture, colourful pieces of modern art and superb lighting, all work to create an inviting and sophisticated atmosphere.

THIS PAGE (CLOCKWISE FROM TOP): *The reception area—in fact nearly everywhere throughout the building—is bathed in light; the rooftop pool is a remarkable work of design and is one of the best places in the hotel to a view; Bodyna Spa & Sensations.*

OPPOSITE (FROM TOP): *Old arch windows refurbished in glass offer views of the city streets.*

The rooftop terrace offers lovely views of the old part of the city. Santa Bárbara castle stands majestically in the background while you lounge in the solarium sipping a drink, take a swim in the heated pool or languish in the enormous jacuzzi. The castle—with several other symbolic monuments—is beautifully illuminated after dusk, making an evening visit especially memorable. The pool is covered in the winter to ensure a comfortable dip, and hotel guests have exclusive use of the fitness centre and luxurious spa facilities of Bodyna Spa & Sensations, which offers a delightful assortment of oriental treatments. The library and Internet zone off the passageway on the main floor is a brightly-lit corner with plenty of comfortable chairs for reading and enjoying the unsparing menu of CD and DVD titles.

The lobby bar has re-created the friendly ambience of the original passageway and Senzone Tapas Bar, with its dramatic contrasts of red and black, boasts a delicious selection. The gastronomic offerings served in the hotel's restaurant, Senzone, are made from fresh local ingredients and an abundance of seafood and natural produce. Through the imaginative innovation of its expert chefs, lost traditional flavours are rediscovered and transformed into a titillating succession of surprises for the senses. The stylish white-on-white décor of the dining room seems to change in personality throughout the day; fresh and energizing in

THIS PAGE (FROM TOP): The hotel's restaurant Senzone is smartly decked in a pure, minimalist black-and-white scheme; there are several meeting rooms which come fully equipped with superb business facilities and a sharp, polished atmosphere.

OPPOSITE: Modern art and furniture form a central part of the décor.

the morning, crisp and inviting at lunch, it is draped sensuously in sophistication during the evening. Guests may also sample the gourmet menu in the private comfort and convenience of their rooms 24 hours a day.

The hotel's business facilities include a flexible variety of meeting rooms with different capacities that, combined with unique spaces such as the passageway, make the Hospes Amérigo the perfect choice for meetings, small-scale conferences, product presentations and various social events. Another key feature is

the property's location in the heart of the city's historic district near its important monuments—such as City Hall and the Co-Cathedral of San Nicolas—which are also only minutes away from the maritime esplanade and beaches.

It is perhaps apt that a building which once represented the leading edge of modern industrial design in the rapidly-evolving Spain of the mid-19th century has now become a renowned, urbane five-star hotel in a city with a dynamic future. Exactly what we have come to expect from Hospes Hotels & Moments.

FACTS	
ROOMS	77 double • 2 junior suites • 1 suite
FOOD	Senzone Restaurant • Senzone Tapas Bar
DRINK	lounge bar • pool bar • Amérigo Passage
FEATURES	rooftop solarium • heated pool • fitness centre • sauna • massage and treatments
BUSINESS	7 meeting rooms (capacity of 15 to 120) • Internet access
NEARBY	Santa Bárbara Castle • maritime esplanade and beaches • restaurants and bars • shopping
CONTACT	Rafael Altamira 7, 03002 Alicante • telephone: +34.965.146 570 • facsimile: +34.965.146 571 • email: amerigo@hospes.es • website: www.hospes.es

PHOTOGRAPHS COURTESY OF HOTELS + MOMENTS.

Hospes Palau de la Mar

THIS PAGE (FROM TOP): *The grand entrance is brilliantly re-created from the former 19th-century palace's arched carriage port; the organic vegetable garden is a lush display amid stark white.*

OPPOSITE (FROM TOP): *The façade is noble with beautiful fenestration; Bodyna Spa's facilities include a pool, sauna and Turkish bath.*

The impressive record of Valencia's many achievements—which include being host to the 32nd America's Cup in 2007, housing Santiago Calatrava's spectacular City of the Arts and Sciences, and producing a local football team that is a perennial contender in the UEFA Champions League—has helped to catapult this arty regional capital to the forefront of Spain's international fame. This recently acquired reputation as one of the great cities of Europe demanded the presence of a world-class hotel, and the cosmopolitan Hospes Palau de la Mar has stepped up to accept the role with confidence and style.

Located in a small 19th-century palace in the well-heeled neighbourhood of Eixample Norte, the property exudes purity, authenticity and originality in perfect synchrony with the

Eighteen of the guestrooms are located in a separate garden area featuring geometric rows of scented herbs. The tranquillity belies the urban situation of the hotel and these rooms are fast becoming favourites with loyal guests who come back year after year. Five superior double rooms with romantic skylights for gazing at the stars and the magnificent

presidential suite complete the grand array of accommodation available to guests. The large, well-appointed library also serves as an executive business centre and can be set up as a meeting room for 30 people.

Senzone, which means 'a zone for the senses', is the hotel's elegant restaurant and, as guests quickly discover, it definitely lives

exuberant dynamism of the Valencian people and reverence for their tradition. The hotel's façade is elegant, yet discreet, and the grand entrance makes ingenious use of the former carriage driveway. A pure, minimalist design pervades the public areas and soft lighting adds warmth and silhouettes to the taupe-coloured walls which are complemented by tasteful pieces of modern art.

The 66 guestrooms maintain the overall 'less-is-more' theme with dark-stained wooden flooring and furniture that sits in dramatic contrast against the eggshell-coloured walls. The visual impression is one of spaciousness and a strong personality. The amenities are superb—a hallmark of the chain—and each room offers thoroughly luxurious beds laid with plush pillows and linen of the finest quality, flat-screen television, Internet access, wireless telephone, high-capacity safe, and the most comfortable bathrobes and slippers.

up to its name. Everything, from the tables and crystal ware to the lighting and décor, is a veritable feast for the eyes. The cuisine is a bold and inspired fusion of avant-garde techniques and affection for traditional dishes. The superb wine cellar and unparalleled service are additional guarantees that every meal will be a memorable occasion and a real treat for the senses.

The hotel's Bodyna Spa & Sensations comes equipped with a fitness area, pool, Turkish bath and sauna. Furthermore, the Turía Gardens are only a block away—ideal for a jog or ride along the extensive bike trails.

Hospes Palau de la Mar is a short stroll from the city centre, its fashionable shopping streets and the visually stunning City of the Arts and Sciences. Local hero Santiago Calatrava's

THIS PAGE (FROM TOP): **Purity is at the heart of the hotel's design ethos; the interior is based on the time-honoured architectural ideals of utilitas, firmitas, venustas— utility, strength and beauty; each exclusive guestroom is a handsome contemporary affair.**

OPPOSITE: **The presidential suite retains an air of neo-classicism.**

Palace of the Arts will amaze even the most jaded critic. Resembling an enormous futuristic luxury liner that has somehow beached itself in the former riverbed, its grandeur is matched by an unprecedented concert schedule that promises the world's finest orchestras and conductors. The proximity of the similarly conceived but smaller Hemisphere and the Science Museum combine to form one of the most impressive architectural groupings in the world today. The Oceanographic Park is a must-see; the final element of the ambitious redevelopment that has placed Valencia at the forefront of Spanish cities.

Each year during the week ending March 19, Valencia celebrates the Fallas. Activities begin with the ear-shattering Mascletà at noon before City Hall and end with spectacular fireworks. The Fallas—which are large castle-like structures built of wood, styrofoam and papier-mâché—are populated by whimsical characters called ninots, and competition for the annual prizes is fierce. The conclusion of the celebrations is dramatic—setting the Fallas ablaze on the eve of St. Joseph in a ritual of purification and springtime renewal.

Another sensational element of the Fallas is the colourful traditional costumes worn by local women, especially during the floral tribute to the Virgin of the Defenceless. The elaborate braided hairpieces and stunning brocade dresses are truly magnificent; the epitome of elegance, purity and authenticity— the very attributes that inspired and, indeed, define the Hospes Palau de la Mar.

FACTS

ROOMS	60 double • 5 superior double • 1 presidential suite
FOOD	Senzone Restaurant: avante-garde/traditional
DRINK	lobby bar
FEATURES	Bodyna Spa & Sensations • garden rooms • modern art •
BUSINESS	meeting rooms (capacity of 30 to 200) • Internet access
NEARBY	City of Arts and Sciences • Hemisphere • Science Museum • Oceanographic Park • shopping • running and biking trails
CONTACT	Navarro Reverter 14, 46004 Valencia • telephone: +34.96.316 2884 • facsimile: +34.96.316 2885 • email: palaudelamar@hospes.es • website: www.hospes.es

PHOTOGRAPHS COURTESY OF HOTELS + MOMENTS.

Hotel Neptuno

At the turn of the last century, Las Arenas in Valencia was a jumble of modest cottages and run-down warehouses that mostly faced away from the Mediterranean Sea. That all changed, however, when some imaginative and dynamic families began to establish a number of cosy restaurants and small hotels along the beaches. It wasn't very long before the incomparable seafood and paellas turned the area into a popular holiday destination for savvy locals. Today, even foreign visitors know that the tastiest versions of Valencia's famed rice dishes are to be found in the area.

A hundred years after its big turnaround, Valencia is now about to experience an even greater boom as it gets ready to host the 32nd America's Cup in 2007, and the stylish Hotel

THIS PAGE (FROM LEFT): *One of the suites, which opens onto a large private terrace, outdoor jacuzzi and breathtaking sea views; rooms have been aptly designed in a contemporary Nordic style.*

OPPOSITE (FROM LEFT): *Amid such vast sky and sea, it is easy to imagine being on the deck of a ship far out in the middle of ocean; as its décor suggests, Tridente serves designer and avant-garde Mediterranean fare.*

Neptuno is a star example of the spectacular changes taking place. The property is well anchored at the end of the row of restaurants facing Las Arenas beach and is just across the new America's Cup Port, where many of the activities will take place. As its name suggests, there is a distinct nautical theme about the hotel's design; beginning with the lobby that is decorated with large, dramatic photographs of challenger boats in action at sea. The glass-enclosed elevators provide a soothing view of the central patio, with water gently cascading down a three-storey wall of grey slate.

Most of the 45 standard rooms offer stunning views of the beach or the America's Cup Port and common décor elements include pinewood floors and darker ash furniture set against cream-coloured walls finished with sleek light-grey metal trim—the overall effect is an almost Nordic style. The bathrooms feature Spanish marble and jacuzzis, and

...sunrises over the sea...palm-lined promenade along the beach...the perfect scene.

every room comes with a flat-screen television, minibar, free high-speed Internet and a safe large enough for laptops. Two spacious suites on the upper level each has a private rooftop terrace complete with a large outdoor jacuzzi. The en-suite spa showers promise everything from a soothing massage to aromatherapy.

Tridente restaurant offers expansive views of the beach, attentive service and, with world-class Chef Josemi Bielsa at the helm, the menu promises exquisite fresh seafood

and traditional regional dishes. The wine menu is also well-conceived, with a comprehensive selection of mostly renowned Spanish labels; and the comfortable lobby bar offers a lighter menu and a pleasant environment for cocktails.

Outside, the sunrises over the sea and the palm-lined promenade along the beach set the perfect scene for a leisurely morning stroll. Nearby are the spectacular City of the Arts and Sciences, and El Saler shopping centre.

FACTS

ROOMS	45 standard • 3 junior suites • 2 full suites
FOOD	Tridente: avant-garde Mediterranean
DRINK	lobby bar
FEATURES	spa • roof deck • library • plasma television • free high-speed Internet access
NEARBY	Las Arenas beach • America's Cup Port • City of the Arts and Sciences • El Saler
CONTACT	Paseo de Neptuno 2, 46011 Valencia • telephone: +34.963.567 777 • facsimile: +34.963.560.430 • email: reservas@hotelneptunovalencia.com • website: www.hotelneptunovalencia.com

PHOTOGRAPHS COURTESY OF HOTEL NEPTUNO.

andalucía

Portugal

Castilla y León

Madrid

Aragón

Extremadura

Castilla-La Mancha

Valencia

Murcia

• Córdoba

> Hospes Palacio del Bailío

Andalucía

> AC Palacio de Santa Paula
> Hospes Palacio de los Patos

• Seville

> Casa del Maestro
> Hacienda Benazuza
> Hospes Las Casas del Rey de Baeza

• Granada

> Hacienda de San Rafael

• Málaga

> Hotel La Fuente de la Higuera

Cádiz •————> Villa Jerez

• Marbella

> Don Carlos Beach + Golf Resort Hotel
> Gran Hotel Guadalpin Banús
> Gran Hotel Guadalpin Marbella Spa

Isla de Alborán

Morocco

andalucía

It's almost a cliché: burning hot sun, cicadas, a strumming guitar, a gut-wrenching voice, olives, jamón, beer, wine and the click-clack stamp of flamenco dancers. Fire, passion, high colour and emotions. This is the heart and soul of that great swathe of southern Spain, Andalucía. Al-Andalus was originally the Moorish name for their entire Iberian territory before it shrank with the Reconquista's advance. By 1492 the last corner, the kingdom of Granada, fell, but the name Andalus stuck, a clear indication of the region's indelible Arab roots. Today this diverse belt of gently undulating land veers from horizons of olive groves to arid lunar landscapes near Almería or fertile pastures for fighting bulls near Cádiz. Just as beguiling as it was centuries ago, Andalucía's cultural appeal peaks in three remarkable cities: Córdoba, Granada and Seville, with Málaga now an additional magnet due to its intelligent reinvention. These are rivalled by the idyllic valleys of the Sierra Nevada, the Pueblos Blancos route and a few stretches of coast that have kept development at bay.

moorish imports

Above all, Andalucía is shrouded in the relics of its 800-year Moorish past: architecture, cuisine, crafts, music and fiery dark eyes are the obvious legacies. Over centuries, these astute settlers brought new agricultural methods as well as acres of olive and lemon groves, date palms, almonds and sugarcane. In fact, any Spanish food title beginning with 'al' derives from their presence. The aridity of the land was something the North Africans knew only too well, so irrigation became a prime concern. Today some might feel nostalgia for this era as, in tandem with climate changes, desertification is advancing alarmingly fast. Agriculture increasingly occurs inside immense plastic hothouses blanketing—and scarring —huge areas of eastern Andalucía and tended by armies of underpaid North Africans. It is said, but difficult to confirm, that they now extend so far that they are visible from the moon. Much of northern Europe's supply of avocados, artichokes, tomatoes and green beans is thus produced on a year-round basis. Olives are, however, product number one, and the area between Jaén and Córdoba is where the top quality is produced.

PAGE 168: Detail of the original Almohad palace in Seville.

THIS PAGE (FROM TOP): Flamenco footwork—heartbeat of Andalucía; crimson bougainvillea thrives in the region's hot, dry climate.

OPPOSITE: The Fountain of Doves in Seville's Parque de María Luisa, its intricately handpainted tiles and semi-permanent visitors.

tales of the alhambra

The historical heart of Andalucía is indisputably Granada. This magical town perched up in the shadow of peninsular Spain's highest mountains, the snow-capped Sierra Nevada, reeks of Moorish artistry and imagination. This is where the magnificent Alhambra Palace regally surveys its former territory in the plain below. Such an extraordinary complex of palaces, patios and gardens epitomizing Moorish architectural style never fails to seduce, the only drawback being its popularity. From the walls of the 9th-century Alcazaba, the original fortress, to the delicately carved archways and domes of the magnificent Nasrid Palace and the summer palace and gardens of the Generalife, it feels like paradise on earth. And this was precisely the aim. Every sense is ignited by a subtle combination of light, colour, sound and smell created by trickling fountains, reflective pools, cool shade and fragrant flowers such as roses, jasmine and honeysuckle. Nor is the intellect ignored, as lines of poetry are carved into numerous surfaces.

The walls once enclosed a self-contained community of palaces, workshops, baths, workers' houses, a madrasah (Islamic school) and mosques and, although several have disappeared, the surviving buildings exercise an incomparable magic. Even the Bourbon Carlos V succumbed and chose to live in Nasrid Palace, constructing an incongruous adjacent palace for ceremonies. Most photographed of all is the Patio de los Leones, a colonnaded courtyard that, in traditional Islamic style, is divided by water-channels which symbolize the four rivers of life. Three surrounding halls display breathtaking workmanship, from exquisite stucco ceilings and domes to walls tiled in dazzling colours and patterns.

Altogether the Alhambra is a hard act to follow, yet its impact is everywhere. On the hillside opposite lies the Albaycín, the former Moorish residential quarter. Here the structure and atmosphere of an Arab médina is preserved in a maze of narrow streets and steep alleyways threading their way past walled gardens, patios and Mudéjar details. Every corner brings a fabulous viewpoint, something the local gypsies are only too aware of for peddling their wares and wiles, and garden restaurants have made full use of. Although churches all over Spain were built on the foundations of mosques, contemporary Granada

THIS PAGE: *Classic perspective of the 14th-century Court of the Lions in Nasrid Palace within Granada's magnificent Alhambra.*

OPPOSITE (FROM TOP): *A sweeping view across the Albaycín, the old Moorish quarter of Granada; Guillermo Vázquez Consuegra's refurbishment of La Cartuja in Seville has transformed the old monastery and ceramics factory.*

has not ignored its burgeoning Muslim population, building a brand new mosque on the hilltop. Downhill, another reflection of the town's enduring North African links is Calderería Nueva, a street lined with charming Moroccan pastry shops and tearooms. Granada's favourite spot for an outdoor drink is at the base of the Albaycín beside the Darro river, overlooked by the towers and walls of the Alhambra high above.

the other granada

Besides a converted caravanserai, Arab baths and La Madraza (a 14th-century Islamic college), the rest of Granada is very much a Renaissance and baroque city. Everyone in town pays homage to the Catholic kings, Ferdinand and Isabel, who have lain entombed for five centuries in the royal chapel of the city's grandiose cathedral. Vying with their regal presence is the sacristy where an impressive collection of ecclesiastical glitter joins Isabel's art collection—spot the Botticelli and the Memling. Granada's other major Catholic sight is the monastery of La Cartuja, on the northern edge of town. Although the Carthusians aimed to live austerely, they did not hold back on ornamentation, and La Cartuja reveals a mind-boggling interior of gilt, mirrors and marquetry—with cherubim revelling in it all.

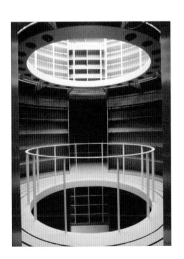

Despite this weight of history and pomp, Granada is a youthful city. Fifty thousand students keep the nights and tapas bars alive and there is no shortage of cultural events—without counting the permanent flamenco strumming up in the gypsy quarter of Sacromonte. The summer festival is one to aim for as concerts are held in the evocative gardens of the Generalife. Shoppers also have a field day in Granada, snapping up ornate fans and local ceramics in the touristy Alcaicería—the rebuilt Moorish soukh next to the cathedral—antiques near the Plaza Nueva or fashion and shoes in the avenues and streets to the south. There are even a few Arab-style hammams to recover in. Literati will head for the birthplace of Federico García Lorca, one of Spain's greatest poet-playwrights who met with a tragic and brutal end at the hands of Franco's troops in 1936. Despite the subsequent prohibition on his works by the fascist government, Lorca attained an almost mythical status, and a visit to his family farmhouse has now become something of a literary pilgrimage.

córdoba's big mosque

Córdoba presents a very different atmosphere and character. Less extroverted, more soulful and much smaller, its fame comes from an extraordinary Muslim-Catholic hybrid structure as well as some champion bullfighters and flamenco artists. Yet Córdoba had incredibly illustrious beginnings; its 10th-century zenith making it the envy of Europe. Philosophers, poets, mathematicians and doctors thrived in this intellectual hothouse (a word that can be applied literally when the summer heat soars). After being reconquered in 1236, Córdoba slumped into somnolence and its 1,000-odd mosques vanished—all except La Mezquita.

This massive edifice towering over Guadalquivir river opposite a Roman bridge is the absolute jewel in Córdoba's crown. One of the largest in the world and the only one left from medieval Spain, its construction spanned 200 years from the 8th century. Today the rhythmical horseshoe arches and their 824 columns (each distinct) give the same sense of infinity that its architects wished to convey in harmony with Islamic belief. It is a masterpiece—save for its carbuncle, namely the Renaissance-baroque cathedral built smack in the middle of the mosque. There could be no better symbol of the Reconquista than this.

Then there is the fortress-palace, Alcázar de los Reyes Cristianos, with its lovely water-gardens and maze of backstreets packed with delightful patios. These come into their own each May during the Feria, when contests are held for the prettiest. Feria also sees taking to the arena, Córdoba's formidable bullfighters—the legendary Manolete hailed from here and is adulated by younger generations. An offshoot of this is Museo Taurino, where suits of light and memorabilia give great insight into this controversial, highly theatrical sport.

A different sense of the golden days of Islamic Spain lies a few miles west of Córdoba at one of Spain's most important archaeological sites, the Médina Azahara. These are the atmospheric ruins of a vast 10th-century palace of a Caliph of the Umayyad dynasty, built in honour of his favourite wife Al-Zahra ('orange blossom'). At the time it was an even more sumptuous structure than was to appear later in Granada. Marble of all hues, ebony, ivory and precious stones figured among the materials, and it is said that some 10,000 workers were employed. Yet Islam, like Christianity, has its variants, and after only 70 years, the lavishly decorated palace was destroyed by a more puritanical wave of rulers.

sevillian hedonism

Back in the present, Seville is easily Andalucía's most enjoyable theatre set, a playful, fun-loving regional capital. Spread out along the banks of the Guadalquivir river, it manages to combine a rich history going back to the Phoenicians and Romans with a passion for food and the arts. It is no surprise that two famed literary legends were born here: the serial heart-breaker Don Juan, and that firebrand Carmen, who stomped her feet and nursed her divided heart while working in Seville's old tobacco factory—then entered operatic history.

Like Córdoba, Seville's inhabitants are addicted to bullfighting and flamenco, but you can add two more: tapas and sherry. All of these combine marvellously during the Feria de Abril, when thousands of traditionally dressed locals converge on the fairground to party, and indulge, day and night. In contrast, Seville's other big calendar event, Semana Santa, is one of the most moving in Andalucía along with Málaga's, filling streets with processions, penitents and religious statues—interjected by the occasional grito, a gut-wrenching howl.

THIS PAGE (FROM TOP): The ornate façade of the Plaza de España; sunflowers colour the fields in southwestern Andalucía.

OPPOSITE: The belltower of Córdoba's cathedral started life as a minaret towering over the mezquita in Moorish Spain.

Twice over in the 20th century, Seville has entered the world spotlight: firstly as host to the 1929 Latin American Expo which left pavilions in the Parque de María Luisa, then as the site for Expo '92. This world fair bequeathed a string of white elephants on Isla de la Cartuja, a trail-blazing bridge by Santiago Calatrava, 70 km (43½ miles) of new streets, and the high-speed train AVE to Madrid. Since then Seville has concentrated on upgrading the town centre in more subtle ways, and there have been no great urban projects comparable in Spain's other major cities. Yet Seville remains a perennial favourite, as much for its strikingly varied monuments as for its atmospheric patio hotels and trail of enticing bars and restaurants.

As the main port for expeditions to the Americas, the city of Seville has reaped its rewards. Columbus, Magellan and Elcano all set sail from here and the ensuing two-way trade brought a steady flow of gold and silver into the city. The result was a plethora of churches and monasteries gleaming with baroque gilt and alive with carved angels, as well as a notable school of baroque painting. Francisco Pacheco was its father, and the great Diego Velázquez was one of his pupils. Another was Murillo, but his diaphanous renderings of beatific virgins in clouds of cherubim are a lot less compelling.

Seville's towering Giralda is the number-one sight, now attached to the massive cathedral. Once again Moorish Spain re-emerges, as the tower served originally as a minaret, its interior ramp for the muezzin (the crier) to ascend on horseback to make the call to prayer. The cathedral itself is no less impressive as it is the world's third largest after St. Peter's in Rome and St. Paul's in London; one century was just about long enough for its construction, so giving it a late-Gothic and Renaissance style. For a true embodiment of Latin American riches, the high altar takes the biscuit as it is said to incorporate 2.5 tonnes (5,500 lb) of the precious metal from Mexico and Peru. Stunning craftsmanship is joined by Columbus' alleged tomb and a sacristy packed with treasures. Right opposite stands the celebrated Alcázar of Seville, another feast of Moroccan carved stucco and tile-work with a typically relaxing garden.

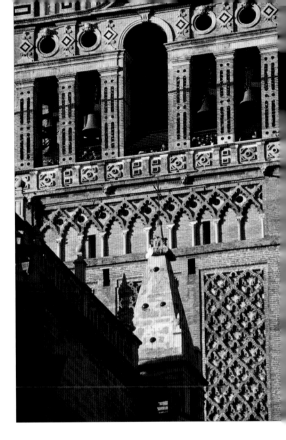

Out on the streets, Seville's most obvious area to explore lies in wait just east of the cathedral, in Santa Cruz. This attractive web of streets, once the Jewish quarter, is today heavily geared toward visitors, yet still retains much of its charm—from flowery patios to traditional tapas bars. The real Seville lies further north in the tiny, narrow streets and little plazas between the historical Centro and the wide esplanade of Alameda de Hércules (named after Seville's mythical founder). This is a place to get lost in, to enjoy its quaint specialist shops and markets, and to sample tapa after tapa. Triana, too, across the river from La Maestranza and once a workers' suburb, is witnessing a new flourishing wave of well-designed venues and tapas bars.

tapas territory

Seville is widely claimed to be where tapas were invented. Who knows if this is true, but the explanation—a tapa ('lid') of cheese or sausage covering a glass of fino to keep the flies off—does ring relatively true. At any rate, the city now boasts a deluge of over 1,000 tapas bars, and several of these are coming up with a multitude of thoroughly original and revolutionary dishes. Gone are the days when you were served a saucer of fried whitebait or olives to help your beer down—and encourage the next round. Today tapas have changed spectacularly, and have even become an art in themselves.

Throughout the year people spill onto the pavement or squeeze up to a sherry barrel to wolf down ever more varied composite lunches. Gazpacho, chilled soup that came to Andalucía with the Moors, assumes numerous guises and develops into thicker salmorejo, a delicious tomato cream laced with garlic or ajo blanco, a classic of almonds and grapes. Chicken thighs are baked in a honey and mustard sauce or stuffed with prunes and nuts then served with a blackberry sauce. Potatoes are mashed with diced green pepper and onions and doused in litres of heavenly virgin olive oil. If anything is the secret of Andalucian cuisine, it is their access to divinely fresh, top-grade ingredients, as well as a historical grounding in fearless combinations of sweet and salty flavours.

THIS PAGE (FROM TOP): *Delicate brick-work and blind arches front La Giralda—Seville's iconic minaret and belltower—erected by the Almohads in the 12th century; with emerging combinations of new techniques and flavours, the tapas tradition is changing shape at a remarkable pace.*

OPPOSITE (FROM TOP): *Esparto grass blinds, ideal for keeping out the sweltering heat, at the Hospes Las Casas del Rey de Baeza; patio of legendary 10th-century Hacienda Benazuza.*

picasso, son of málaga

Andalucía's indisputable creative giant was none other than painter and sculptor, Pablo Picasso. Born in central Málaga in 1881, Picasso spent the first decade of his life in this luminous, exuberant port, thematically absorbing an obsession with bullfighting as well as his iconic dove of peace. Although he never returned to his hometown after a brief visit in 1900, Málaga never forgot him. Finally, in 2003, the much overdue Museo Picasso opened its doors to reveal a stupendous collection of around 250 major works, donated and loaned by Christine Ruiz-Picasso, his daughter-in-law, and Bernard, his grandson.

In order to reintegrate their prodigal son, the Andalucian government invested nearly 70 million euros in this landmark in the heart of old Málaga, just a few minutes' walk from the artist's birthplace in Plaza de la Merced. It joins a handful of major sights clustered around a hill which overlooks the port: a Roman theatre, the much-renovated 11th-century Alcazaba and, high above, the ruins of the 14th-century Gibralfaro castle. All are striking relics of Málaga's long history—a factor that delayed the museum schedule by over two years when Phoenician walls were uncovered in its foundations. Now spotlit as artworks in themselves, these walls lie below a beautifully renovated Renaissance mansion. Locked into this edifice is an intelligently designed extension by New York architect Richard Gluckman and Spanish architects Isabel Cámara and Rafael Martín Delgado.

Thus Málaga, a seaside town not previously associated with a strong cultural agenda, now claims not only the Museo Picasso, but also a slick contemporary art centre, the CAC, and a sharply designed museum illustrating the town's history. As a result, instead of speeding from the airport en route to the sybaritic delights of Marbella or north to the towering splendour of the Alhambra, many people are now giving more time to this extroverted Andalucian crossroads. Art aside, Málaga is an unpretentious place for enjoying tapas bars, pedestrianized shopping streets, breezy seafood restaurants and a few city beaches. Easter Week brings stirring nocturnal processions and crowds of thousands without any aggression, and in August, the Feria keeps the town and its fairground buzzing on a 24-hour basis.

THIS PAGE (FROM TOP): Olives, the economic mainstay of Andalucía, blanket the hillsides between Jaén and Córdoba; a street scene in Málaga, home to the Picasso Museum and one of Spain's most exuberant summer ferias.

OPPOSITE (FROM LEFT): Quintessential Andalucian—whitewashed walls, tiled roof and geraniums; the Pueblos Blancos route of striking hill-towns stretches from Cádiz to Málaga.

andalucía's hidden secrets

THIS PAGE (FROM TOP): The Virgen del Carmen, the patron of fishermen, is enthusiastically paraded and celebrated every July 16 in fishing-villages and ports throughout Andalucía; Cádiz cathedral stands on a peninsula first visited by the Phoenicians in 1100 BCE.

OPPOSITE: Rippling sand dunes, lagoons, maquis and herons contribute to the beauty and biodiversity of Donaña National Park in the region's far west.

However captivating they may be, Andalucía's cities are also gateways to vast stretches of relatively unspoilt and addictive interior. Even there, between herds of bell-tinkling goats and pottery shops, a new sophistication is creeping in; many country cortijos are now the pastoral settings for some wonderful guesthouses and hotels. The terraced foothills of the Sierra Nevada and the Alpujarras, which lie between Granada and Málaga, have in recent years lured waves of expatriates in search of rural bliss and idyll. Here, you will find goats, jamón, almonds and yoga classes belonging in tandem.

Another area experiencing a surge in popularity is Costa de la Luz, south of Cádiz and Jerez. This greener side of Andalucía boasts some stunning hilltop villages (Vejer de la Frontera being particularly entrancing), breathtaking sandy beaches and strong Atlantic winds—Tarifa, its southern tip, is one of Europe's best windsurfing spots. Further west to the Portuguese border lies yet another surprise, the Doñana National Park, where shifting sand dunes and riverside pastures nurture one of Spain's richest wildlife populations.

And then there is eastern Andalucía between Granada and Almería, traditionally much poorer but catching up fast. Despite encroaching coastal development around Mojácar and Roquetas, there remains one unspoilt corner: Cabo de Gata Natural Park. Beyond a blight of plastic hothouses, it conceals a host of unexpected sights—derelict gold mines, tiny fishing-villages, deserted beaches, volcanic rock formations and the farmhouse scene of the crime of passion that inspired García Lorca's *Blood Wedding*.

Further inland, desert-like crests and valleys of karst and shale are pockmarked with caves which still function as desirable residences—and replete with satellite dishes. This ambivalent corner of Andalucía could be North Africa, the Middle East or the Wild West, and as such has been targeted by many filmmakers. *Lawrence of Arabia* (1962) started the trend, but it was Sergio Leone who multiplied the screen presence of these landscapes in his 1960s-to-1970s spaghetti westerns, with Indiana Jones and many others following suit. Proof that, whatever the clichés and in spite of an ever-increasing stream of tourists, Andalucía is perhaps Spain's most evocative region.

Fire, passion, high colour and emotions.

AC Palacio de Santa Paula

Spain offers a wonderful treasure trove of former palaces, monasteries and noble estates to explore and sleep in; a cultural experience much appreciated by visitors from abroad. Yet it takes great vision and a delicate touch to successfully convert a historic monument into a luxury hotel, and even more so when the project involves architectural gems as precious and revered as the magnificent 16th-century

Santa Paula Convent and 14th-century Casa Morisca in the city of Granada. The meticulous restorations that now form the heart and soul of the enchanting Palacio de Santa Paula are of the same excellence that we have come to expect from the AC Hotels group, but what makes this property distinct is its perfect blend of modern design and ancient splendour. The result is an exceptional hotel that has already found a place of pride in the rich architectural patrimony of this legendary city.

The buildings' mixture of singular spaces has allowed the design team to create several distinct room types. The hotel's standard rooms are found in the modern part of the hotel and offer the full range of amenities that AC guests have become accustomed to—complimentary minibar, wireless Internet and a selection of sublime pillows. The superior rooms, featuring the same amenities, offer the added charm of being located in the atmospheric convent or

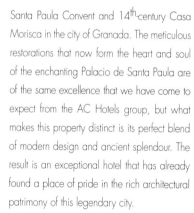

...perfect blend of modern design and ancient splendour.

Casa Morisca. The junior suites, housed in the latter, feature luxurious parquet floors and high wood-beamed ceilings, each suite replete with a separate lounge area and VIP amenities.

The convent's cloister is the crown jewel of the establishment, adding luminosity and an air of grace and tranquillity. The former library adjoins the area and has been converted into a magnificent restaurant—El Claustro—which serves lunch, dinner and a fabulous breakfast buffet featuring homemade pastries for which the hotel's kitchen is justifiably well-renowned. Connoisseurs will appreciate the restaurant's exquisite gourmet menu inspired by traditional cuisine of the region, as well as the extensive list of excellent Spanish wines.

Legend has it that the last Sultan of the city, sent into exile by the Catholic Kings with the fall of Granada in 1492, wept when he gazed upon his beloved city for the last time. Guests should not be surprised nor saddened if they experience a similar reaction after a sojourn at the AC Palacio de Santa Paula; just remember, you can always come back.

FACTS		
ROOMS	standard • superior • suites	
FOOD	El Claustro: gourmet regional	
FEATURES	fitness centre	
BUSINESS	4 meeting rooms • high-speed Internet • audiovisual equipment	
NEARBY	city centre • the Cathedral • El Alhambra	
CONTACT	Gran Vía de Colón 31, 18001 Granada • telephone: +34.958.805 740 • facsimile: +34.958.805 741 • email: psantapaula@ac-hotels.com • website: www.ac-hotels.com	

Casa del Maestro

The worlds of flamenco and the bullring have always shared deep roots, and in no place is this truer than in Seville. This close relationship is symbolized by the two colours ochre and dark red; an old combination commonly seen throughout the city. The ochre is called 'albero' in Spanish—the name of the clay that is used in the bullring; the red represents blood, passion and drama. The perfect synthesis of these essential elements of Andalucian temperament can be found in the exquisite Casa del Maestro, shyly tucked away on tiny Almudena Street in the historical centre of the city.

It is no coincidence that the name of the property begins with 'casa'—this is just exactly the impression everyone has when they arrive. The balconies with potted geraniums, the imposing wooden door, tiled entranceway and delightful patio, all make it look like one of the many late 19th-century homes in the neighbourhood. 'Maestro' is a special tribute, a reference to the house's long association with legendary flamenco guitarist, El Niño Ricardo, who lived there most of his life.

The owners have taken great pains to maintain the original style, respecting both the character and architecture of the building.

THIS PAGE (FROM TOP): *With its old photographs, wooden windows and doors and beautiful mosaic floor, the house has been lovingly maintained with its history and architecture in mind; cool drinks are served while guests lounge on the sunbeds; rooms are naturally lit and offer views of the lively streets below.*
OPPOSITE: *The hotel's old, modest interiors evoke nostalgia for a world in a different time.*

The result is 11 charming bedrooms, each proud and distinct with evocative names such as 'Memories of Seville' and 'Flamenco Nostalgia'. The rooms are compact, artfully decorated and lacking in none of the amenities one would usually expect.

Old photographs adorn the public areas, and on each level is a glass display with a different 'suit of light'—a bullfighter's dress—donated by famous matadors who are friends of the family. The rooftop terrace offers splendid vistas over the sea of red-tiled roofs that is old Seville, punctuated by mudéjar-style bell towers of Santa Catalina and San Pedro.

Breakfast is served in a small room with few tables; an affair that sometimes demands patience in this popular establishment. Yet this is precisely the greatest reward offered here—a different sense of time, a relaxed rhythm that allows one to slow down and perceive life in a different manner—a true gift and a rare privilege. Seville and the Casa del Maestro, a perfect combination.

FACTS

ROOMS	11 doubles and singles
FOOD	all-day breakfast on the roof
DRINK	salon
FEATURES	rooftop terrace • Seville-style patio • bullfighting memorabilia
NEARBY	Old Seville • Mozarabic churches of San Pedro and Santa Catalina • Casa de Pilatos • Tetuan and Sierpes: shopping • bars • restaurants
CONTACT	Almudena 5, 41003 Seville • telephone: +34.954.500 007 • facsimile: +34.954.500 006 • email: reservas@lacasadelmaestro.com • www.lacasadelmaestro.com

Don Carlos Beach + Golf Resort Hotel

THIS PAGE (FROM TOP): *One of Don Carlos' several marvellous Beach Suites—each comes with its own private sun terrace, an enormous lounge area and a shared pool; nuzzled delightfully amid palms and gardens and surrounded by Marbella's beautiful coastline, this is the town's trendiest resort.*

OPPOSITE: *Full-length windows, light wooden furnishings and tones of sandy hues give the rooms a fresh, pleasant feel.*

Over the last 50 years Marbella has secured itself as the most fashionable resort get-away in the Costa del Sol. The romantic old town—a maze of cobbled streets, shaded squares, colourful gardens and picturesque houses—is dotted with glitzy restaurants and sophisticated bars catering to a pampered clientele, and luxurious boutiques and international retail brands squeeze into its narrow stone alleys.

Set on the edge of this cosmopolitan parade, yet firmly established within the centre of stylish society, is the five-star Don Carlos Beach & Golf Resort Hotel. Nestled amid lush sub-tropical gardens with exotic flowers and pine woods opening up onto Marbella's finest beach, the property's exclusive grounds encompass gorgeous rooms and suites, bars, restaurants, multiple swimming pools, and its Beach Club where, just next door, you will find the famous Nikki Beach, host to—according to the *Observer*—the world's sexiest parties.

The rooms are modern and spacious, all decorated in a timeless contemporary style. The Mediterranean sunlight pours in through floor-to-ceiling windows and looking out, you'll find stunning views along the coastline. Beach Suites in separate annexes share a private pool and include huge lounge areas, fully-equipped kitchens and private sun terraces.

The main pool offers a tranquil haven for relaxation; with superb views of the ocean and the lush gardens, you can easily spend the day hopping between sunbeds and the bright mosaic bar of Sol y Sombra with its enticing menu of cocktails, snacks and light meals. Set between the wide sandy beach and the hotel's vibrant gardens, the second pool forms part of the Beach Club. During the day Nikki Beach caters to luxury al fresco dining at huge wooden tables amid white cushioned benches and sail-like awnings masterfully tied to palms. Beautiful lounging beds on the beach create a sun-worshipper's paradise and—assuming you can keep awake long enough—you can request for massages to be delivered on your own divan. As the sun dips behind the Mediterranean,

Nikki Beach bursts alive with Marbella's most trendy parties. For a more intimate dining atmosphere, aperitifs on La Terrasse, followed by an elegant dinner at Los Naranjos, offer a sophisticated alternative.

The hotel's strategic location in the heart of the Golf Coast—where over 50 courses stretch between Málaga and Soto Grande—

confirms it as a favourite of golf lovers. The hotel boasts its own Tennis Academy—with 10 courts within the property's gardens—and many beach sports which include windsurfing, sailing, water-skiing and jet-skiing. To wind down after a full day of activities, the hotel's gym comes with a full complement of steam baths, massages and a hydro-massage.

FACTS		
ROOMS	superior • superior sea view • deluxe • suites • 24 Beach Suites	
FOOD	Los Naranjos: à la carte • Bahía: breakfast buffet • Sol y Sombra: light meals	
DRINK	Beach Club • La Terrasse	
FEATURES	pools • beach • gardens • golf • tennis academy • water sports • gym • massages • hydro-massage • steam baths	
BUSINESS	wireless Internet • conference centre • banqueting	
NEARBY	Puerto Banús • Costa del Golf	
CONTACT	Carretera de Cádiz, km 192, 29604 Marbella • telephone: +34.952.768 800 • facsimile: +34.952.833 429 • email: info@hoteldoncarlos.com • website: www.hoteldoncarlos.com	

PHOTOGRAPHS COURTESY OF DON CARLOS BEACH + GOLF RESORT HOTEL.

Gran Hotel Guadalpin Banús

THIS PAGE: The hotel's cheery, brightly-lit suites offer a cosy feeling of home and marvellous views of the Mediterranean.

OPPOSITE (FROM LEFT): Rooms boast a luxurious spread of comforts, but guests usually can't wait to explore the surrounding beach, golf courses and boutiques; day or night, the halcyon sight of swaying trees, vast sky and water from the terrace is lulling.

In the richly diverse region of Andalucía, covering the deserts of Almería and stunning pine forests of Serranía de Ronda, mountains stretch down to the coast, towards its most renowned region, Costa del Sol. Contrary to its gaudy reputation, the area—blessed with a stunning coastline dotted with local fishing villages and sophisticated, picturesque seaside towns—is inevitably one of Europe's most beautiful and frequented tourist destinations.

The exclusive marina of Puerto Banús, only a few kilometres from the historic city of Marbella, is just one of these villages now firmly established among the fashionable elite. It is just 5 minutes from the luxury five-star resort of the Guadalpin; however, passing a row of enticing designer boutiques, the short walk can quickly become an extravagant shopping trip. Luxury yachts are moored alongside the quay, and restaurants and bars line the waterfront in the likes of San Tropez.

...plenty of luxuriating in the Spanish sunshine.

As the mountains disappear into the sky in the background and—on a clear blue day—Africa stirs hazily across the ocean, it is an idyllic setting for a refreshing cerveza.

Back at the hotel, its glistening pool, rustling palm trees and the soft lapping of the sea offer a lovely setting for taking in the Spanish sunshine. A spacious terrace decked with an enormous pool is scattered with stylish sunloungers facing out across its beachfront. The Beach Club serves snacks during the day and is fantastic for sundowners.

A total of 40 golf courses line the coast in the surrounding area; guests are entitled to special rates and tee-off times, and classes can be organized from the comfort of your sunlounger or bar stool. Nearby, sister hotel the Gran Hotel Guadalpin Marbella has an innovative spa with a magnificent pool, individual treatment booths, and a thermal and relaxation room.

With its close proximity to Puerto Banús there's a huge variety of restaurants and bars; the hotel also offers some diverse dining opportunities. La Proa, an exquisite seafood restaurant, serves the finest local catches; the prestigious Ristorante L'Ambasciata offers superb Italian dishes prepared by a worthy 2-Michelin-star chef; Abanda has a menu of rice dishes from around the world and home-style Basque cooking may be tasted at Lorea.

Luxurious rooms with extravagant en-suites outfitted with every modern accessory draw you to sleep after dusk, and the private terraces, looking out onto the Mediterranean, are a perfect setting for a final nightcap.

FACTS

ROOMS	181
FOOD	La Proa: seafood • Ristorante L'Ambasciata: Italian • Abanda: international • Lorea: Basque
DRINK	Beach Bar • Sofia Cocteles • Boulevard Cafe
FEATURES	pool • beach • golf facilities • spa (sister hotel Marbella) • business facilities
BUSINESS	3 modern halls
NEARBY	Puerto Banús • Marbella
CONTACT	Edgar Neville s/n, Nueva Andalucía, Marbella • telephone: +34.952.899 700 • facsimile: +34.952.899 701 • email: reservas@guadalpin.com • website: www.granhotelguadalpin.com

PHOTOGRAPHS COURTESY OF GRAN HOTEL GUADALPIN BANÚS.

Gran Hotel Guadalpin Marbella Spa

Luxury has been the most important commodity in Marbella, Spain's jet-set destination on Costa del Sol, ever since Prince Alfonso von Hohenlohe and other visionaries began to promote the sun-drenched coastal resort over 50 years ago. The architects and designers of the Guadalpin Marbella never lost sight of that fundamental truth, and the result is a universe of opulence and comfort, a guarantee of a truly unforgettable experience.

There are a total of 127 luxury rooms and suites to select from, most of them with splendid views of the Mediterranean, refined décor, and all the comforts that you would expect in a deluxe property. Most of the suites have two or three bedrooms, each with a private bathroom and lounge, while all have a fully-equipped kitchen or kitchenette and a private terrace or balcony. Many also have a jacuzzi, a solarium or an extra large terrace.

...a universe of opulence and comfort...a truly unforgettable experience.

Restaurants play a fundamental role in the Guadalpin Marbella experience, with award-winning Chef Ramón Freixa in command at Aralia serving Mediterranean-inspired dishes, and Mesana, which offers gourmet cuisine with all the latest trends and innovations. Taro Guadalpin provides the exotic touch with renowned Chef Masao Kikuchi delighting diners with exquisite Japanese cuisine and the finest sushi around. The Pool Bar features a wide selection of cocktails and tropical fruit juices.

Health and beauty are in expert hands at the 1,200 sq-m (12,916 sq-ft) Guadalpin Spa, which houses a dynamic pool and four different sections—individual treatment cabins, an area for taking the waters, a thermal and a relaxation area. The Fitness Centre, located on the first floor of the hotel, offers ample facilities with plenty of natural light and magnificent views.

For golfers, the area around Marbella has the highest number of courses in Europe. The Golf Department offers guests special rates on most courses and the possibility of booking a tee-off time and private instruction.

Of course, after all that activity you will want to book an appointment at the hotel's exclusive hair salon, Cebado. Additional services include manicures, pedicures, make-up and hair-removal treatments. The hotel houses a shopping mall, Boulevard Guadalpin, featuring prestigious designers such as Andalucian Victorio y Lucchino. And of course, there is always the beach.

THIS PAGE (FROM TOP): Guadalpin Spa is unsparing in its range of facilities and dedication; to match their laudable service are fine restaurants and a Pool Bar for drinks and snacks.

OPPOSITE (FROM TOP): Breakfast on the terrace with an uninterrupted vista of open land and clear sky; the dazzling lapis lazuli waters of the pool offer a cool respite.

FACTS		
ROOMS	127 luxury rooms and suites	
FOOD	Aralia: Mediterranean • Mesana: gourmet • Taro Guadalpin: Japanese	
DRINK	Pool Bar	
FEATURES	dynamic pool • fitness centre • Guadalpin Spa • Cebado hair salon • exclusive shopping mall • shuttle to Puerto Banús	
BUSINESS	meeting rooms • business centre with Internet access	
NEARBY	Golden Mile of Marbella • shopping • bars • cafés • beaches • golf • sailing	
CONTACT	Blvd. Príncipe Alfonso de Hohenlohe, 29600 Marbella, Málaga • telephone: +34.952.899 400 • facsimile: +34.952.899 401 • email: info@granhotelguadalpin.com • website: www.granhotelguadalpin.com	

PHOTOGRAPHS COURTESY OF GRAN HOTEL GUADALPIN MARBELLA SPA.

Hacienda Benazuza

There are hotels built upon legends, others that were constructed by legends, many which have hosted legends, and those that aspire to become legends; then there is the Hacienda Benazuza. There is an indefinable magic that envelops this magnificent Andalucian estate with more than a millennium of history to its name. Perhaps it is the spirits of the Saracen princes, sainted kings and medieval counts, legendary bullfighters, Hemingway and other modern potentates who have strolled through her exquisite gardens and patios. Then again it may also be the alchemy of Ferran Adrià, super-star chef who has somehow transferred the aesthetic behind his world-famous cuisine to a hotel experience. The combination is a perfect recipe, and the result is pure gold.

Forty-four extraordinarily beautiful rooms and suites await the privileged guest; each is exquisitely decorated with valuable antiques and artworks. Many feature wooden beams, canopy beds and painted vault ceilings, and the windows open onto cool interior patios or exterior gardens scented by orange blossoms and jasmine. The amenities are exactly what discerning travellers would expect of a hotel in this category, where nothing has been left to chance. The common areas are just as resplendent, and the restored architecture is truly sublime. The service is both exceptional and discreet. As one soon discovers, this is a hotel in a league of its own.

Guests have exclusive use of the pool at Belmonte Terrace, a jacuzzi, daybeds in quiet shaded areas and private patios. Strolling through the French Gardens is a delight any time of the day and a visit to the beautiful 17th-century chapel is a must. There are also tennis and paddle tennis courts on the estate and a horse riding range near the hotel. For those who can't leave business behind, there are five meeting rooms of various capacities equipped with the latest technology.

There are three restaurants which include two-Michelin-star La Alquería, where you can try Ferran Adrià's recipes from the acclaimed El Bulli. Next to the pool, La Alberca is an open-air alternative that offers an Andalucian menu by Chef Rafa Morales. Sample tapas at La Abacería for a true Seville experience. Guadarnes Bar, a salon in equestrian décor and access to the French Gardens, is the perfect place for drinks. In the summer, El Sur Bar offers a romantic ambience by the pool and the opportunity to watch a silent movie.

When asked "why a hotel?" Ferran Adrià answered, "perhaps because cuisine is not something to be had, but a state to be in." The Hacienda Benazuza is not just a hotel, but rather, a veritable catalyst for that state.

THIS PAGE (FROM TOP): Guestrooms are awe-inspiring with details such as this dome mural; elements of fantasy are to be found throughout the hacienda.

OPPOSITE: The courtyard has an air of magic to it—not at all surprising for this 10th-century Moorish farmhouse which has seen the footsteps of historic legends from medieval royalty to bullfighters and Hemingway.

FACTS	ROOMS	single • double • superior double • junior suites • master suites • special suites
	FOOD	La Alquería • La Alberca: Andalucian • La Abacería: tapas
	DRINK	Guadarnes Bar • El Sur
	FEATURES	gardens • pool • olive oil museum • art • antiques
	BUSINESS	5 meeting rooms • audiovisual equipment • private heliport • limousine service
	NEARBY	Seville • Atlantic coast • La Doñana Biosphere Reserve • golf • horse riding • hot-air ballooning • winery tours • Flamenco shows
	CONTACT	41800 Sanlúcar la Mayor, Seville • telephone: +34.955.703 344 • facsimile: +34.955.703 410 • email: hbenazuza@elbullihotel.com • website: www.elbullihotel.com

PHOTOGRAPHS COURTESY OF HACIENDA BENAZUZA.

Hacienda de San Rafael

Andalucía undisputedly offers a feast for the eyes and a banquet for the mind. Equally impressive is the tapas of languages with cadences of Spanish, Catalan, Basque and Galician. This Moorish region's history of unrelenting poverty is counterpoised by its cultural treasures—Velázquez, Picasso, Lorca, flamenco, fiesta and, surely, bullfighting.

In the beautiful agricultural patchwork between the cities of Seville and Jerez lies a grand, traditional estate. The 300-year-old Hacienda de San Rafael is a former olive farm, with lands quenched by Guadalquivir river. Its serene, whitewashed homestead is adorned with a gorgeous bougainvillaea-drenched courtyard, a characterful wrought-iron well, three pools and a panoramic view over palm trees and plains. In this carefully preserved, rustic environment, the dramatic arrival of a liveried messenger on horseback would probably not raise an eyebrow.

In an area renowned for bullfighting, exclusive visits to breeding ranches come highly recommended. Exhilarating private horseback safaris as well as yachting and shooting parties are only a mere suggestion away. Alternatively, a restful afternoon might be spent savouring the rarefied atmosphere and reserves at a local sherry bodega.

Afterwards, retreat to the sanctuary of the Hacienda de San Rafael, with its tempting infinity-edge pool and private gardens. The main house and three casitas—intimate, cosy thatched cottages—are a haven for the dreamy escapist. Antiques and paintings bear silent witness to the personal touch that has lovingly brushed each room, a unique fusion of classical-Spanish style and some Eastern influences. Variegated walls of cream and

THIS PAGE (CLOCKWISE FROM LEFT):
Behind the whitewashed front lies a faraway enclave in a distant time and old dreamy settings that legends such as Alfred Noyes' Highwayman are made of; three sequestered casitas offer privacy and countryside views; sunloungers to revel in the sights.

OPPOSITE: The stone-clad pool is guests' only reminder that they are really strolling through the garden in the 21st century.

ochre lead the eye first down to the burnt-sienna flagstones, then gradually up to the elaborate beam and thatch-work of the ceilings. Spiral staircases, archways, shaded verandahs and galleried bedrooms with crisp white linen complete the charming, rustic idyll.

The best way to take in the exquisite settings of Andalucía's sultry summer nights is to dine al fresco. Be it the restaurant or the courtyard, or under the sombrajo in the east garden, the delicacy and excellence of both cuisine and service will not fail to impress, just

as they did back in the halcyon days, when haciendas were regarded esteemed bastions of self-sufficiency, luxury and status. At the Hacienda de San Rafael, not only does this golden era continue to reign; like a truly fine wine, it improves with age.

FACTS		
	ROOMS	11 deluxe • 3 casitas
	FOOD	restaurant: Mediterranean • patio and gardens: al fresco options
	DRINK	Luna Bar • Sunset Bar
	FEATURES	3 pools • private gardens • paddle tennis • massages • yoga • Wi-Fi access • boutique shop • private chauffeur service • private guides
	NEARBY	White Villages • Jerez • Seville • Costa de la Luz • Coto Doñana National Park • golf • sailing • hot-air ballooning • horse riding • bird watching
	CONTACT	Apartado 28, Carretera N-IV, 41730 Las Cabezas de San Juan, Seville • telephone: +34.95.587 2193 • facsimile: +34.95.587 2201 • email: info@haciendadesanrafael.com • website: www.haciendadesanrafael.com

PHOTOGRAPHS COURTESY OF HACIENDA DE SAN RAFAEL.

Hospes Las Casas del Rey de Baeza

In the 18th century, much of the working class of Seville lived in tenement buildings constructed around spacious, open patios that became the focal points of a remarkably rich communal lifestyle. This shared living experience, deeply ingrained over the centuries, helps explain the friendliness and highly developed sociability of the people of this city. The unique architectural legacy that it left behind was the inspiration for the delightful Hospes Las Casas del Rey de Baeza; and the result is a superb boutique hotel that wraps its guests in a cultural and sensory blanket as inviting as the Egyptian cotton sheets and terry-towelling robes it provides. The historical authenticity of the property, its modern amenities and attention to detail promise that your stay will be both a revelation and a transformation.

The 41 spacious rooms, including five suites, are beautifully distributed around a series of quaint cobble-stoned patios that overflow with potted plants, Andalucian charm, and a bright, airy atmosphere. Wrought iron tables and chairs offer the opportunity for a romantic evening cocktail under the stars with the sweet smell of jasmine or a leisurely outdoor breakfast perfumed by the scent of orange blossoms. Large antique ceramic pots are set against genuine Roman columns supporting the tiled balconies that provide access to the rooms on the second and third levels. The blue paint on the wooden beams and railings provides a fresh, pleasing contrast against the creamy whitewashed walls. The windows of the guest rooms lining the corridors are covered on the outside with typical woven grass shades that roll up when not in use. Before the advent of air-conditioning, they were wetted down with water and lowered to cool hot summer breezes blowing through the window.

THIS PAGE (CLOCKWISE FROM TOP): **The charming cobbled-stone patio is a lovely corner for a short rest; a quaint old chimney sits on top of the bright creamy façade; beamed corridors and grass shades are living traces of a delightful architectural tradition.**
OPPOSITE: **The rooftop pool offers captivating sights of old Seville.**

All of the rooms' interiors feature noble materials such as slate on the flooring and cool marble in the bathrooms. The décor is reminiscent of a fine country estate with period furniture, leather sofas, framed prints and homey beds with cushy pillows and soft linen spreads. Of course, with the Hospes chain, historical integrity does not mean sacrificing any modern conveniences. Each room is equipped with panoramic television, DVD player, bathrobes, slippers and Internet.

The rooftop swimming pool is the perfect place to relax after a day of sightseeing or shopping expeditions, especially with an iced bottle of dry sherry. The panoramic vista of the old part of the city is wonderful, and even more appreciated with your toes dangling in the cool water. The number of bell towers will amaze you, and most people easily recognize the profile of the famed Giralda of the Cathedral of Seville. Try to catch the view after sunset when many of the monuments are beautifully illuminated.

Apart from the terrace, the atmospheric, ample common areas include the elegantly decorated library on the ground floor that can be converted into a meeting room with a capacity of 25 people. The more intimate Hearth Room has quiet corners for relaxing with a good book and the Games Room is the ideal spot to gather with friends for a cocktail before dinner. The hotel's restaurant,

converts the fortunate guests of Las Casas del Rey de Baeza into privileged front-row witnesses to one of the world's most truly remarkable cultural traditions. Just to the left on Santiago Street, you will discover the Corral del Conde, a wonderful example of the typical tenement building. If luck smiles on you and the door is open, step inside and take a peak at the flower-strewn patio.

Many popular attractions are only a short stroll from the hotel, such as the beautiful 15th-century palace of the Dukes of Medinaceli, Casa Pilatos. Plateresque in style, it features stunning mozarabic tiles, exquisite gardens and an important collection of antiques from the Roman ruins at Italica. Francisco Pacheco painted the frescos on the upper level in 1603. Also worthy of a visit are the nearby

Senzone, offers an enticing menu of simple, light dishes featuring fresh local ingredients transformed by the delightful imagination and sensitivity of its kitchen's expert chefs.

As every guest soon discovers, there is magic in Las Casas del Rey de Baeza. The dust of centuries impregnates the air, invisible yet as real as the weight of the antique wooden cross hanging in the large patio. The gurgling of the fountain is hypnotic and mixes with the intoxicating fragrance of orange blossoms; one would be forgiven for never wanting to leave. Hospes understands.

Yet when you do decide to explore old Seville, you will realize that the hotel is conveniently located in the very heart of the old part of the city. The adventure starts as soon as you set foot outside. Just to the right you will find the entrance to the 18th-century parish church of Santiago with interesting paintings by Spanish artist Francisco Pacheco, better known as the teacher and father-in-law of Velázquez. The church is also the home of the brotherhood of Christ of the Redemption, which makes its procession on Monday of Holy Week and in the process

...one would be forgiven for never wanting to leave.

parish churches of Santa Catalina and San Esteban. There are bicycles available for guests who wish to explore further afield. Every Thursday there is a flea market on Feria Street and the trendy shops of Sierpes and Tetuan streets are temptingly close.

Without a doubt, Seville is a treasure chest waiting to be discovered and Las Casas del Rey de Baeza is the very distillation of her style, culture, history and tradition. Like a fine perfume, the impressions of your discoveries here will linger on long after you depart.

FACTS

ROOMS	36 double • 5 suites
FOOD	Senzone Restaurant: Andalucian/avant-garde
DRINK	library • Chimney Room • patios
FEATURES	rooftop terrace and pool • Old Seville • patios • solarium
BUSINESS	meeting room/library (capacity of 25) • Internet access
NEARBY	Mozarabic churches of San Pedro, Santa Catalina and San Esteban • Casa de Pilatos • cathedral and Alcázar • shopping • bars • restaurants
CONTACT	Santiago, Plaza Jesús de la Redención 2, 41003 Seville • telephone: +34.954.561 496 • facsimile: +34.954.561 441 • email: reydebaeza@hospes.es • website: www.hospes.es

Hospes Palacio del Bailío

THIS PAGE: A colour theme of white, black and gold creates a contemporary feel of regality.

OPPOSITE (FROM TOP): Room service is available 24 hours a day; the restoration and design team has kept as much of the original architectural details as possible, from the layered stone walls to the detail of the stiled windows.

The enchanting patios of Córdoba are a vestige of Roman architecture adapted to the sometimes harsh climate of this beautiful Andalucian city, and a fundamental element of myriad buildings from grand palaces to cloistered monasteries and tenement blocks to hospitals. Typically they have a trickling fountain, stone basins for washing, orange and lemons trees for shade, creeping vines of jasmine to perfume the evening breezes and thick stone walls, their rough edges softened by countless layers of whitewash splashed with brilliant splotches of red and purple geraniums like drops of paint fallen from the palettes of the gods. For centuries these patios were the centre of communal

Wherever possible, the design team has incorporated original architectural elements —such as ancient stone walls and arches— complemented by a minimalist design and handcrafted stucco wall murals evoking the distinct textures and colours of old Córdoba. The finest expression of the team's efforts is the airy, romantic grand suite loft that boasts expansive views over the Patio of Orange Trees. Each room features a writing desk and reading chairs, Wi-Fi connection, state-of-the-art plasma television, a minibar, safe,

lovely Egyptian cotton sheets, plush bathrobes, towels and slippers, amenities of natural essences, and bathrooms wrapped in gorgeous local Sierra Elvira marble.

There are two rooms which are worth mentioning for their special characteristics. The first, located on the main floor, has a unique oval shape and is decorated with late-19th-century wall frescos highlighting scenes from Cervantes' *Don Quijote*. The second is located directly above and consists of two rooms separated by a gilded plaster

living and the womb that nurtured flamenco. Their crucial role in the culture and traditions of Córdoba's people is proudly reflected in the Festival of the Patios held every year in May. The event was first conceived in 1925 to help conserve the increasing number of these historic spaces which had been left in abandonment and crumbling into ruin. Like many of the large homes once owned by noble families of the city, the Hospes Palacio del Bailío was built around several patios that might well have been lost for all time if it were not for the magnificent efforts of the Hospes Hotels & Moments group, who has restored them to their beauty and made them the heart and soul of a new luxury hotel.

The property has a total of 53 rooms, spread across three separate buildings and situated around four exquisite patios—the Patio of Orange Trees, the Fountain Patio, the Roman Patio and the Patio of Lamps.

portico with Corinthian columns. The frescos on the walls depict episodes in the life of the Gran Capitan, Gonzalo Fernández de Córdoba, which include the fall of Granada and the taking of Naples.

The scenic Patio of Orange Trees offers an inviting outdoor pool shaded by orange, lemon and palm trees, embraced by fragrant flowers. This space is an alluring setting for Bodyna Spa & Sensations, located in the former Roman baths where guests can soak in an indoor pool and indulge in a myriad of massage and beauty treatments amid a rare historical ambience. The 18th-century Fountain Patio illuminates a long hallway decorated with plaster motifs reminiscent of the city's famous monuments, and a door opposite the patio provides access to a salon that serves as the library and Internet corner. The décor is inspired by one of the side chapels in the Mezquita of Córdoba.

The dramatic arched main entrance, in true Renaissance style, leads directly to the reception area and the Patio of Lamps at the end of the former coach lane. There is a public entrance to the Senzone Tapas Bar for light meals, and the elegant Senzone Restaurant, which offers gourmet cuisine based on a fusion of traditional influences and the touch of an avant-garde edge. Senzone Lobby Bar is located in the Roman Patio with a unique glass floor covering

the remnants of Roman ruins which were discovered during previous restorations and very delicately conserved in situ. The hotel's various tantalizing gastronomic offerings can be enjoyed in all the patios, in an intimate corner for two, or through the convenience of its 24-hour room service.

The friendly and well-informed staff are always at hand and happy to share with visitors fascinating facts about the palace which, in many ways, mirrors the very history of Córdoba itself. Of particular intrigue are the many magnificent coats of arms—above the doorways lining the two blocks of Torres Cabrera and Ramírez de las Casas Deza streets—which symbolize the noble families associated with the property over centuries. In its long history, the palace has seen all sorts of occupants, once house to the Office of Public Works and, in the 19th century, even suffering the ignominy of being rented out. Over the years, many families have also lived among its former splendours. The staff involved in the palace's restoration and the hotel's construction recall a constant stream of locals—mostly elderly—who stopped by periodically to check on the progress of the works. Many would recollect fondly that they had been raised in the palace or played among its patios as children. The captivating air of nostalgia emanating from the previous incarnations of the Hospes Palacio del Bailío remains very much alive, and its guests too will be certain to feel a sense of home here.

THIS PAGE (FROM LEFT): **The smartly-clad Senzone Tapas Bar; walking through the palacio's main entrance is an experience evocative of antediluvian times and certainly conjures beautiful tapestries in the imagination.**
OPPOSITE: **Rooms are infused with an air of old world romance.**

FACTS		
	ROOMS	38 double • 10 superior • 4 junior suites • 1 grand suite loft
	FOOD	Senzone Restaurant: traditional/avant-garde • Senzone Tapas Bar
	DRINK	Senzone Lobby Bar
	FEATURES	Bodyna Spa & Sensations • outdoor pool
	NEARBY	historic centre of Córdoba • The Mezquita • Sephardic heritage routes • restaurants • bars
	CONTACT	Ramírez de las Casas Deza 10–12, 14001 Córdoba • telephone: +34.957.498 993 • facsimile: +34.957.498 994 • email: palaciodelbailio@hospes.es • website: www.hospes.es

Hospes Palacio de los Patos

Spain has such a vast patrimony of ancient buildings—being endowed with everything from the spectacular ancient engineering of the Roman era to the towering spires of great Gothic cathedrals—that it would almost be too easy to overlook the comparatively recent architecture of the late 19th century; especially if it wasn't designed by the likes of Antoni Gaudí. A perfect example is Granada, a city blessed with treasures such as its beloved Cathedral, the Royal Chapel, the Arab baths, the Monastery of La Cartuja, and crowned by the timeless beauty of the Alhambra. The extraordinary transition of the country from a medieval agrarian society to an emerging industrial powerhouse—reflected in the civil architecture of the period—played almost as important a historical role as the fall of the Moorish Caliphate to the Catholic Kings in 1492; and that is precisely what makes the Palacio de los Patos such a valuable addition to Granada's list of restored monuments and to the Hospes Hotels & Moments collection.

The late-19th-century mansion that forms the centrepiece of this outstanding property is a wonderful example of the era's refined bourgeoisie taste that successfully mixed old-world elegance with elements of aborning industrial design. The building, which has always been a favourite of the locals, is surrounded by a stately wrought-iron fence with two gates marked by pillars of stone that lead to the grand entrance covered by an elaborately decorated porch, also in wrought-iron. Once inside, the main floor is dominated by a magnificent and imperial staircase in polished marble that invites your gaze upward toward the stunning cupola,

delicately filigreed by a ring of windows that bathe the spacious interior in natural light. A warm welcoming smile directs you to the minimalist reception area where you are offered a refreshing drink; the formalities of registration are a mere blur as you take in the abundant details of the intricately decorated plaster ceiling and mouldings.

The 42 guestrooms are divided between the restored mansion and a complementary contemporary structure—which boasts a truly arresting façade of alabaster—that houses Senzone Restaurant. Each room in the original structure is unique due to the loving respect shown for the building's historical integrity. The high white ceilings, elaborately carved mouldings, fine wood detailing and mosaic-tile floors blend perfectly with a confident contemporary décor that proudly cedes prominence to that which was avant-garde in a not so distant age. The result is a design excellence that imbues every room with a distinctive charm and which reaches its highest expression in the palatial presidential suite; guests will love such details as the tall faux marble columns with Ionic capitals and friezes in Room 20, or the lovely, authentic rose window in the former dovecot.

Every room features high-speed Internet, plasma television with DVD player, minibar, luxurious Egyptian cotton sheets, plush terry towelling robes and slippers. Truly amazing are the exquisite washbasins of Italian design, hand-painted in gold and silver reflected in beautifully carved mirrors of polished metal. The complement of bathroom amenities offers a full sensory experience with delights such

as lemon body milk, vanilla and cinnamon bath gel, rice protein shampoo and whole-wheat face soap. If they whet your appetite for a complete and thoroughly luxurious spa treatment, the hotel boasts the exclusive Bodyna Spa & Sensations, which offers a lavish range of massages and treatments. There is also an indoor pool, fitness centre, sauna and vapour bath, all devoted to the sole pleasure of the hotel's guests.

Palacio de los Patos is renowned for its gourmet breakfast. An alternative and more imaginative start to the day would be the

exquisite spread of avant-garde Andalucian cuisine offered in Senzone Restaurant. Enjoy aperitifs in the restaurant's bar or sip a cool after-dinner refresher under the stars in the Arabian Gardens. The patio—a convenient link between the two edifices—is a pleasant space for dining al fresco in the summer.

There are two rooms ideal for meetings and special events, an Internet corner in the library and all of the services that discerning travellers have learned to expect of Hospes' hotels—24-hour room service, complimentary local, national and international newspapers, an impressive selection of DVDs and CDs,

and, of course, the much-appreciated pillow menu. Also offering secure private parking, Palacio de Los Patos is a convenient walk from the main shopping area of town and close to monuments such as the Cathedral.

Just in case you were wondering about the hotel's appellation—Spanish for 'Palace of the Ducks'—it comes from the fountain in front of the main entrance where white marble statues of a handsome pair of swans stand gracefully. After staying at the hotel, one might be inclined to think of it as the exquisite and dearly-loved *Swan Lake*; a classic truly worthy of a standing ovation.

FACTS		
ROOMS	21 double • 11 superior double • 5 junior suites • 3 suites • 1 grand suite • 1 presidential suite	
FOOD	Senzone Restaurant: avant-garde Andalucian • Senzone Pool Bar (summer)	
DRINK	Library Bar • lounge bar	
FEATURES	Bodyna Spa & Sensations • Arabian gardens	
BUSINESS	2 meeting rooms • Internet access	
NEARBY	Alhambra • Sierra Nevada ski resorts • shopping	
CONTACT	Solarillo de Gràcia 1, 18002 Granada • telephone: +34.958.536 516 • facsimile: +34.958.536 517 • email: palaciopatos@hospes.es • website: www.hospes.es	

PHOTOGRAPHS COURTESY OF HOTELS + MOMENTS.

Hotel La Fuente de la Higuera

In a renovated olive oil mill, overlooking the neat rows of olive trees and mountainous Spanish firs, Hotel La Fuente de la Higuera provides the ultimate rural retreat. Located in the valley of Los llanos de la Cruz, facing the nature park, Sierra de las Nieves, and the Moorish town of Ronda that towers over the gorge of El Tajo, this laid-back country hotel offers gorgeous views and absolute reprieve from the bustle of the surrounding cities of Seville, Granada, Córdoba and Málaga. Whether it's a siesta under the acacia tree, a leisurely swim in the sparkling waters of

the turquoise pool or reading a good book in the library next to the open, roasting fire, La Fuente de la Higuera has every means to keep you busy doing nothing. With a rustic Mediterranean restaurant opening onto a beautiful shaded terrace that looks out over the garden and a panorama of breathtaking mountain views, this sanctuary provides an authentic and luxurious Spanish break.

The entrance is reminiscent of a grand private home with a stunning double-vaulted, galleried hallway, stone pillars and antique furniture. Each suite and bedroom bears a distinctive character and the individual rooms range from the grandiose—with rich period furnishing, aged rugs, upholstered armchairs

and four-poster beds—to the contemporary, with painted wooden floorboards and light wicker furniture. Every guestroom is designed to be an exquisite individual private escape, each complemented with a large bathroom and access to a private garden or terrace.

The property also offers a private house, comfortably sleeping 12, for hire through all the seasons. Set within a 9-hectare (22-acre) land with incredible views across Sierra de las Nieves, the vast, picturesque garden has its own private pool. An attentive personal chef and maid ensure guests are well taken care of; or guests may choose to dine in the Fuente's exclusive restaurant which offers fine traditional Mediterranean fare. Each of the six bedrooms has its own terrace or garden for absolute privacy; outside these individual personal havens, a large sitting room, library and multiple terraces are accessible to all guests of the Fuente. You will also delight in the property's spa, which includes a Turkish bath, hydrotherapy and lavish massages.

Nearby, Ronda holds the oldest and largest bullfighting ring and is host to many cosmopolitan bars and restaurants. Within driving distance is the famous Andalucian coastline and its enticing historic cities, and for a day-trip to the Rock, Gibraltar is just less than 90 minutes away by car.

THIS PAGE: The Fuente's terrace is possibly one of the most enviable settings in Málaga where fine al fresco dining is accompanied by an astounding panoramic vista.

OPPOSITE (FROM TOP): A brightly lit atrium is a quintessential element of old Andalucian architecture; access to a terrace or garden from each guestroom promises a private hideaway even within the hotel's pastoral grounds.

PHOTOGRAPHS COURTESY OF HOTEL LA FUENTE DE LA HIGUERA.

FACTS		
ROOMS	3 standard • 1 junior suite • 3 suites • 1 double suite • 2 deluxe suites • 1 artist's suite	
FOOD	Mediterranean	
DRINK	Honesty Bar	
FEATURES	spa • pool • library	
NEARBY	Ronda • Seville • Granada • Córdoba • Málaga • Gibraltar	
CONTACT	Partido de los Frontones, 29400 Ronda, Málaga • telephone: +34.952.114 355 • facsimile: +34.952.165 609 email: info@hotellafuente.com • website: www.hotellafuente.com	

Villa Jerez

Jerez is globally renowned for its sweet wines, which adopted the town's name. The British pronounced it 'sherry'. With such a claim to liquid fame—coupled with its location in the heart of Andalucía—touristic artifice is simply not necessary. The region has a flair for nurturing fine dancing horses and flamenco singers of the highest calibre. The manifold cultural celebrations offer ample opportunities to enjoy such diversions. The town's extended name, Jerez de la Frontera, evokes the period when Jerez formed the frontier between Moorish and Christian realms, the architectural legacy of which lives on.

One building steeped in the tradition and design influences of this era is the Hotel Villa Jerez. This dignified mansion is an exclusive paradise in the centre of Jerez, sequestered from the outside world with undulating, terracotta-topped walls. Nestled in 4,000 sq-m (43,055-sq-ft) of landscaped gardens, the building's lemon façade and confident stature rise up behind its veil of palm trees. The refreshing saltwater pool is cloistered by latticed walls that frame traditional statues, while remarkable and contemporary sculptures of birds and swans grace the verdant gardens. Intricate details

THIS PAGE (FROM TOP): The noble entrance is elegant and inviting against its creamy yellow walls; dining al fresco is a must within the quaint, beautiful grounds; a beautiful façade and palms make for an atmospheric arrival.

OPPOSITE: On top of an outdoor pool and lush inviting gardens, the Villa Jerez also offers a full complement of thermal baths, hydro-massage and a variety of body and beauty treatments.

of wrought-iron work, iconic of the region, are dappled throughout the mansion and its surrounding lush gardens.

These enchanting vistas can equally be appreciated from the privacy and absolute comfort of Villa Jerez's suites. The spacious rooms all incorporate traditional elements of interior design, with vertical stripes, soft drapes and summery hues of peach and pale orchid which enhance the polished woods and spotless brass. The addition of expedient business facilities and luxuries—which include hydro-massage and thermal baths—layers new-world convenience onto a timeless and romantic atmosphere.

As the evening shadows lengthen, meander through the distinctly aristocratic squares of Jerez proper, and indulge in a tour of a sherry bodega. The allure of Villa Jerez's restaurant, Las Yucas, will soon draw you back with its delectable selection of tapas, regionally and internationally inspired dishes, as well as the fine sherry on offer.

The gorgeous evening sun pours through generous windows to warm the light woods and creams of the intimate dining room. Alternatively, enjoy an al fresco supper on the colonnaded terrace as the gentle aromas of the garden mingle with those rising from your elegantly laid table.

As the sun sets over the historic buildings of Jerez, trail along the smooth pillars, ornate banisters and quaint archways of this stately mansion. As you glide through the lobby in the direction of sleep, linger a moment longer to marvel at how this air of old world charm has been so stylishly preserved at Villa Jerez.

FACTS

ROOMS	18
FOOD	Las Yucas • terrace
DRINK	Las Yucas • terrace
FEATURES	climate control • gardens • gym • saltwater pool • thermal baths • massages • hydro-massage • hair and beauty salon
NEARBY	Seville • Málaga • Gibraltar
CONTACT	Avda de la Cruz Roja 7, 11407 Jerez de la Frontera, Cádiz • telephone: +34.956.153 100 • facsimile: +34.956.304 300 • email: reservas@villajerez.com • website: www.villajerez.com

PHOTOGRAPHS COURTESY OF HOTEL VILLA JEREZ.

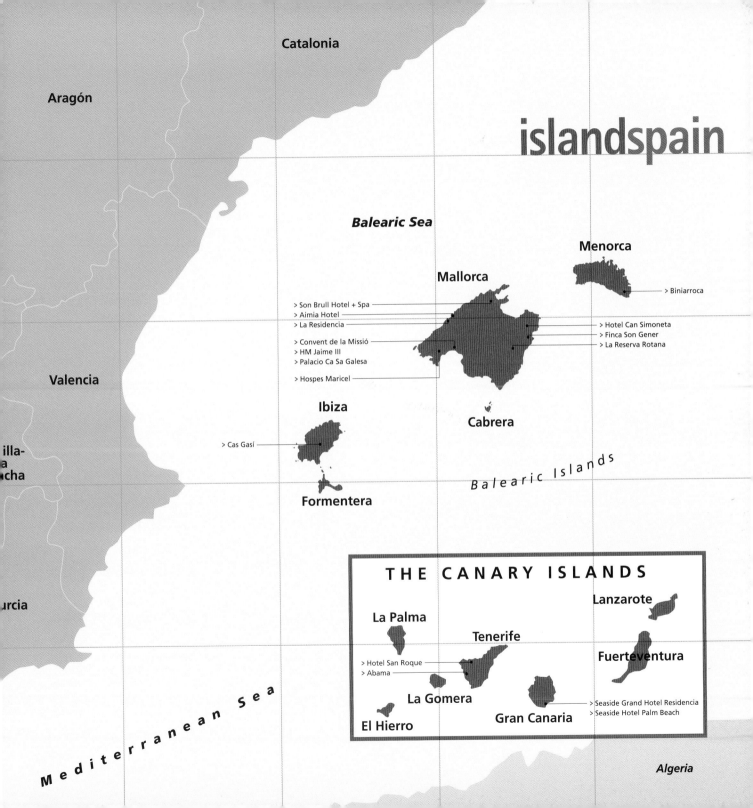

Catalonia

Aragón

islandspain

Balearic Sea

Menorca

Mallorca

> Son Brull Hotel + Spa
> Aimia Hotel
> La Residencia

> Hotel Can Simoneta
> Finca Son Gener
> La Reserva Rotana

> Convent de la Missió
> HM Jaime III
> Palacio Ca Sa Galesa

> Hospes Maricel

Valencia

> Biniarroca

Ibiza

illa-
a
cha

> Cas Gasí

Cabrera

Balearic Islands

Formentera

urcia

THE CANARY ISLANDS

Lanzarote

La Palma

Tenerife

Fuerteventura

> Hotel San Roque
> Abama

La Gomera

Gran Canaria

> Seaside Grand Hotel Residencia
> Seaside Hotel Palm Beach

El Hierro

Mediterranean Sea

Algeria

island spain—balearics

Flung into the Mediterranean like four very unequal pearls, the Balearics have long been classics in the farniente—ships, sailing and maritime—stakes. At the most, activity involves grabbing a tiller, unfurling the sails and heading for a cove. Mallorca, Menorca, Ibiza and its afterthought, Formentera, form this idyllic group, each one different in nature, history and culture. From Mallorca's moody, mountainous backbone, coves and literary associations to Menorca's emerald-green pastures and prehistoric relics, from the hopping nightlife of Ibiza to tiny Formentera's omnipresent turquoise sea, they are all equally enchanting.

What binds them together—apart from sensational beaches and clear, calm sea—is a sense of a separate identity to Catalonia and, more generally, to Spain. The Balearic language may be derived from Catalan, but it preserves ancient roots, and the mentality is certainly more laidback, some would say less pretentious, than in mainland Catalonia. These are, after all, islands where, until a few decades ago, agriculture was the mainstay —with commerce, fishing and shoe-manufacturing close behind. Today, although sun, sea and sand rule the economy, each island claims its own stimulating features.

early days

Tourism being king here, there is an uneven level of activity and population throughout the year. Once the season ends in late October, the islands are left to their 870,000 residents—whether local or expatriate—and Palma's international airport, designed to cater for 3 million passengers, certainly echoes to their absence.

Mallorca has a long and illustrious history of writers and artists being drawn to its shores, from Robert Graves to Chopin and Georges Sand, Joan Miró (himself a native of Barcelona) and—a more recent arrival—rock-singer Annie Lennox. Despite the foreign influx and developments, some villages in the untouched interior carry on as if no one other than Catalans (and Mallorcan at that) existed. Ibiza came to prominence as the hippie-dippy island of the 1960s and 1970s, something of an artists' hideaway that was big on beads and baskets. There is still a strong sense of this alternative culture, although

PAGE 212: Take the plunge…into the ultramarine Cala Figuera at Mallorca's Cap de Formentor, the ever-increasingly popular northern haunt of the island.

THIS PAGE: A plane of azure at the Hospes Maricel, looking right out to sea, just west of Palma.

OPPOSITE: The monastery of Lluch, founded in the 12th century, nestled in a quiet valley of the dramatic Tramuntana mountains. Inside is a revered statue of La Moroneta (the Black Virgin), Mallorca's patron saint.

understated sophistication lurks there too. Ibiza's offshoot, Formentera, is like an appendix or a far-flung comma; with similar rocky terrain and powdery white beaches yet poised in miniscule scale, it commands a faithful following. Mellow, discreet and laudably more concerned by the environment than by tourism, Menorca is an anomaly. It has inland and coastal areas of great beauty, forts, prehistoric settlements and the Balearics' best cheese, yet somehow remains one of those 'best kept secrets'.

mallorcan schizophrenia

Mallorca, the largest island, is easily the most diverse, something which is, of course, no secret to millions of tourists. Through an ambitious programme of self-improvement, it has successfully raised its profile from the mass-tourism morass of a decade or so ago. Palma gets slicker by the minute as new galleries, museums, boutiques and restaurants fling their doors open. The inevitable label of 'the new Barcelona' has been mooted, but, for the moment, this city of 335,000 souls has a long way to go.

Many measures have been successful, not least the traffic flow through this town that sweeps proprietorially around a generous bay. A vast marina, spiked with thousands of masts, fronts rows of high-rise apartment blocks, typical of the 1960s and 1970s when development was in full swing. Palm trees —no surprise in a town with this name—are of course, omnipresent. From here, over 20 km (12½ miles) of seafront hotels and apartments extend west to the mass-tourism black spots of Magaluf and Palmanova, and east to quieter beaches much favoured by capital-dwellers.

It was in these waters where, in 1229, the Aragonese king captured Mallorca after 400 years of Muslim rule and kick-started a strange history that at one time united Mallorca with Montpellier and Roussillon in France. A striking relic of those days is the circular Castell de Belver overlooking the harbour; this medieval building built by Jaime II served as both a royal residence and royal prison—somehow typical of Mallorca's schizophrenic

THIS PAGE (FROM TOP): A bookshop in the culturally-oriented old quarter of Palma de Mallorca; Belvedere castle, one of Palma's landmarks, was originally built as a summer residence for the Mallorcan kings before transmuting into a prison.

OPPOSITE (FROM TOP): The cathedral of Palma glows in the setting sun with the burgeoning marina in the foreground; Forn des Teatre, the island's most prestigious pastry shop, specializes in ensaimadas (a light spiral roll) and cocas (meat pies).

nature. Palma's heyday came in the 16th to 18th centuries when Mallorca was part of the powerful Mediterranean empire which united Barcelona and Valencia with Naples and Sicily. In time, the resultant population of wealthy merchants left a clear and distinguished seigneurial stamp on the old town.

to the patios

Up in the old town, Palma's architectural beauty is announced by the Almudaina, an official royal residence that goes back to the Moors, and, above all, the adjacent cathedral. This impressive Gothic masterpiece crowns the town by day or by night, when its biscuit-coloured limestone walls and pinnacles are dazzlingly spot-lit. Inside, humans are dwarfed by the immense scale even though it has a light, airy feel to which Gaudí contributed during its early-1900s restoration. Behind this magnificent mammoth, a labyrinth of narrow backstreets and freshly re-plastered façades actually smells of renovation. Beautiful patios with marble columns, sweeping stairways, loggias and potted plants are visible through archways and ironwork gates: this is where the elegant Mallorcan style took shape in the 18th century. This network of over 150 patios is a delight and is unique in Spain; those of Andalucía have a very different scale and decorative style. Most patios are still private, but if the gates are open, admirers can enter for a peep.

Palma's surprising wealth and diversity of architecture continues in the elegant Passeig del Born, a wide tree-lined rambla which runs from Avenida Jaime III down to the water-front. These two arteries are where the city's best designer labels and shopping are found, running the whole gamut from Loewe to Zara. Boutiques continue uphill in the fascinating web of narrow streets surrounding the Plaça Major, although quality varies considerably. Mallorca's homegrown names are above all leather-based; shoe labels such as Farrutx and Camper have achieved international renown.

art + design

Cultural status means contemporary art, and that Palma has by the bucketload. Number one is the Fundació Pilar i Joan Miró on the western outskirts of Palma. Not only is this an eye-opener on Miró's huge studio—movingly left as it was when he died in 1980—and its innovative 1950s design by his great friend Josep Lluís Sert, but it also has a superbly designed museum by Rafael Moneo and lush gardens. Particularly striking are Moneo's alabaster windows and water features—even spilling across the roof. A recent rival is the contemporary art museum, Es Baluard, built into the old walls to offer a scenic stroll round the ramparts—but with sadly limited art. More form than substance? The small collection includes Mallorca's contemporary star, Miguel Barceló, but is strongest on its vast sculpture terraces. It is worth indulging in a breezy Mediterranean fusion lunch in the museum restaurant to enjoy the views at length.

Far more artistic meat is found at the foundation set up by the late Mallorcan banker, Juan March, in an immaculately restored 18th-century mansion. Less avant-garde, more modern, this first-class collection focuses on works by Picasso, Miró, Dalí, Juan Gris and Tàpies. Equally coherent is the Fundació La Caixa, housed in a lavish Modernista edifice by Domènech i Montaner that was Palma's original Gran Hotel. Temporary exhibitions of museum quality range from Japanese photography to contemporary African art. Add to this, exhibitions at the lovely Casal Solleric and a number of private art galleries tucked down the backstreets, and an aesthetic feast is assured.

to the hills + coves

A breakout from Palma's captivating centre inevitably leads upward into the glorious hills surrounding Valldemossa, Deià and Sóller. Dramatic vistas unfold between switchbacks and vertiginous drops, while pine trees perfume the air. This is where the nobility of Palma built themselves palatial summer villas, and where French writer Georges Sand and her lover Chopin famously canoodled one long winter at Valldemossa's monastery. Hourly piano concerts (the composer need not be specified) ensure that they are never forgotten.

Near here too are the beautifully lush gardens of Alfàbia, surrounding what was once a Moorish palace. Deià, above all, has always attracted a cosmopolitan, creative crowd. Numerous bars and restaurants cater for these discriminating, offbeat clients, and low-key design highlights the bucolic setting and fabulous views.

Mallorca's northern promontory of Formentor curves round the Bay of Pollença, with the walled town of Alcúdia and Pollença (claiming its very own Mount Calvary) the main focal points. To the east, the marshes of S'Albufera attract more than 230 species of birds, while the neighbouring plain of Sa Pobla is where to try counting hundreds of windmills. It is, however, the indented sweep of the east coast that has made Mallorca's reputation. This is where transparent turquoise and emerald waters lap crescents of white sand in idyllic coves or calas. Caves, watchtowers, serpentine dry-stone walls, white fincas (old farmhouses) and the odd megalithic site all add to the rural appeal. The coast itself is by no means untouched by development, but there are enough coves to go around.

menorca—pastures greener

If Mallorca is the big brother, Menorca is the little sister of the Balearics. It is unexpectedly and brilliantly green, like a pocket of Cantabria tossed into the Mediterranean, complete with healthy, cud-chewing cows. In 1992, the entire island was declared a biosphere reserve centred on S'Albufera des Grau—an area of heathland and marshes where birds are in their vociferous element. Bicycle and hiking trails round the island are well-marked, making this a perfect place to recover from gastronomic excess. And if Menorca lags behind in the nueva cocina stakes, it certainly makes up for it in seafood and cheese.

Menorcan cow's cheese is arguably the best in Spain and, like manchego, improves vastly with age. Sopa de langosta (crayfish stew) is the local speciality, along with others shared with Mallorca: sobrassada (a paprika-rich sausage) and ensaimada (a large flat cake). Add to this mayonnaise, famously named after the capital, Maó (or Mahón, from which 'Mahon-ese' was then coined), where it was invented during France's short rule of Menorca, and gin, a legacy of English rule, and you have a pretty varied dining table.

THIS PAGE (FROM TOP): Deià, the artists' and writers' town for decades, still maintains an inimitable atmosphere; prehistoric menhirs stud Menorca's beautiful interior.
OPPOSITE: A biker enjoys the view on one of Mallorca's cliff edges.

One main road runs 45 km (28 miles) east to west from the capital Maó to Ciutadella. Minor roads trace leisurely trails north and south, with a few ending at beautiful coves or more developed resorts such as Cala Galdana or Binbequer. Between them, undulating meadows are dotted with an estimated 500 megalithic sites or talayots. These intriguing stone structures throw up the usual enigma, that is, how such massive stones were moved without mechanical means. Trepuco, south of Maó, is particularly impressive—composed not only of a watchtower and worship enclosure with a towering taula (T-shaped structure), but also of remains of homes. Thought to date from 1400 BCE, Trepuco was abandoned after the Roman conquest, in 123 BCE.

urban island life

Prehistory aside, Menorca's most elegant architecture is at Ciutadella, the island capital under Moorish rule. Teetering above an inlet and harbour lined with seafood restaurants, Ciutadella hides its finest old buildings in a web of tiny streets behind the Plaça des Born. Palm trees, mimosa and scarlet hibiscus give this imposing square that typical Menorcan soft touch. Although the cathedral dates from the 14th century, the mansions are mostly of the 17th to 19th century, their façades often creamy yellow or pink ochre.

THIS PAGE: The blissfully turquoise waters of Sa Caleta lie just around the corner from Menorca's lovely old capital, Ciutadella.

OPPOSITE (FROM TOP): The attractive waterfront of multi-tiered Maó is lined with bars, seafood restaurants and yachts; a stroll up the steep cobbled streets of Ibiza's old town is the thing to do on a balmy summer's evening.

Maó, too, conceals a wealth of periods and styles in its vertiginous, much coveted site high above the 5-km- (3-mile-) long inlet that made its fame. Here the quays are one long excuse for restaurants and bars. Up above, the easygoing town stretches almost to more tourist-oriented Es Castell. Nearby, surveying the mouth of the inlet, is the castle of Saint Felipe and also Fort Marlborough—the most outstanding relic of England's century-long occupation of the island. That period was not all military however, as rumour has it that Lord Nelson and Lady Hamilton indulged their tryst nearby.

Other highlights include the appealing old fishing-village of Fornells and neighbouring Cap de Cavallería, a rugged, windswept promontory whose lighthouse marks Menorca's northernmost point. Enchanting calas and sandy beaches lie elsewhere, some completely wild and accessible only on foot or by bike—Menorca still feels wonderfully somnolent.

ibiza—hopping by night

The same cannot be said about Ibiza, or Eivissa as it now calls itself. Hot in temperature and mood through July to August, it magnetizes planeloads of youth in search of eternal partying. Sant Antoni on the west coast is the clubbers' capital, so best avoided in season. This is also the main terminal for ferries to Formentera and Denia on the mainland. The north of the island around Sant Joan has some beautiful wild landscapes along its coastline, only interrupted by the family resort of Portinatx. In the south, the salt-flats and nature reserve of Ses Salines are a great magnet for migrating waders and water-fowl, while the east coast claims Santa Eulàlia, its high-rise seafront hiding an old quarter. Cosmopolitan (including the odd ageing hippy) with a steady year-round population, it is allegedly the richest town in Spain per capita, and where some of the island's best restaurants are found.

Ibiza's big surprise, however, comes in its capital in the Dalt Vila (old town) perched above the harbour, encircled by Renaissance walls. Dominating it from afar is the cathedral, below which a labyrinth of stone steps and cobbled passages connect elegant mansions. A few good restaurants, boutique hotels and shops have found their way up here, but it remains delightfully calm, as the main commerce is concentrated in the 'new' town below.

The character and appearance of Ibiza is light years from greener islands, Mallorca and Menorca. Here, being much closer to the Valencian coast, the landscape echoes that of Andalucía and is noticeably drier and rockier, studded with simple whitewashed cubes clustered around towering churches. Long ago, these were fortified to shelter inhabitants against pirate attacks. Some farmhouses have become rural restaurants, offering relaxed settings to tuck into a rice and pork dish or a sofrit payés—a filling, aromatic peasant stew combining chicken, pork, sausages and potatoes. Swimming to little Formentera could be the solution to work it all off.

island spain—canaries

Far closer to Africa than to Spain, the sub-tropical Canary Islands are, like the Balearics, known for their budget sun and sand—although, as they are volcanic, the latter is often a rather uninviting shade of charcoal. Solutions have been found by importing golden sand from the Sahara 200 km (124 miles) away, and by building saltwater lidos. Nonetheless, the balmy year-round climate, cooled to a steady 25–30°C (77–86°F) by marine currents, has ensured that these seven islands have not only fabulously lush vegetation, including a surfeit of bananas, but also a constant flow of visitors. The majority are attracted by resorts such as Tenerife's Playa de las Americas, yet their tarnished reputations—complete with satellite football and fish and chips—eclipse dramatic and incredibly varied scenery. This ranges from Tenerife's cloud-forest and Teide volcano (Spain's highest peak) to the canyons of Gran Canaria, the lush interiors of La Palma and La Gomera, the simmering craters and lava-fields of Lanzarote, or the windswept rock-formations of tiny El Hierro.

Two capitals serve the archipelago: Santa Cruz de Tenerife and Las Palmas on Gran Canaria. Santa Cruz, a lively town with a 500-year history and a gigantic port, is famed for its exuberant February carnival which is massively fuelled by Gran Canaria's excellent wines. A more sober policy has produced a spectacular new opera house courtesy of Santiago Calatrava. This ambitious architect has, once again, hit the headlines with a sculptural design which resembles the Sydney Opera House. Herzog & de Meuron are

meanwhile, hard at work on a new cultural centre in the centre of town. Similarly sleek, contemporary design approaches throughout the island have converted typical tinerfeño farm-estates into compelling specialist museums devoted to ethnography, ceramics, and wine. All this is a sign that the islands, far from being culturally isolated, have caught peninsular Spain's self-renewal bug.

manrique's pools

However, the undisputed king of Canarian design is César Manrique (1920–1992). This exceptional artist and designer from Lanzarote was truly far in advance of his time, as by integrating art and landscape, he raised local environmental awareness. "Man in New York is like a rat. Man was not created for this artificiality." His words encapsulated his belief. Lanzarote's Museum of Contemporary Art, converted from a castle in the capital, Arrecife, was Manrique's brainchild, while the north of the island boasts his Jameos del Agua (a saltwater lagoon in a volcanic cave) and the clifftop Mirador del Río. The César Manrique Foundation, built by the artist in 1968 at Teguise, exemplifies his far-sighted ideas and also houses a fine collection of Spanish art. Tenerife too, claims its Manriques, notably at Puerto de la Cruz, the oldest resort on the island where a couple of delightful 19th-century hotels are all dark varnished wood, carved shutters, ornate balconies and potted palms. With Puerto's development in the 1960s to 1970s came Costa Martiánez, a landscaped seawater lido of seven pools to which over 1 million people flock yearly. A similar, smaller lido lies on Santa Cruz's coast near the new auditorium.

big canary

The most populated and visited island among the Canaries is Gran Canaria, mainly due to its breathtaking and incredibly diverse landscape. Naturalists head for the Parque Rural del Nublo on the flanks of Pico de las Nieves, to track down the largest number—and amazing variety—of endemic species in the archipelago. However, the biggest card is the seemingly endless beach—in fact about 17 km (10½ miles) long—of Maspalomas

THIS PAGE (FROM TOP): Rainbow-hued houses in Gran Canaria's Las Palmas, which shares capital status of the Canaries with Santa Cruz de Tenerife; Lanzarote's dramatic volcanic rocks reflected in a cool pool.

OPPOSITE: A black volcanic beach with Tenerife's Los Gigantes cliffs in the background.

on the south coast. Shared by four resorts, Maspalomas' natural highlight is a spectacular protected area of undulating sand dunes dotted with oases of palm trees. These dunes are home to many rare plant species—as well as nudists enjoying the idyllic seclusion—and can only be crossed on foot or by camel, an enlightened measure.

Las Palmas, the sprawling capital and port, dates back to 1478 and its old quarter of Vegueta reverberates with the memories of four stopovers by Christopher Columbus en route to the Americas. The Casa de Colón (in the governor's palace where he stayed in 1502) outlines the great navigator's expeditions. Yet Las Palmas is as feisty, dynamic and forward-looking as Santa Cruz, impressively straddling the Guiniguada ravine and the Isleta peninsula for 10 km (6 miles), with a buzzing city beach. Like Santa Cruz, Las Palmas too has a museum, which pays homage to the archipelago's indigenous inhabitants, the Guanches, who were still in the Stone Age when the Spaniards arrived. Little is known of their origins and primitive lifestyle other than their mummification techniques.

THIS PAGE (FROM TOP): Endemic flora of El Teide includes white broom, violets, Viper's bugloss and, at the base, caña de blanca, which is unique to this zone; dromedaries in Lanzarote's Timanfaya Park.

OPPOSITE: Lava stacks announce Spain's highest peak, the volcano of Teide.

gastro canaries

With such abundant flora and a long agricultural tradition, it is hardly surprising that the islands have produced a cuisine worthy of their landscapes. Unctuous dipping-sauces made from olive oil and either coriander (mojo verde) or paprika (mojo rojo) are omnipresent on restaurant tables, while papas arrugas—wrinkled little potatoes cooked in massive doses of salt (weighing a quarter of the weight of the potatoes)—accompany much of the fresh seafood. Roast goat with almonds, rabbit stew, lamb with honey and mint sauce, sancocho (stewed grouper with bananas and potatoes) or grilled cheese drizzled with miel de la palma (a dark sweet liquid from the palm tree) are just some of the archipelago's unique specialities. Tropical fruit piles onto plates in the form of mangoes, guavas, papayas and, of course, those small Canarian bananas. To wash it all down, there is an ever-increasing variety of quality wine whose cultivation goes back centuries. Its praise was even sung by no less than Shakespeare in *Henry IV* and *As You Like It*. Part of his annual stipend was a barrel of his beloved 'malmsey', also known as 'canary sack'. Praise indeed.

...the islands, far from being culturally isolated, have caught peninsular Spain's self-renewal bug.

Aimia Hotel

Port de Sóller is the only natural port along Mallorca's northwestern coastline. Dominated by the dramatic Serra de Tramuntana mountain range, it is surrounded by wonderfully quaint villages and valleys that contribute to its fascinating charm. Tucked away quietly within these enchanting surrounds is the four-star Aimia Hotel.

Opened in summer 2004, Aimia is a chic hideaway that has been thoughtfully equipped with modern conveniences of the highest order. Think wireless Internet access throughout its reception area and terrace, serviceable business facilities, a state-of-the-art gym, and televisions that double as computers and game consoles.

Check into Aimia's junior suite, located at the top floor of the hotel. Here is a paradise unto itself with breathtaking views of the Port de Sóller. Blonde woods and soft furnishings bestow a sense of peace and relaxation, while crisp white sheets on its delightfully soft beds beckon for a lazy lie-in. Its large deck area is the perfect place to take in the spectacular sights, while your personal jacuzzi virtually ensures hours of

liquid pleasures. Aimia's superior and standard rooms are equally well turned out, with the same blonde wood and white palette, with accents of biscuit and plum.

Should you decide to leave the plush comforts of your room, the hotel boasts a terrace pool where you can soak peacefully in its aquamarine waters. Further beyond, the island's famous beaches offer a myriad of activities from fishing and diving to languorous hours of sun worshipping.

At Aimia's Blue Spa, cyclonic showers, saunas, Turkish baths and jacuzzis are all at hand to help calm your body and mind. Other spa services, like massages, algae-based cleansing treatments, facials and capillary massages are also available and administered by expert hands using St. Barth's natural range of skincare products which are made in the French Caribbean.

At Airecel restaurant, signature local dishes are served with a fine selection of wines from Spain and the Balearic islands.

Through Airecel's glass curtain wall, gaze at Aimia's opulent gardens or head outside to the terrace to enjoy the balmy temperatures of Serra de Tramuntana.

Post dinner, Aimia's sultry cocktail bar is the perfect place to end the day. Sink into its dark plum sofas and pick from an unending list of cocktails that will no doubt leave you with a delicious buzz.

THIS PAGE (TOP): Cool aquamarine waters of the terrace pool make a soothing evening freshener after a day out in the sun.

OPPOSITE (FROM TOP): Spacious chambers and softly lit furnishings in burnt sienna promise a languid afternoon; Airecel restaurant offers a simple yet elegant ambience for fine wines, personable service and local cuisine.

FACTS		
ROOMS	43	
FOOD	Airecel restaurant • room service	
DRINKS	cocktail bar	
FEATURES	spa • gym • multipurpose room • 1 outdoor pool • wireless Internet access	
NEARBY	Serra de Tramuntana	
CONTACT	Santa María del Cami 1, 07108 Port de Sóller, Mallorca • telephone: +34.971.631 200 • facsimile: +34.971.638 040 • email: info@aimiahotel.com • website: www.aimiahotel.com	

PHOTOGRAPHS COURTESY OF AIMIA HOTEL.

Hotel Can Simoneta

On Mallorca's northeastern coast within the nature reserve of Serra de Llevant, protected for its astounding nature and beauty, lies Can Simoneta, magnificently exposed on the edge of a cliff overlooking the small bays and wide beaches along the rocky coastline.

This lovely, charismatic countryside hotel comprises two adjacent historic buildings built from old local materials over 140 years ago. Can Simoneta—just 14 m (46 ft) from cliff's edge—houses a small number of rooms, all offering magnificent sea vistas; the larger Can Nofre is home to the fine restaurant, reception area and remaining rooms.

Facing east onto the Bay of Canyamel, opening your windows early in the morning and taking in the fresh sea air, you can watch fishing boats sparkling on the phosphorescent sea as the glowing sun creeps up behind he horizon. Steps cut into the cliff give you direct access to the sea and a quiet, sandy bathing cove. On the way down, you'll even walk past a delightful natural seawater pool.

The hotel's land stretches 600 hectares (1,483 acres) along and back from the long coastline. With much of it being used by local farmers growing varying crops, Can Simoneta is literally hemmed in by the beauty of nature. The breathtaking garden has a pool and sun terrace, paths along the cliff edge and shaded hammocks for a peaceful afternoon siesta.

Only 5 minutes away from the hotel is the lovely village of Canyamel, whose main attraction is the 13th-century tower that has

borne witness to major historical events in the region over the last 700 years. The narrow streets, local shops, restaurants and its weekly market offer a lively, fun atmosphere.

Other quaint attractions nearby include a beautiful church in the ancient town of Artá and the medieval castle in Capderpera. Four major golf courses are within 8 km (5 miles) of the hotel, and the attentive Can Simoneta staff will happily book you the perfect tee-off time. Alternatively, they can help arrange for a wide variety of sports and other leisurely ways to spend the day—from tennis, fishing, hiking and horse riding, to a myriad of water sports and beach activities which include kite boarding and windsurfing.

THIS PAGE (FROM TOP): Tucked in a nature reserve and sequestered on one end by Mallorca's coast, Can Simoneta is truly a haven; the pool and sun terrace beckoning amid a vast expanse of verdant plains and clear sky.

OPPOSITE (FROM LEFT): A magnificent and enthralling vista over and beyond the cliff edge where Can Simoneta is quietly perched; tree-shaded hammocks make for a lazy and memorable nap.

The hotel's restaurant offers home-cooked Mediterranean cuisine. In the summer you can dine on the terrace where the sea sparkles in the background and the night is blanketed with stars. In winter, the elegant dining room is centred round a huge stone chimney where a bright, crackling fire warms the entire room.

Each guestroom has been created with a unique character; old wood beams arouse a cosy country atmosphere and marble adorns the bathrooms, yet they are, at the same time, contemporary in feel. Some offer terraces or sea views and others look out onto the scenic landscape surrounding this stunning hotel.

FACTS

ROOMS	18
FOOD	home-cooked Mediterranean
DRINK	bar
FEATURES	pool • sun terrace • hammocks • garden • farmland
NEARBY	beach • Canyamel • Artá • Capdepera
CONTACT	Carretera de Artá a Canyamel, km 8, Finca Torre Canyamel, 07580 Capdepera, Mallorca • telephone: +34.971.816 110 • facsimile: +34.971.816 111 • email: info@cansimoneta.com • website: www.cansimoneta.com

PHOTOGRAPHS COURTESY OF HOTEL CAN SIMONETA.

Convent de la Missió

In the old town of Palma sits an ancient church, the Convent de la Missió. Beside it stands a monastery of the same name, surrounded by narrow cobbled streets and gardened patios. In the 17th century, the monastery was dedicated to the education of missionary priests. Today, it has been transformed into Palma's most fashionable hotel, with 14 exquisitely styled suites that draw the rich, famous and discerning.

Its owners—who are also behind the très chic Son Gener in Mallorca—took three years to restore this old gem. The result is a truly breathtaking masterpiece; a fusion of modern minimalism and carefully preserved 17th-century ecclesiastical architecture.

Pass through its opaque glass entrance to witness its spectacular lobby, undoubtedly a study in the exceptional use of light and space. Its designers retained the original

high vaulted ceilings and limestone walls, fusing them with cutting-edge design, natural materials and massive windows.

All 14 guestrooms are white sanctuaries of calm, softened by fine muslin and smooth oak floors. All are spacious, especially the suites with their modern four-poster draped in swathes of white. The public spaces are simply heart-stopping with natural light drenching the rooms in a sense of peace and calm. In the sitting room, ergonomic beanbags make funky substitutes for armchairs, and glossy design books make the perfect page-turners

before the log-fire on winter days. Conversely, the room becomes a comforting respite from the heat during the sweltering summer months.

Up on the roof, the Zen-inspired solarium is a fabulous space for those in need of solitude, while down in the old crypt is a spa, complete with jacuzzi, sauna and Turkish bath. There is also a brilliant art gallery, which features exhibitions of paintings, sculptures, photography and ceramics.

Convent de la Missió is also famous for its restaurant, Refectori—one of the best in town—endowed with the same delicate sense of aesthetics. Housing a dining room and terrace replete with waterfall and palm trees, it serves sumptuous nouvelle cuisine.

Just beyond the hotel are historical sights and trendy bars, not to mention hip boutiques and the international marina.

Convent de la Missió is still one of those secret places shared by a knowing few and it would be worthwhile to languish in its relative anonymity before the hordes discover it.

THIS PAGE (FROM TOP): The eminent lobby keeps the original high ceiling and walls, complemented by a dramatic interplay of light, space and a spartan interior; in keeping with the designers' minimalism, the guestrooms are brightly-lit and well-defined by clean lines and furnishings.

OPPOSITE (FROM TOP): The church's old crypt has been converted into a spa facility complete with jacuzzi, sauna and Turkish bath; a fireplace offers warmth and a stark contrast in the sitting area.

FACTS		
	ROOMS	14 suites
	FOOD	Refectori: nouvelle cuisine
	BUSINESS	convention hall (capacity of 100) • audiovisual equipment • Internet connection
	FEATURES	spa • Turkish bath • sauna • jacuzzi • art gallery • terrace
	NEARBY	historical sights • shopping • international marina
	CONTACT	Carrer de la Missió 7A, 07003 Palma de Mallorca • telephone: +34.971.227 347 • facsimile: +34.971.227 348 • email: hotel@conventdelamissio.com • website: www.conventdelamissio.com

PHOTOGRAPHS COURTESY OF CONVENT DE LA MISSIÓ.

Finca Son Gener

Mallorca, largest of the Balearic Islands, reclines in the Mediterranean Sea to the east of Spain. Made famous as a beautiful island of soul-stirring natural beauty and artistic inspiration by painters who sojourned here many years before, its magnetic allure is both multifaceted and captivating—from pristine bays to the intriguing cave systems that inspired Jules Verne's epic, *Journey to the Centre of the Earth*, Mallorca constantly reveals magical new surprises.

One such surprise, nestled between the quaint villages of Son Servera and Artà, is the intimate hideaway retreat of Finca Son Gener. Dating back to the 18th century, the property was originally used for the production of oils and grains. A nod to this history can be found in Son Gener's distinct logo, whose symbol represents the way in which olive oil production was traditionally measured—a line for each barrel would be etched onto the wall, and carefully scored

Mediterranean light, the modern minimalism effortlessly accentuating the use of natural materials and antique furnishings. Indeed, Son Gener's interior is a celebration of light and form, an exemplary study of elegant restraint. Thoughtfully selected sculptures embellish its rooms, while lush plants and well-placed tables and lamps seem to create

THIS PAGE (FROM TOP): *Son Gener's interior is a beautiful blend of tradition and the contemporary; the lapis lazuli of the pool's waters is a spectacular sight.*

OPPOSITE (FROM TOP): *The original stone façade of the old country house is virtually unchanged; rustic furniture and potted plants create a warm, idyllic feel.*

through once a full ten barrels were filled with the valued commodity. This beautifully designed boutique hotel is the kind of secret you want to keep all to yourself, yet cannot resist sharing with anyone who will listen.

The charming country estate lay in ruin for many years until designer Antonio Estevas Cañellas arrived; the architectural equivalent of a knight in shining armour. He rekindled the romantic feel of the historic and, at the same time, breathed an altogether new spirit into the property, creating the breathtaking rustic-meets-contemporary jewel it is today. While Antonio is to be credited with this remarkable design transformation, his wife Catin runs the show with her warm and impeccably trained staff.

Few other Mallorcan accommodations have been designed with such impassioned artistry, and this personalized feel is in no way a purchased commodity. Finca Son Gener's furniture was designed by Antonio himself and carved in Mallorca's second town, Manacor. The interior is awash with

a backdrop for its walls and the structure of the buildings. From the terraces and patios to the lounges and halls, the fine equilibrium between space, purity of line and décor is exquisitely maintained. The unique ceramics, art and woodcraft are in perfect harmony with their settings, never overpowering, but subtle and complementary.

Wooden-beamed ceilings crown each of Finca Son Gener's suites, each designed to combine an almost meditative, Buddhist simplicity with rustic chic. Walls, gossamer-thin drapes and soft furnishings are bathed in hues of buttercream, orchid white and cinnamon to complement the deeper tones of the hand-crafted wooden furniture. Inviting armchairs encourage contemplative views over the surrounding countryside, in which everything from megalithic monuments to picturesque fishing villages reside.

Astounding though Son Gener's location and panoramic vistas are, it is perhaps the building's infrastructure itself that creates the most indelible impression. The glassy calm of the indoor pool is surrounded by unusual walls of wood, placed so that details of the grain and inner patterns are visible. These soothing elements serve as reminders of the

THIS PAGE (FROM TOP): *A dining area; stone work exposed between the smooth cream walls add a feel of the contemporary; each guestroom is a private haven with high ceilings, soft earthy tones and natural light streaming through sheer drapes.*

OPPOSITE: *Space and light have been well-utilized in the design.*

breathtaking natural environment into which the property sympathetically blends. Similarly, layers of intricate stonework are exposed amid the otherwise smooth, colour-washed walls, highlighting the idyllic and timeless character of the old country house. Its stark beauty lies, quite literally, within.

Finca Son Gener's estate is embraced by verdant gardens and beautiful almond, carob and olive trees. An authentic olive press is displayed prominently on the patio, which is surrounded by sweet-smelling fruit trees at the edge of an organic vegetable garden. The garden's neat rows are pregnant with vine-ripened tomatoes, glossy aubergines and fragrant herbs and spices. The hotel's kitchen is self-sufficient, using the garden's produce and sewing these ingredients into dishes that incorporate freshly caught fish and locally cured meats which are served in Son Gener's homely restaurant. Visit the underground wine vaults to choose the ideal complement to round off each meal.

If you can possibly bring yourself to step out of the pastoral confines of this heavenly retreat, visit the nearby ruins of an ancient Talayotic settlement—one of the myriad cultures to have inhabited Mallorca in the course of its animated history. Four kilometres (2 miles) from Son Gener is Manacor, famous centre of the world's trade in artificial pearls of the finest quality. Avid golfers are also well-catered for, with several high-calibre courses such as those of Pula, Costa de los Pinos and Canyamel within easy reach of the property. And of course, sun seekers are handsomely rewarded with some of the most exquisite virgin beaches on the island, found in the bays of Alcúdia and Pollença.

FACTS

ROOMS	10 junior suites
FOOD	dining room
DRINK	dining room
FEATURES	spa • pool • jacuzzi • sauna • hamman • gym • body treatments
NEARBY	Manacor • bays of Alcúdia and Pollença • golf: Pula, Costa de los Pinos and Canyamel
CONTACT	Ctra. vieja Son Servera, Artà, km3, 07550 Son Servera, Mallorca • telephone: +34.971.183 612 • facsimile: +34.971.183 591 • email: hotel@songener.com • website: www.songener.com

PHOTOGRAPHS COURTESY OF FINCA SON GENER.

Hospes Maricel

Mallorca has been a tourist magnet ever since the phenomenon of international travel began, and with very good reason indeed. The island's visually contrasting assets range from the towering heights of the Tramuntana Mountains to the beautiful cerulean depths of the Mediterranean Sea which surrounds them, and from its ancient hilltop fortresses,

old villages and olive estates to the bustling capital of Palma de Mallorca. The delicate spires of La Seu Cathedral preside gracefully over the city, its old harbours and environs. Taking almost 400 years until its completion in 1601, this magnificent Gothic architectural masterpiece confirms the wise, time-honoured Mallorcan belief that if something is worth doing, it's worth doing very well. This brings us to the awe-inspiring Hospes Maricel.

The stately edifice of the Maricel stands magnificently in haute style with noble, eye-catching Balearic elements of the typically Mallorcan building, built on a promontory jutting out into the spectacular waters of the Mediterranean. The archways, arcades and pillars hewn from marble and stone hold truly enviable views over the vast, breathtaking sea,

while the neoclassical lines of the grand entrance whisper in the sombre regional style of the 16th and 17th centuries.

Further inside, echoes of an antediluvian past reverberate, proudly complemented by contemporary design principles that attract the modern-day jetsetter. Stark, neutral tones and textures, a sharp minimalist edge and a remarkable use of light inform its décor, creating gorgeous juxtapositions against the old architecture. Alongside the maximization of light, comfort and space are the other tenets by which the interior has been designed. The guestrooms are washed in pristine white and warmed by dark leather accents and blonde wooden floors. In the common areas, furnishings made of natural materials create a breezy yet luxurious feel.

A unique focal point of the Maricel is its collection of naturally-created caves where Bodyna Spa & Sensations is housed. Here in its calm, cool cocoons, oriental massages may be enjoyed. Alternatively, for an equally mellow experience, slip into and silently break the surface of the secluded infinity-edge pool, whose brilliant cerulean shade perfectly melts into the Mediterranean sky. Choose a sleek wooden deck chair to call your own and while away the hours gazing at the captivating and ever-changing view of the waters. Sip from a flute of champagne from Senzone Cocktail Bar and enjoy the

palette. Let your footsteps mingle with those of others who have trodden these ancient roads to admire the timeless sights. Reflected in the city's architecture and culinary variety is the diversity of cultures—from the Greeks and Phoenicians to the Roman and Muslim empires—which have called Mallorca their home. If having to face such a plethora of choices is debilitating, fret not. Back at the hotel, relax as the master chefs at Senzone Restaurant prepare fresh, absolute highlights of Mallorcan cuisine and bring them right to your table—there is no need to move one single sun-bronzed, massaged muscle.

Senzone Restaurant serves a delightful array of sumptuous dishes, either indoors or al fresco. Its gourmet breakfast was named 'Best Breakfast in the World' at Madrid's 2004 International Gastronomic Conference. This award-winning spread contains eight sets of dishes—including melon and ginger

sight of sky and sea fusing into the other, as you ponder the great plethora of enticing options for lunch and dinner.

Head into the charming capital, Palma de Mallorca, to choose from a wide selection comprising over a thousand eateries, each well-qualified to please the most discerning

A magical finishing touch to the already flawless Hospes Maricel experience is the exciting option of arriving via private yacht and mooring alongside at the property's exclusive pier. Approaching the island from the sea is rewarding in other ways, offering as it does unrivalled vistas of Palau de la Almudaina and La Seu Cathedral; vividly sun-bleached by day and breathtakingly lit by night. It would be a good arrangement to appreciate and absorb such sights and wonders before arriving at the hotel. For, once settled within the luxurious, baronial confines of the Hospes Maricel, you will feel tempted to languish there, quite powerless to leave the pools, terraces and impeccable service for even a moment. To that end, a collection of DVDs has been thoughtfully stocked, and each beautifully appointed suite offers two televisions and high-speed Internet access. After all, even the very most dreamy and committed of romantic travellers must stay in touch with the world.

THIS PAGE (FROM TOP): Pure tones and clean lines are the perfect modern complement to the old wooden beams and laid marble; attached bathrooms are inviting and thoroughly well-equipped.

OPPOSITE PAGE (FROM TOP): Drinks are served on the ground terrace; the guestrooms are decorated in an elegant contemporary style.

juice, sobrassada, kiwi and cheese ice-cream, and a wide selection of pastries such as plum cake. The breakfast is neither served as a buffet; nor is there a menu. Instead, a very well-informed waiter will talk you through the dishes in detail before catering to your order.

FACTS

ROOMS	24 double rooms (6 with mountain view, 14 with sea view and 4 with terrace) • 4 suites • 1 terrace suite
FOOD	Senzone Restaurant • Senzone Pool Bar
DRINK	Senzone Cocktail Bar
FEATURES	Bodyna Spa & Sensations • infinity-edge pool • massages • private jetty
BUSINESS	Internet access • meeting rooms
NEARBY	Palma de Mallorca • La Seu Cathedral • Es Baluard Contemporary Art Museum • Golf Bendinat • Golf Son Vida
CONTACT	Carretera d'Andratx 11, 07181 Calvià, Mallorca • telephone: +34.971.707 744 • facsimile: +34.971.707 745 • email: maricel@hospes.es • website: www.hospes.es

PHOTOGRAPHS COURTESY OF HOTELS + MOMENTS.

HM Jaime III

Palma's rich and colourful history as the major port city between Europe and Africa has created a strong Moorish influence manifest in its magnificent architecture. The old centre is a maze of narrow lanes that lead down to the stunning, ancient cathedral and to the harbour itself. Set in this atmospheric landscape is the city's modern centre, filled with smart shopping malls, offices and an abundance of bars and restaurants. This contrast of crumbling history and towering modernity is what gives Palma its unique and vibrant spiritedness.

HM Jaime III sits in the middle of this buzzing core, making it an ideal location to wander around the fascinating old streets and to gaze at one of the country's most majestic cathedrals—which took an astonishing 500 years to build. The exclusive Avenida Jaime III is also just minutes from the hotel, offering designer boutiques and a profusion of enticing restaurants where a wealth of seafood, tapas and international cuisine may be savoured along with popular local Mallorcan dishes such as sobrassada and the ensaimada.

The hotel itself has a feel of eclectic and contemporary minimalism to it, with dramatic modern artworks and photography displayed throughout the reception area and hallways, as well as in the quirky reading, music and contemporary art library. The guestrooms are

modern and spacious, furnished in bold red and dark woods. In the pair of junior suites, a comfortable living area is elegantly separated by a glass partition. Large-screen televisions and Sony music systems are just the beginning of the impressive inventory of gadgets that have been fitted out in each room.

The hotel's well-equipped health club is decked in spanking cool white and features an ultra-sleek, sophisticated Turkish bath. Built entirely from slate, it is a most luxurious way to detoxify and rejuvenate after a night out among Palma's groovy in-crowd. The health

club also boasts a jacuzzi, sauna and the most comfortable massage beds, promising a worthwhile and truly gratifying extravagance.

The hotel's Constanza Café-Restaurant is a popular nightspot with Palma's local crowd and hotel guests alike. The menu changes with the seasons, ensuring that the freshest ingredients are always served and that organic ingredients are supplemented by an impressive menu of coffees, teas, and even water. After dinner, the hotel's ever-bustling and characterful bar offers fun surroundings for an evening of happy mingling.

FACTS

ROOMS	88 (including junior suites)
FOOD	Constanza Café-Restaurant
DRINK	Constanza Café-Restaurant
FEATURES	spa with thermal bath • sauna • jacuzzi • reading, music and contemporary art library
BUSINESS	meeting room (capacity of 70)
NEARBY	Casal Solleric • Es Baluard Contemporary Art Museum • Plaça la Feixina • Old Town • marina of Palma
CONTACT	Paseo Mallorca 14B, 07011 Palma, Mallorca • telephone: +34.971.725 943 • facsimile: +34.971.725 946 • email: recjaimeIII@hmhotels.net • website: www.hmhotels.net

PHOTOGRAPHS COURTESY OF HOTEL JAIME III.

La Reserva Rotana

Golf enthusiasts form the bulk of visitors to Mallorca, which makes playing a quiet game on a spectacular course a growingly difficult endeavour. At La Reserva Rotana, guests not only enjoy the luxury of their own private nine-hole course with a course length of 2,815 m (1.8 miles), they can also play at their leisure, sans tee times, green fees and haughty members. Set on a gentle hill near Manacor, this 17th-century mansion boasts its own vineyard and olive grove. Guests can immerse themselves in wonderful isolation, making the idyllic Reserva Rotana a favourite hideaway for international celebrities.

The 202-hectare (500-acre) property is reserved exclusively for hotel guests. And since there are only 22 guestrooms within the property, there is plenty of space for everyone to enjoy their own slice of golfing paradise. A putting green and driving range are also available for those in need of a little practice, and resident PGA-Pro David

McGinness is always on hand to offer tips to those looking to improve their game, or to coach newbies on the art of a good swing.

Golfing aside, there is much to gush over at La Reserva Rotana. Each room has been individually designed with romantic four-poster beds, sumptuous textiles and beautiful marble bathrooms. Every piece of furniture in the hotel was handpicked by owner Juan Ramon Theler and his wife, and a large family portrait hanging in the restaurant evokes the sense of lounging as a guest in a resplendent family home.

At the restaurant, La Reserva Rontana's Chef Jörg Kocher serves excellent cuisine based on the freshest Mallorcan ingredients available. Sup on elegant dishes like himmel und erde of black pudding with foie gras, lax trout stuffed with spinach and saffron, or warm chocolate tart with orange ragout and rum ice-cream. Take your cue from the well-informed maitre d' who will recommend the perfect wine to accompany each course.

When you're not dining or golfing or admiring the landscape from the terrace, laze by the pool, get a massage or enjoy the myriad fitness facilities—from tennis courts to a well-equipped gym. Alternatively, drive 15 minutes to the coast and get in on the bevy of water sports or simply immerse yourself in the calming waters of the ocean.

For a spot of quiet time, La Reserva Rotana's shaded terrace is quite possibly the most romantic place in the world, with its swinging king-size bed floating amid lush greenery. Under the glow of moonlight, toast the intoxicating sense of being in one of the world's most dreamy getaways and prepare to do it all over again the following day.

PHOTOGRAPHS COURTESY OF LA RESERVA ROTANA.

FACTS

ROOMS	double • suites
FOOD	La Reserva Rotana: Mediterranean
DRINK	La Reserva Rotana
FEATURES	golf • tennis • pool • sauna • fitness centre • massages • heli-pad
NEARBY	golf: Capdepera, Vall d'Or and Pula • horse riding • hiking • cycling • hot-air ballooning • water sports
CONTACT	Cami de s'Avall, km3, 07500 Manacor, Mallorca • telephone: +34.971.845 685 • facsimile: +34.971.555 258 • email: info@reservarotana.com • website: www.reservarotana.com

La Residencia

La Residencia is quite possibly the best-known hotel in the Balearic Islands. Besides the fact that Richard Branson used to own it —it is now owned by Orient-Express—this sprawling property offers a level of comfort and service that is unsurpassed in the area, earning itself a spot on the must-visit list of discerning travellers. La Residencia is seated in the idyllic coastal mountain village of Deià, Mallorca, once home to the famous writer Robert Graves. Today, Deià counts among its residents writers and artists who settle here to be inspired by its scenic surrounds.

Nestled between the Mediterranean Sea and the Tramuntana Mountains, every season casts a magical glow here. In summer, the coast is inviting, beckoning with its brilliant sunshine, azure blue waters and picturesque landscape. In the cooler months, wander the beautiful hills and mountains with a hike or climb, depending on your capabilities.

The property is made up of three main buildings—two which date back to the 16th and 17th centuries and one farther up the hill from the 18th century. These were first converted into a hotel in 1984, retaining as

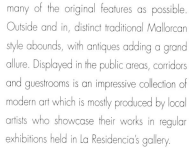

many of the original features as possible. Outside and in, distinct traditional Mallorcan style abounds, with antiques adding a grand allure. Displayed in the public areas, corridors and guestrooms is an impressive collection of modern art which is mostly produced by local artists who showcase their works in regular exhibitions held in La Residencia's gallery.

The guestrooms are large and airy, with cool linen sheets and white cotton-sheathed furniture thoughtfully placed so they never obscure the views of the breathtaking landscape beyond the large windows. The suites are spacious and sumptuously furnished with palatial bathrooms and various luxuries such as plasma-screen televisions.

The property's verdant exterior grounds are linked together by a network of cobbled and paved pathways, which make the ideal setting for a curious saunter around. These are bound by an ambience of serenity and quiet, as La Residencia's dedicated staff pad around with peaceful, tranquil smiles, lulling guests into a happy, relaxed state.

Visitors to La Residencia seldom leave its pastoral premises, and it is easy to see why. There are two irresistible blue pools to languish by with a cocktail, a beauty salon with six treatment cabins offering a myriad of beauty treatments and body massages, a luxurious spa with an indoor pool, a sauna, a steam room, a jacuzzi and a fitness area boasting some of the most spectacular views you could possibly ask for.

Dining options are just as exquisite, with the hotel's elegant restaurant, El Olivo, for romantic, indulgent meals or Son Fony for a more casual setting. Even where to take breakfast can be a tough choice, as the extensive buffet is served either by the pool or on the terrace. Which, really, is reason enough to stay at La Residencia for a little bit longer.

THIS PAGE (FROM TOP): *The fair countenance of La Residencia, sand-hued and dappled by picturesque trees and flowers; perched on a hilly terrace, the estate keeps all the charm of an old Mallorcan village and is an idyllic haven despite its renown.*

OPPOSITE (FROM LEFT): *Rooms are delightful with four-poster beds to match the cottage-style décor; tiny romantic corners abound, with cobbled grounds and stone walls embraced by lush foliage.*

PHOTOGRAPHS COURTESY OF LA RESIDENCIA.

FACTS		
ROOMS	4 single • 9 classic double • 23 superior double • 17 junior suites • 2 superior suites • 4 luxury suites (three with pool and one with plunge pool)	
FOOD	El Olivo • Son Fony	
DRINK	lounge bar • pool bar • beach bar	
FEATURES	1 indoor pool • 2 outdoor pools • spa • gym • sauna • jacuzzi • tennis • art gallery	
BUSINESS	business centre • conference facilities (indoor and outdoor) • laptop rental • audiovisual equipment	
NEARBY	golf	
CONTACT	Son Canals s/n, 07179 Deià, Mallorca • telephone: +34.971.639 011 • facsimile: +34.971.639 370 • email: reservas@hotel-laresidencia.com • website: www.hotel-laresidencia.com	

Palacio Ca Sa Galesa

Palacio Ca Sa Galesa isn't just one of Palma's most exquisite hotels. It is a symbol of how the city has changed since this restored old manor opened its doors in 1995. Credited with introducing a whole new concept for city hotels in Europe, this five-star treasure trove in the heart of Palma dates back to 1576.

From the outside, Palacio Ca Sa Galesa looks like a modest old town house with somewhat forbidding gates. But venture inside and you'll find a place of perfect proportions, anointed with a wonderful collection of arts and crafts. Paintings—including originals by Joan Miró—and sculptures line the walls. Under its 16th-century ceiling, Palacio Ca Sa Galesa's décor combines Mallorcan, French, Italian and English style to evoke a sense of understated grandeur. French clocks from Imperial times, wooden furniture from the end of the 17th century, and walls made from now extinct Mallorcan palm trees all create the feeling of a private museum.

THIS PAGE (FROM TOP): Elegance and eclectic old-world style reflect the hotel's long history; artwork and antiques from the hotel owner's private collection deck the halls of the hotel.

OPPOSITE (FROM LEFT): In true Mallorcan style, the hotel houses a beautiful courtyard; the patio provides privacy and a place to relax in the sun; downstairs, the pool sits among the arches. Heated in winter and cooled in the summer, its benefits are felt all year round.

...a place of perfect proportions, anointed with a wonderful collection of arts and crafts.

On its floor of common rooms is a bar decked with furniture from the 17th and 19th centuries. There is also a library, complete with an old-fashioned chimney—a fabulous place to curl up on winter nights with a good book, a drink or a Cuban cigar. The star of the floor is undoubtedly the Cocina Monet or Monet Kitchen. A replica of the French Impressionist painter's kitchen, it is clad in sunny yellow and serves tea and coffee in the afternoons, along with the best Mallorcan cakes in town.

There are only 12 rooms in the hotel (seven suites and five double rooms), each decorated in its own theme and named after famous musicians. Sumptuous silk completes the opulent décor, while in the bathrooms, special mosaic tiles and Mallorcan stones have been painstakingly applied by hand.

Up on the hotel's roof terrace are views of the bay of Palma and the gothic cathedral. Framed by nature's shades of brilliant blues, it is often hard to distinguish where the sea ends and the sky begins.

Palacio Ca Sa Galesa is home to the Old Town's only indoor swimming pool, located in the cellars, along with the gym and sauna.

A stone's throw away from the hotel is the walled battlement of the old citadel. Explore its historical wonders and then stroll around the gardens that surround the cathedral. Also, the outdoor market and the city's main shopping streets, including top designer names and a massive El Corte Ingles department store, are all within a 15-minute walk from the Old Town.

FACTS

ROOMS	7 suites • 5 double rooms
FOOD	Café Rick's
DRINK	bar • Cocina Monet, library
FEATURES	spa • indoor pool
NEARBY	The Cathedral • outdoor markets • shopping streets
CONTACT	Carrer de Miramar 8, 07001 Palma, Mallorca • telephone: +34.971.715 400 • facsimile: +34.971.721 579 • email: reservas@palaciocasagalesa.com • website: www.palaciocasagalesa.com

PHOTOGRAPHS COURTESY OF PALACIO CA SA GALESA.

Son Brull Hotel + Spa

Near the foothills of the mountain range of Tramuntana, on the island of Mallorca, Son Brull Hotel & Spa is a veritable shrine to urban chic. Nestled amid 40 hectares (99 acres) of verdant landscaped gardens, this 18th-century former monastery has been transformed into an airy, minimalist space with accents of its rich heritage embedded within its décor. Designed by Ignasi Forteza, a young Mallorcan designer and personal friend of the property's owners, Son Brull's

interiors combine clean and modern design with historic Mallorcan features. The 23 guestrooms boast pristine white walls, stone floors and works by regional artists specially commissioned for the hotel. Of these, two boast wide terraces, and one a large jacuzzi from which guests can gaze at superb views of the Bay of Pollença. The common areas are wonderfully spacious; an idyllic mix of ancient walls and contemporary design. A beguiling inner courtyard bestows upon the property a charming old world feel, and is the ideal place to sit back and take in the tranquillity of these surrounds. Run by the Suau family, who has been in the

...a veritable shrine to urban chic.

Mallorcan cuisine based on traditional and modern recipes from the region. Post-dinner, head to the bar, sleek with contemporary furnishings and home to an olive press from the 19th century. Sip special cocktails made from the cactus fruit and groove the night away, before retiring to your divine beds to sleep the slumber of the blissfully satiated.

hospitality business for over 50 years, the service at Son Brull is fittingly warm and genial. The family lives by their philosophy that their guests are their best ambassadors, and true to this belief, every effort is made to satisfy and exceed guests' expectations.

A host of facilities and activities abound within and around the hotel. The library's open fireplace makes for the perfect spot to curl up with a book in winter. Soak up the summer sun by the large outdoor pool or indulge in the comfort of the heated indoor

pool when the temperature dips. Son Brull is conveniently located on the edge of the nine-hole Pollença Golf Course, and a quick drive will take you to Alcanada Golf Course. For the less sportive, Son Brull's spa offers a range of treatments and massages, a Turkish bath, and luxurious jacuzzis and saunas to ease the assaults of everyday living.

When hunger strikes, head to the hotel's restaurant, 365—the island's very first non-smoking restaurant with a Cigar Corner—where expert chef Juan Marc Garcías serves

FACTS

ROOMS	double superior • double deluxe • junior suite
FOOD	Restaurant 365
FOOD	u-bar
FEATURES	outdoor pool • heated indoor pool • spa • tennis court • library
BUSINESS	indoor and outdoor conference facilities • laptop rental • audiovisual equipment
NEARBY	Palma de Mallorca • Port of Pollença • golf • hiking • cycling • mountain-biking • horseback riding • water sports • helicopter rides
CONTACT	Carretera Palma-Pollença, PM 220 WM 49, 8, 07460 Pollença, Mallorca • telephone: +34.971.535 353 • facsimile: +34.971.531 068 • email: info@sonbrull.com • website: www.sonbrull.com

PHOTOGRAPHS COURTESY OF SON BRULL HOTEL + SPA.

Biniarroca

THIS PAGE (FROM TOP): *Guestrooms are furnished in country-manor style and retain a historic feel; one of the two pools amid a charming setting of marble statues and bougainvillea.*

OPPOSITE (FROM TOP): *Biniarroca is surrounded by lush gardens and stone sculptures which create an air of magic and romance; the restaurant serves Menorcan cuisine made from fresh produce specially grown in the garden.*

Owners Lindsay Mullen and Sheelagh Ratliff spent five years painstakingly renovating and breathing renewed life into Biniarroca, which stands today as an absolute work of love and beauty. Using their diverse creative vision as a post-impressionist artist and fashion designer respectively, they have shaped a dilapidated 15th-century farmhouse into one of Balearic Islands' most renowned, picturesque boutique hotels; the perfect secret sanctuary for dreamy romantics and honeymooners.

Retaining all its old rural enchantment, the hotel and restaurant can be found down a bumpy, curving narrow lane in the heart of Menorca's countryside. Set within walking distance from the quaint, tiny villages of San Luís and El Castell, and only a 10-minute drive to the island's foremost attractions—a stretch of rugged, sandy beaches and the beautiful historic city of Mahón—Biniarroca's location, while tucked away in rustic and peaceful surroundings, is also convenient.

Inside the charming house the ground floor, laid throughout in its original flagstone, comprises a drawing room, library, sections of the restaurant and Lindsay Mullen's art gallery, where you can view a permanent collection of her work. Upstairs, each of the hotel's bedrooms is uniquely and stylishly decorated. In keeping with the traditional country-manor style the beams, curves and

...the perfect secret sanctuary for dreamy romantics and honeymooners.

metres from your room, yet drawing residents and visitors alike from across the island. The atmosphere is close to magical as candlelit tables perch outside on levelled terraces of the rose gardens. Indoors, slanting stone flooring, wooden beams and low ceilings create a rich, heady ambience. Resident Chef Dean Lafosse has built a reputation unrivalled on the island for his exquisite cuisine, which includes gourmet Menorcan specialties and inventive vegetarian dishes cooked from fresh herbs and myriad ingredients grown organically in Biniarroca's lush, ambrosial gardens.

crannies of a typical 15th-century cottage have been lovingly restored, adding to the delightful individuality of each room.

Embracing the hotel in verdant splendour are captivating gardens which promise a truly tranquil hideaway and the ideal setting for a garden wedding or private party. It's easy to lose yourself—in all senses of the word—amid the beguiling rose gardens, scented lavender bushes and striking bougainvillea clambering along the whitewashed walls. The suites and deluxe rooms are nestled in these enthralling surroundings; and two pools part enclosed by an old stone wall and heavy-lidded statues tempt you farther into secret reverie.

In the evening, finding the perfect place to dine requires almost no deliberation, with perhaps the best restaurant on the island only

FACTS		
	ROOMS	single • double • deluxe • suites • guests' minimum age requirement: 16
	FOOD	Biniarroca Restaurant: Mediterranean
	DRINK	poolside bar
	FEATURES	pools • art gallery • library • gardens • weddings and celebrations • massages • hair salon
	NEARBY	golf • cycling • horse riding • sailing • wind surfing • scuba diving • archeological sites • museums
	CONTACT	San Luís, Menorca • telephone: +34.971.150 059 • facsimile: +34.971.151 250 • email: hotel@biniarroca.com • website: www.biniarroca.com

PHOTOGRAPHS COURTESY OF BINIARROCA.

Cas Gasí

The town of Ibiza is better known as a hotbed for trendy young clubbers in search of dance-till-dawn fun. Beach resorts abound, drawing hordes of party travellers who revel in the festive atmosphere. However, if you're not that sort of traveller, yet are headed to the Spanish island, there is a pocket of tranquillity that you could call your own for the length of your stay.

Just 12 minutes away from Ibiza, Cas Gasí is an oasis of calm, surrounded by lush orchards, olive groves and fragrant fruit trees. This 19th-century manorial hacienda is all traditional stonewalls with a brilliant whitewashed façade. Typical of a house of its time, it oozes rustic charm with flora adding splashes of bright, happy colour.

Its owners, Margaret von Korff and Luís Trigueros, acquired the house several years ago and have taken great care to maintain the authenticity of a typical Mediterranean home. Warm hues of cream, blue, ochre and lime are paired against wooden beams, hand-painted tiles and Moroccan-style carpets. Every room bears its own little surprises, from antique furniture to local handicrafts. All are immaculately decorated, with beautiful brass beds, hand-painted wall tiles and terracotta tile floors.

Even the geography of the house has been well thought out—the summer sun reigns here, while winter winds are kept at bay. In the hot season, guests lounge on the porches and terraces, taking in the bucolic view while basking in the sun. When the temperature dips, there is nothing like the toasty warmth of the living rooms and its roaring fireplace.

THIS PAGE (CLOCKWISE FROM TOP): The hotel boasts two pools, each hemmed by a terrace of foliage; lovely linen and cream hues in the bedrooms set a warm Mediterranean ambience; in winter, guests gather together before the fireplace in the cosy, stone-walled sitting area.

OPPOSITE: Nestled in a small valley, Cas Gasí is an authentic Ibicencan-style country house with charming orchards, almond trees and its very own organic vegetable garden—a veritable pastoral sanctuary.

Like a country resort, Cas Gasí boasts two swimming pools at different levels, each hugged by verdant garden terraces. From here, guests can gaze at Sa Talaia, the island's only mountain. Breakfast is taken on the terrace, while dinner should be ordered in advance if you intend on partaking of the delicious fresh produce picked straight from the hotel's own organic vegetable garden.

With Ibiza just a stone's throw away, guests can take advantage of the sights and attractions, which include the fine beaches and quaint towns nearby. Otherwise, they would do just as well relaxing in the hotel and enjoying a languorous massage, steeping in the hotel's whirlpool or reading a book in its very well-stocked library.

If the mood strikes, there is nothing to stop you from heading to a throbbing nightclub in Ibiza to dance the night away. The best part of the evening will be knowing that when you return to Cas Gasí, peace and quiet will undoubtedly be restored.

FACTS

ROOMS	8 double • 2 suites
FOOD	restaurant • organic vegetable garden
FEATURES	2 pools • spa • fitness room
BUSINESS	business lounge
NEARBY	Ibiza Town and beaches
CONTACT	Cami Vell a Sant Mateu s/n, Aptdo. 117, 07814 Santa Gertrudis, Ibiza • telephone: +34.971.197 700 • facsimile: +34.971.197 899 • email: info@casgasi.com • website: www.casgasi.com

PHOTOGRAPHS COURTESY OF CAS GASÍ.

Seaside Grand Hotel Residencia

This picturesque boutique hotel sits amid a 1,000-year-old palm oasis and nature reserve, a stone's throw from the beautiful stretch of beach and dramatic sand dunes of Maspalomas on the southern tip of the island of Gran Canaria. Built in Spanish-Moorish fashion by French designer and architect Alberto Pinto, the hotel is made up of elegant and rustic two-storey villas.

Each villa is nestled into beautiful, lush gardens; palm trees and bright plants and flowers create a private pastoral sanctuary. Gorgeous views look out over the sand dunes ahead and the jagged mountains of Gran Canaria behind. In the heat—which pervades all year round—a freshwater swimming pool hemmed by the sun terrace and blossoming garden makes for a cool, refreshing reprieve from the hot, arid air.

Furnished in authentic Moorish style, all the rooms offer a balcony or private patio with charming teak-wood furniture. The presidential suite boasts its own remarkable 420-sq-m (4,520-sq-ft) private garden.

The Grand Hotel Residencia is perfectly located for experiencing the multitude of attractions Gran Canaria has to offer. The stunning, diverse landscape offers plenty of exhilarating outdoor activities—mountain-biking through scented pine forests, climbing down dramatic volcanic craters, taking a jeep safari across moon-like lava terrain, scrambling through cave passages or a convertible tour through the banana and tomato plantations dotted around the island.

Not far from the hotel is Puerto de Mogán, often referred to as 'Little Venice on the Atlantic', a picturesque fishing village

THIS PAGE (FROM TOP): The Therapy & Wellness Centre offers age-old cleansing rituals in a rasul or Arabic steam chamber; spa treatments include luxurious baths in comfortable settings; the freshwater swimming pool is bordered by a sun terrace.

OPPOSITE (FROM LEFT): The reading room is a restful and cosy area for drinks and a game of chess; the guestrooms are bright and in homely tones of blue and white.

...a pastoral private santuary.

Golfers can take delight in six golf courses, all within easy reach of the hotel. After a round of 18 holes, guests can relax in the Therapy & Wellness Centre where the heated saltwater pool with underwater massaging jets, sauna and steam bath will eliminate any aches or pains. Spa treats include a hydro-massage and mud bath.

with canals meandering through its maze of narrow, bustling lanes. Home to one of the finest yachting marinas in the Canary Islands, teeming with local fishing boats and passing yachts, the lively village has some of the best seafood restaurants on the island. Closer by, the hotel's in-house restaurant serves exquisite fresh seafood and also specializes in authentic Canary Islands cuisine. A cosy patisserie, also located within the hotel, offers delicious homemade cakes and sweets.

FACTS		
ROOMS	standard • junior suites • master and presidential suites
FOOD	international/traditional • patisserie
DRINK	pool bar • piano bar
FEATURES	Therapy & Wellness Centre • pool • beauty salon • hair salon • golf • mountain-biking • sailing • diving • camel safaris
NEARBY	Las Palmas beach • Playa del Inglés • Puerto de Mogán
CONTACT	Avenida del Oasis 32, 35100 Maspalomas, Gran Canaria • telephone: +34.928.723 100 • facsimile: +34.928.723 108 • e-mail: info@grand-hotel-residencia.com • www.grand-hotel-residencia.com

PHOTOGRAPHS COURTESY OF SEASIDE HOTELS.

Seaside Hotel Palm Beach

Gran Canaria is a part of the gorgeous Canary Islands, lapped by the warm waters of the Gulf Stream. Far-celebrated for their astounding natural beauty and shores, these breathtaking islands share the Macaronesia stretch of the Atlantic Ocean with famous and exclusive island destinations such as the Azores and Madeira. Gran Canaria itself has become known as 'the small continent',

being blessed with topographical features ranging from dramatic canyons, towering volcanic peaks and valleys to verdant tropical forests, mysterious Saharan sand dunes and pristine coastlines. The island's lush vegetation whispers the secrets of its cosmopolitan past and present, with colourful flora from Europe, America and Africa flourishing side by side.

On the beautiful southern tip of Gran Canaria is the resort town of Maspalomas, an area renowned for its phenomenal sand dunes and the 19th-century lighthouse, Faro de Maspalomas, which stands proudly on Europe's most southerly promontory. It is here on this frontier that Gran Canaria's first designer hotel, the Seaside Hotel Palm Beach, famed for its innovation and design, is situated. The hotel stretches the boundaries of unobtrusive luxury, its myriad facilities and indulgences outshone only by the region's gentle sun, which maintains an average temperature of 22°C (72°F) in the balmy winters, and upwards of 30°C (86°F) at the height of the lengthy, languorous summers.

The Seaside Hotel Palm Beach was built in the 1970s and recently enjoyed a post-millennial refurbishment masterminded by Alberto Pinto, revered French architect and interior designer. He has preserved and successfully reinstated endearing elements of the building's original character, while cleverly re-styling and modernizing the whole. Installed with every imaginable modern amenity, the Seaside Palm Beach's style remains distinctly reminiscent of the 1970s, dominated by retro décor and confidently contrasting colour direction. Pinto has not so much reinvented as reinvigorated and enhanced its natural, unique appeal and exuberance. Assertive contemporary infrastructural materials such as chrome, glass, marble and mirrors form the elegant background into which the attractive, multi-hued rooms blend comfortably.

The luxuriously decorated, well-appointed rooms and suites come with every modern convenience, including climate-control and satellite television (which should preferably remain switched off, to do justice to the breathtaking panoramas and skyscapes). The guestrooms are designed around four mood-spanning colour themes, which include

The pull-factor generated by the Seaside Palm Beach's impressive array of facilities is considerable—if not insurmountable. Succumb to a day of soaking up positive energies in the oasis that is the Spa & Wellness Centre. As the sun's beneficial rays ricochet from the stunning blue mosaics framing the pools, the indulgent will gravitate towards the heated freshwater and seawater pools featuring stimulating underwater massage functions for added reinvigoration. This innovative and state-of-the-art garden of health has been most thoughtfully designed to tease out all the knots in your mind, body and soul. Within the harmonious, conducive surrounds of a 1,000-year-old palm garden, participate in tai chi or water gymnastics, or choose from a menu of baths and treatments. Rasul, Cleopatra and hammam baths, massages,

reef-inspired coral and blue, soothing tones of violet and green, uplifting hues of yellow and turquoise, as well as a more muted but equally alluring scheme of beige and brown. The walls are suffused with warm shades redolent of an unforgettable sunset, while the flooring is boldly patterned in aquamarine and white to create a cool feel evocative of sea and sand, which are, of course, a mere stone's throw from the hotel.

With the diversity of a continent literally just on the doorstep, it would seem almost ungrateful not to immerse oneself in every opportunity available for exploration. A 6-km (4-mile) beach is within easy reach from the hotel and golf lovers can take advantage of the Salobre Golf or Campo de Golf courses, where the favourable trade winds add to the relaxing nature of the game.

THIS PAGE (FROM TOP): All guestrooms are specially themed by colour; the hotel's interior is decked in retro style and vibrant colours.

OPPOSITE (FROM TOP): Façade of the hotel's Spa & Wellness Centre; nestled within the embrace of a millennium-old palm garden, the spa centre is an idyllic haven for enjoying the range of treatments.

If Gran Canaria is a full continent in miniature, then the Seaside Hotel Palm Beach is itself a microcosmic oasis within. With globally-inspired dining, health treatments drawn from across continents and centuries, and ground-breaking innovation masked behind a retro façade, this design hotel has everything the discerning guest could possibly desire. And with an enviable track record of almost 365 days of sunshine every year, the attraction of this oasis is difficult to assuage.

thalassotherapy, algae mineral baths and saunas—Turkish, Finnish, dry and steam—are just a few recommendations.

After a day of relaxation, head to the Gran Restaurante for a huge four-course feast. The excellent quality of the dishes—all prepared by world-class chefs—is paralleled by opulent burgundy and cream furnishings,

with eye-catching jet ceramics showcased seductively in decorative niches. For a lighter alternative, sample the Italian cuisine at the sleek La Trattoria, or go for the à-la-carte menu at the glamorous Orangerie, its walls decked with mirrors aplenty. For cocktails, the Salón Bar beckons with live music and passionate tones of purple and red.

FACTS

ROOMS	standard • luxury corner double • junior suites • suites • master suites
FOOD	Gran Restaurante: four-course meals • Trattoria: Italian • Orangerie: à la carte • Snack bar/Terrace: seaside lunch buffet
DRINK	Salón Bar • Africano Bar
FEATURES	Spa & Wellness Centre • thalassotherapy • diving • golf • tennis • archery • airgun shooting • gymnastics (open-air and water) • boutiques • hair salon
NEARBY	Palmitos Park • volcanic scapes at Barranco de Tirajana valley
CONTACT	Avenida del Oasis s/n, 35100 Maspalomas, Gran Canaria • telephone: +34.928.721 032 • facsimile: +34.928.141 808 • email: info@hotel-palm-beach.com • website: www.hotel-palm-beach.com

PHOTOGRAPHS COURTESY OF SEASIDE HOTELS.

Abama

Like a phoenix rising out of the rubble of volcanic stone, Abama occupies a truly privileged eyrie perched majestically above the azure waters of the Atlantic. Surrounded by swaying palm trees, lush tropical gardens and a blanket of emerald-green grass, the bold outlines of the hotel's Citadel might seem like a mirage at first glance. But guests soon realize that they have arrived, instead, at an oasis of unprecedented luxury and calm; enough to sate even the most seasoned world traveller.

The guestrooms are generous in proportion and many offer gorgeous ocean vistas from spacious balconies. The Citadel boasts 300 rooms; or guests may prefer the privacy of the exclusive Abama Villa rooms and suites. Every room includes fine Egyptian linen, luxe pillows, large flat-screen television, safe, minibar, terry bathrobes, leather-soled slippers and a marble-lined

bathroom with a separate glass-enclosed shower. The public areas are even more impressive, with the grandeur of an Arabian palace flooded with light and sensuality.

Although the décor can best be described as Moroccan, the surprising number of dining options is your passport to a world of culinary delights. Try the avant-garde cuisine of famed Spanish chef Martín Berasategui in El Patio, or skip across Europe to enjoy traditional Italian dishes in Verona. Right next door you'll find yourself in Argentina at La Pampa, specializing in grilled meats. Abama Kabuki, decorated in a

dramatic minimalist style, offers a fusion of traditional Japanese and local products. Sitting on the terrace of El Mirador Restaurant, Gomera Island seems so close that you'll want to reach out and touch it while you enjoy superb rice dishes and seafood. For a lighter menu the best options are Abama Beach Club at the edge of the surf or Los Chozos next to the main pool.

The elegant Lobby Bar has live piano music and looks over the Koi lagoon. Try original tapas washed down with select wines at the Wine Bar. The Tanganika Cocktail Bar takes you to deepest Africa with an atmosphere so authentic you wouldn't be surprised to bump into Humphrey Bogart. Jazz lovers won't want to miss the Morocco Jazz Club if they can tear themselves away from the Abama Sports Bar with large-screen plasma televisions.

The athletic will appreciate the 18-hole golf course designed by Ryder Cup team member Dave Thomas and the opportunity to improve their swing at the Abama Golf Academy. Abama has seven tennis and four paddle courts and a Fitness Centre run by top professionals. After a tough match, the Spa & Wellness Centre awaits with over 2,500 square metres (26,909 square feet) of modern installations devoted exclusively to pampering your body.

With so much to enjoy during your stay, you won't want to leave. It's OK. The best thing about Abama is coming back.

THIS PAGE: Abama's sensuous Citadel rooms open onto wide balconies overlooking a spectacular panoramic ocean vista, kissed by Atlantic breeze.

OPPOSITE (FROM TOP): A marriage of Moroccan architecture and island fantasy, Abama is like a dreamy Arabian palace in the middle of vast ocean; its world-class golf course is complemented by an equally professional golfing academy.

FACTS		
ROOMS	Citadel: 300 rooms & suites • Abama Villas: 120 rooms & suites • Presidential Suite	
FOOD	El Patio • Abama Kabuki • El Mirador • La Pampa • Los Chozos • Verona Abama Beach • La Veranda • Golf Club House • Abama Spa Café	
DRINK	Lobby Bar • Wine Bar • Tanganika • Abama Sports Bar • Morocco Jazz Club	
FEATURES	golf course • tennis courts • Fitness Club • spa • pools • sailing • deep-sea fishing • Abama Beach • jetty • Kids Centre • boutiques • Art Gallery	
BUSINESS	10 meeting rooms • VIP reception • wireless Internet • limousine service • heliport	
NEARBY	El Teide National Park • Playa San Juan • banana plantations • Los Gigantes	
CONTACT	Ctra. Gral TF 47, km 9, 38687 Guía de Isora, Tenerife • telephone: +34.922.126 000 • facsimile: +34.922.126 100 • email: info@abamahotelresort.com • website: www.abamahotelresort.com	

Hotel San Roque

The transformation of Tenerife into a major international tourist destination has brought innumerable benefits to both its residents and visitors. Today it is Europe's winter playground; a tropical paradise with modern infrastructure and perennial spring. Sadly, little remains of the island's traditional lifestyle and architecture, which is what makes a trip to the small port of Garachico a delight and a must for tourists. Snuggled on the lower slopes of El Teide—Spain's highest mountain—and guarded by the 16th-century fortress San Miguel, this quaint municipality has received several awards for its continued efforts to preserve its patrimony of mansions, convents and churches.

Several highly symbolic buildings—Casa de Ponte, Las Conceptionistas Francisco and the former convent of San Julian—are located along the cobble-stoned Esteban de Ponte.

In the heart of this historical enclave, the 18th-century mansion at number 32, lovingly restored by the Carayón family, stands as the alluring Hotel San Roque today. The 20 rooms and common areas were designed with scrupulous attention to the original architecture and decorated with a contemporary flair that incorporates a truly impressive collection of Bauhaus furniture and original works of art by luminaries such as Marcel Breuer, Mies Van der Rohe, Le Corbusier, J. Hoffman and Isamu Noguchi. Unique pieces by Carmen Calvo, Gonzalo González, Susy Gómez, Cristina Gámez and José Noguero add a modern colour to the old building. In this successful design concept, the blending of modern with traditional mirrors Garachico's fast-growing reputation as an artistic centre.

Each of the air-conditioned rooms has a distinct personality, but they all offer the same high level of comfort with jacuzzi bathtubs,

THIS PAGE (CLOCKWISE FROM LEFT): *A breathtaking panorama awaits beyond the rooftop terrace wall; visitors will not be able to resist taking to the old cobbled lanes; a shaded corner of the patio.*

OPPOSITE: *The entire property is a work of art in itself, beautifully restored from an 18th-century mansion and given a modern edge with arresting sculptures and a furniture collection by the likes of Mies van der Rohe.*

terry robes, slippers, safe, Internet and satellite television. Many open onto the pool area or the main patio, where a soaring modern sculpture by Mikel Navarro is surrounded by aged wooden columns over 300 years old. The impressive tri-level Tower Suite boasts magnificent views of the town and the coast.

Anturium Restaurant offers a fusion of the best of island cuisine with a Mediterranean touch. The tables are located on the terrace beside the pool and the excellent year-round climate is complemented by Chef Pep Nogué's delectable creations and an exquisite wine list to create an incomparably romantic dining experience. Hoffman bar, named after the artist whose pieces decorate the room, is the perfect place to enjoy a cocktail before or after dinner in an intimate, elegant setting.

Encapsulating the quintessence of old Tenerife, Hotel San Roque is a rare jewel and a unique sanctuary—beautiful, elegant and tranquil, it is an ideal refuge for savouring the best of the island's old and new worlds.

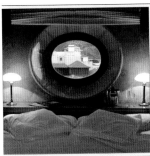

FACTS		
ROOMS	8 standard • 8 duplexes • 2 junior suites • 2 suites (including one tower suite)
FOOD	Anturium Restaurant: local/Mediterranean
DRINK	Hoffman Bar
FEATURES	pool • sauna • rooftop terrace • solarium • digital entertainment library • Internet access • modern art • Bauhaus furniture • mountain-biking • fishing
NEARBY	beach • natural tidal pools • El Teide National Park • golf
CONTACT	Esteban de Ponte 32, 38450 Garachico, Isla Baja, Tenerife • telephone: +34.922.133 435 • facsimile: +34.922.133 406 • email: info@hotelsanroque.com • website: www.hotelsanroque.com

PHOTOGRAPHS COURTESY OF HOTEL SAN ROQUE.

Andalucía Itinerary

Many foreigners say that Andalucía is the region that comes closest to their preconceptions of Spain. It is an incredible pastiche of whitewashed villages looking like strings of sun-bleached islands in a sea of olive trees, the visceral staccato rhythms of flamenco, the passion and splendour of Holy Week processions, the life and death struggle in the bullring and the extraordinary luminosity that has haunted the souls of artists for centuries and, if one is not careful, will capture your heart forever. The culture is a seductive blend of Christian, Moorish, Sephardic and gypsy traditions forged over a millennium of shared history and reflected in the dark, handsome features and enigmatic personality of its people. There is a distinct pace to life in the south that quickly seduces visitors and will have you running to the nearest Renfe office to extend your stay. It's no problem, they are used to it.

Highlights of the region:

Seville • Córdoba • Flamenco • World Heritage sites

Suggested itinerary

- Fly into Madrid international airport.
- Transfer to Madrid for a one-night stay at either Bauzá Hotel & Restaurante (see pages 30–1), De las Letras Hotel & Restaurante (see pages 32–3), Hotel Urban (see pages 34–7), Hotel Villa Magna (see pages 38–9) or Hotel Villa Real (see pages 40–3) to get over your jet-lag in style and then take in the exhibits at the city's stunning collection of world-class art museums.
- Morning trip to Seville on the high-speed AVE train then a two-night stay at the Casa del Maestro (see pages 184–5), Hacienda Benazuza (see pages 192–3) or the Hospes Las Casas del Rey de Baeza (see pages 196–9). Visit the Cathedral and the Alcázar palace (both of them World Heritage sites), tour the city on a horse and buggy, enjoy a cool glass of sherry and a selection of tapas at a terrace by the river, then take in a late-night flamenco show.
- Transfer to the Santa Justa train station and pick up a jar of Seville marmalade made by the monks. Arrive in Córdoba in a wink onboard the convenient connector service on the AVE line. Transfer for a one-night stay at the Hospes Palacio del Bailío (see pages 200–3). Tour the stunning Mezquita (a World Heritage site), wander through the narrow streets of the Jewish Quarter on the hunt for souvenirs, take a relaxing soak in authentic Arab baths, then a romantic stroll along cobble-stone streets on the way to a dinner followed by a glass of sweet Montilla wine.
- A short taxi ride to the train station and return on the AVE to Madrid.

Available train services:
AVE • Altaria • Alta Velocidad • Andalucía Express • García Lorca •
Train Hotel (Trenhotel)

renfe For more information call +34.902.240 202
or visit www.renfe.es

Catalonia Itinerary

There has always been a certain degree of rivalry between Madrid and Barcelona, capital of the Catalonian region, but most foreign visitors are blissfully unaware, and just as apt to raise their glasses and shout 'viva la diferencia' in celebration of the cultural and linguistic diversity that makes a visit to this dynamic region an absolute must on any trip to Spain. Most tourists tend to dedicate most of their time to Barcelona with its abundance of world-famous attractions such as the Modernista buildings of native-born architect Antoni Gaudí, his still unfinished but no less inspiring church of the Sagrada Família and the stunning Palace of Music by his contemporary, Domènech i Montaner. The city also has a well-earned reputation as a centre of design excellence and offers unlimited shopping possibilities. Still, any visit to the region would be sadly incomplete without seeing other areas such as the rugged Costa Brava with its world-class restaurants, fabulous ceramics, picturesque fishing villages and the Dalí museum in Figueres. Catalonia has one of the most impressive patrimonies of Romanesque art in all of Europe, both in situ in tiny rural villages in the Pyrenees and preserved in any of the wonderful museums in Vic, Girona or Barcelona. The Roman ruins at Tarragona and the nearby wine growing regions of Priorat and Penedès are just some of the attractions for visitors in the southern part of the region where tourists flock to the Monastery of Poblet—a UNESCO World Heritage site—and the Crusader castle at Montblanc. Mix the superb gastronomy with history, culture and breathtaking natural beauty and it's a recipe for a repeat visit.

Suggested itinerary

- Take the Altaria train from Madrid on comfortable high-speed service that will deposit you in the very heart of Barcelona. Transfer for a three-night stay at the Hotel America Barcelona (see pages 60–1), Hotel Claris (see pages 62–5), Hotel Condes de Barcelona (see pages 66–7), Hotel Cram (see pages 68–9), Estela Barcelona Hotel del Arte (see pages 70–1), Hotel Gran Derby (see pages 72–3), Hotel Granados 83 (see pages 78–9), Neri Hotel & Restaurante (see pages 84–5), Hotel Omm (see pages 88–91) or Hotel Pulitzer (see pages 96–7).
- Tour Gaudí's Sagrada Família and the Parque Güell. Reserve ahead for the guided tour of the Palace of Music. Alternate shopping with snapshots of the Modernista buildings on the Paseo de Gracía. Visit the trendy Port Nou (new port) for an IMAX movie and lunch. Enjoy a cool glass of horchata, people-watching and the amazing buskers on the Ramblas.
- Use Renfe's regional service for a day trip to Girona with its impressive cathedral and Jewish quarter. Lunch at Can Roca with two stars in the Michelin guide.
- Renfe's frequent commuter service will take you to the trendy port town of Sitges for a relaxing day on the beach.
- Optional trip by regional service to El Vendrell for a two-night stay to pamper your body and soul in the fabulous Hotel RA Beach Thalasso-Spa (see pages 98–9).
- Rent a car for a two-day optional trip to visit the Dalí museum in Figueres, shop for ceramics in La Bisbal and stay for two nights at the ultra luxurious Alva Park Resort & Spa (see pages 56–9) on the Costa Brava, and try your luck getting a table at such culinary temples as Ferran Adrià's El Bulli and Santi Santamaría's Racó de Can Fabes.
- Begin a diet and relax on the return trip to Madrid on Renfe's super smooth Altaria service.

Available train services:
Altaria • Catalunya Express • Regional • Costa Brava • Mare Nostrum

renfe *For more information call +34.902.240 202 or visit www.renfe.es*

THIS PAGE (FROM TOP): **The view from Condes de Barcelona over La Pedrera and the hotel's impressive vista; for those who have booked far enough in advance, the view from Ferran Adrià's El Bulli restaurant is breathtaking.**

OPPOSITE: **Gaudí's dreamy La Pedrera, with Hotel Omm nearby.**

Galicia Itinerary

Galicia has an irresistible appeal that stems partially from the fact that it is so different from what most people expect. Everything, from the lush green countryside to the sound of bagpipes, from the legends of fairies and little people to quaint country villages where time seems to stand still, will both surprise and delight the first-time visitor. For centuries, pilgrims have endured the physical hardships and the dangers of wolves and robbers to walk the Way of St. James, fuelled by the fervent desire to arrive at Santiago de Compostela and visit the tomb of the Apostle. There has been a remarkable resurgence in this tradition in the past decade and, once again, tens of thousands of pilgrims make the trek annually despite the discomfort of blisters and frequent cold showers. Fortunately, Renfe offers a less arduous manner to visit the region with the popular train hotel that will rock you gently to sleep in a comfortable and private compartment and then bid you farewell early the next morning, rested and refreshed, at the Santiago de Compostela train station. Passengers can be confident they will have plenty of time to get to the Cathedral before the first wave of pilgrims arrives.

Highlights of the region:

Santiago de Compostela (World Heritage site) • Rías Baixas wineries • Pontevedra • Vigo • Ribera Sacra and Valdeorras wineries

Suggested itinerary

- Train hotel from Madrid to Santiago de Compostela. One-night stay at AC Palacio del Carmen (see pages 128–9). Tour of the Cathedral and attendance at the Pilgrim's mass to see the famed giant censer called the 'Botafumeiro' swing into action. Walking tour of old Santiago declared a UNESCO World Heritage site.

- Optional car rental to visit the end of the world, Fisterra, and enjoy deliciously fresh grilled sardines in the port and watch the sunset over the Atlantic.

THIS PAGE (FROM TOP): A stay at Pazo los Escudos offers total relaxation and sea views; situated in Vigo, the hotel restaurant serves traditional seafood favourites.
OPPOSITE (FROM LEFT): Pazo do Castro's beautiful façade.

- Transfer onto the convenient Renfe regional service to the coastal city of Vigo for a one-night stay at the hotel Pazo Los Escudos (see pages 132–3). Take a boat charter through the spectacular estuary of Vigo filled with platforms for cultivating mussels and visit the beautiful Cies Islands. Tour the wineries in O Rosal and try the sensational local dish pulpo gallego (boiled squid drowned in olive oil and spiced with paprika) washed down with a delicious bottle of ice-cold Albariño wine.
- Optional car rental to visit the typical fishing-villages of Cambados and Combarro located in the heart of Spain's wine country.
- Transfer by regional train from Vigo to O Barco de Valdeorras through the spectacular scenery of the Ribera Sacra and the valley of the Miño river. Enjoy a two-night stay at the Pazo do Castro (see pages 130–1) for a taste of rural life in the luxury of a country palace and the ultimate in local cuisine. Visit local wineries and ancient monasteries.
- Short trip by regional service to Ourense and connection to Madrid.

Available train services:
Train Hotel (Trenhotel) • Regional (Regionales)

renfe For more information call +34.902.240 202
or visit www.renfe.es

index

picturecredits

The publisher would like to thank the following for permission to reproduce their photographs:

Alessandra Meniconzi/Tips Images 168
Andrea Pistolesi/Tips images 20, 22 (top), 118, 121 (top), 123 (below), 124 (top), 127, 156 (top), 179 (below)
Anne Rippy/Tips Images 110 (top), 141 (top)
Cadaphoto/Photo Library 122
Carlos Dominguez/Corbis 26
Chad Ehlers/Tips Images back cover: procession, 8–9, 107 (top), 153 (left)
Charles Mahaux/Tips Images back cover: Gaudí pots, 44, 151 (below)
Chris Sattlberger/Tips Images 138 (right)
Copson Alan/ Jon Arnold Images/Photo Library 106, 109 (below), 112 (top), 113
Dag Sundberg/Tips Images 222
Despotovic Dusko/Corbis Sygma 25 (top)
Erika Ede, FMGB Guggenheim Bilbao Museoa back cover: Guggenheim, 102, 108 (top)
Estela Barcelona Hotel del Arte front cover: wall art
Fernando Alda/Corbis 173 (below)
Ferran Adriá/El Bulli back cover: seascape, 16 (top), 48, 267 (below)
Fiona Dunlop front cover: doorway, 50 (top)
Fridmar Damm/Corbis front cover: yacht, 212
Gary Bedell 21 (top) 22 (below), 54 (below), 121 (below), 123 (centre), 125, 126 (top), 137, 138 (left), 139, 140, 141 (below), 143, 152 (below), 153 (right), 154 (top), 156 (top), 180 (top and below)
Gerard Vandystadt/Tips Images 107 (below)
Glen Allison/Tips Images front cover: casa mila, 46, 175 (top)

Guenter Rossenbach/zefa/Corbis 214
Guido Alberto Rossi/Tips Images 2, 24, 123 (top), 170, 174, 177 (top), 216 (below), 221 (top), 224 (below)
Hacienda Benazuza front cover: dish, 176 (below), 264 (top and below), 265
Hacienda de San Rafael front flap: garden and flowers, 171 (below), 175 (top), 177 (below), 179 (top)
Hans Georg Roth/Corbis 223 (below)
Hans Wolf/Getty Images 178 (right)
Hospes Las Casas del Rey de Baeza 176 (top)
Hospes Maricel 215
Hospes Palacio del Bailio front flap: bedroom, 5
Hospes Palau de la Mar front cover: table setting
Hotel Condes de Barcelona 267 (above)
Hotel Malcontenta 53 (centre)
Hotel Omm back flap, 49 (top), 266
Hotel Trias 4, 53 (top)
Hubert Stadler/Corbis 223 (top)
J.C.Cardenas/epa/Corbis 14 (right)
Jan Baldwin/Narratives 171 (top)
Jochem Wijnands/Feature Contact back cover: bull, matador, 12, 13 (top), 17, 47 (below)
Jon Hicks/Corbis 216 (top), 217 (top), 221 (below)
Jose Fuste Raga/Corbis 148, 151 (top)
Juan Mari Arzak/Arzak 16 (centre), 110 (below)
Kai Foersterling/epa/Corbis front cover: shadow, 15 (top), 150
Laurence Simon/Tips Images 217 (below)
Luis Castaneda/Tips Images back cover: fire, 15 (below), 28, 126 (below), 136, 142 (top), 224 (above)

Mark L Stephenson/Corbis 134
Martin Berasatagui back cover: dish, 108 (below), 111 (top and centre)
Massimo Listri/Corbis 13 (below) 52
Mason Florence/Lonely Planet Images/Getty Images 157
Matteo Brogi 50 (below), 51
Michael Katz 18, 49 (below), 112 (below)
National Tourist Office of Spain 104, 105, 142 (below), 152 (top), 172, 178 (left), 219 (top), 220
Nik Wheeler/Corbis 23 (below)
Palacio del Bailio 5
Paolo Curto/Tips Images 155
Paolo Lazzarin/Tips Images 120
Patrick Ward/Corbis 14 (left), 21 (below)
Pazo do Castro 269
Pazo los Escudos Hotel + Restaurante 268 (above and below)
Pedro Subijana/Akeláre 111 (below)
Peter and Georgina Bowater/Tips Images 47 (top), 173 (top)
Peter M. Wilson/Corbis 23 (top)
Pixers/Tips Images 54 (top)
Renato Valterza/Tips Images 181, 225
Rob Cousins/Getty Images front cover: skirts, 154 (below)
Robert Estall/Corbis 219 (below)
Ruth Tomlinson/Getty Images 55
S. Andreas/zefa/Corbis 218
Sandra Baker/Tips Images 25 (below), 124 (below)
Sandro Vannini/Corbis 16 (below)
Sergi Arola/La Broche 27
Sheraton Bilbao 109 (top)
Stephane Cardinale/People Avenue/Corbis 29
Tibor Bognar/Photo Library 53 (below)

directory

Abama (page 260)
Ctra. Gral TF 47, km 9
38687 Guía de Isora, Tenerife
telephone: +34.922.126 000
facsimile: +34.922.126 100
email: info@abamahotelresort.com
website: www.abamahotelresort.com

AC Palacio de San Esteban (page 144)
C/ Arroyo de Santo Domingo 3
37001 Salamanca
telephone: +34.923.262 296
facsimile: +34.923.268 872
email: psanesteban@ac-hotels.com
website: www.ac-hotels.com

AC Palacio de Santa Paula (page 182)
Gran Vía de Colón 31
18001 Granada
telephone: +34.958.805 740
facsimile: +34.958.805 741
email: psantapaula@ac-hotels.com
website: www.ac-hotels.com

AC Palacio del Carmen (page 128)
Calle Oblatos s/n
15703 Santiago de Compostela, A Coruña
telephone: +34.981.552 444
facsimile: +34.981.552 445
email: pcarmen@ac-hotels.com
website: www.ac-hotels.com

Aimia Hotel (page 226)
Santa Maria del Cami 1,
07108 Port de Sóller, Mallorca
telephone: +34.971.631 200
facsimile: +34.971.638 040
email: info@aimiahotel.com
website: www.aimiahotel.com

Alva Park Resort + Spa (page 56)
Francesc Layret 3–5
17310 Platja de Fenals
Lloret de Mar, Girona
telephone: +34.972.368 581
facsimile: +34.972.364 467
email: mail@alvapark.com
website: www.alvapark.com

Hotel America Barcelona (page 60)
195 C/ Provença, 08008 Barcelona
telephone: +34.934.876 292
facsimile: +34.934.872 518
email: america@hotelamericabarcelona.com
www.hotelamericabarcelona.com

Bauzá Hotel + Restaurante (page 30)
Calle Goya 79, 28001 Madrid
telephone: +34.91.436 4546
facsimile: +34.91.431 0943
email: info@hotelbauza.com
website: www.hotelbauza.com

Biniarroca (page 250)
San Luis, Menorca
telephone: +34.971.150 059
facsimile: +34.971.151 250
email: hotel@biniarroca.com
website: www.biniarroca.com

Hotel Can Simoneta (page 228)
Carretera de Artá a Canyamel, km 8
Finca Torre Canyamel
07580 Capdepera, Mallorca
telephone: +34.971.816 110
facsimile: +34.971.816 111
email: info@cansimoneta.com
website: www.cansimoneta.com

Cas Gasí (page 252)
Cami Vell a Sant Mateu s/n, Aptdo. 117
07814 Santa Gertrudis, Ibiza
telephone: +34.971.197 700
facsimile: +34.971.197 899
email: info@casgasi.com
website: www.casgasi.com

Casa del Maestro (page 184)
Almudena 5, 41003 Seville
telephone: +34.954.500 007
facsimile: +34.954.500 006
email: reservas@lacasadelmaestro.com
www.lacasadelmaestro.com

Hotel Claris (page 62)
Pau Claris 150, 08009 Barcelona
telephone: +34.93.487 6262
facsimile: +34.93.215 7970
email: claris@derbyhotels.com
website: www.derbyhotels.com

Hotel Condes de Barcelona (page 66)
Passeig de Gràcia 73–75, 08008 Barcelona
telephone: +34.93.445 3222
facsimile: +34.93.445 3223
email: info@condesdebarcelona.com
website: www.condesdebarcelona.com

Convent de la Missió (page 230)
Carrer de la Missió 7A
07003 Palma de Mallorca
telephone: +34.971.227 347
facsimile: +34.971.227 348
email: hotel@conventdelamissio.com
website: www.conventdelamissio.com

Hotel Cram (page 68)
Aribau 54, 08011 Barcelona
telephone: +34.93.216 7700
facsimile: +34.93.216 7700
email: info@hotelcram.com
website: www.hotelcram.com

De las Letras Hotel + Restaurante (page 32)
Gran Via 11, 28013 Madrid
telephone: +34.91.436 4546
facsimile: +34.91.523 7981
email: info@hoteldelasletras.com
website: www.hoteldelasletras.com

Don Carlos Beach + Golf Resort Hotel (page 186)
Carretera de Cádiz, km 192
29604 Marbella
telephone: +34.952.768 800
facsimile: +34.952.833 429
email: info@hoteldoncarlos.com
website: www.hoteldoncarlos.com

Estela Barcelona Hotel del Arte (page 70)
Av. Port d'Aiguadolç 8
08870 Sitges, Barcelona
telephone: +34.93.811 4545
facsimile: +34.93.811 4546
email: info@hotelestela.com
website: www.hotelestela.com

Finca Son Gener (page 232)
Ctra. vieja Son Servera, Artá km 3
07550 Son Servera, Mallorca
telephone: +34.971.183 612
facsimile: +34.971.183 591
email: hotel@songener.com
website: www.songener.com

Hotel La Fuente de la Higuera [page 208]
Partido de los Frontones
29400 Ronda, Málaga
telephone: +34.952.114 355
facsimile: +34.952.165 609
email: info@hotellafuente.com
website: www.hotellafuente.com

Hotel Gran Derby [page 72]
Loreto 28, 08029 Barcelona
telephone: +34.93.445 2544
facsimile: +34.93.419 6820
email: granderby@derbyhotels.com
website: www.derbyhotels.com

Gran Hotel Balneario Blancafort [page 74]
Mina 7, 08530 La Garriga, Barcelona
telephone: +34.93.860 5600
facsimile: +34.93.861 2390
email: info@balnearioblancafort.com
website: www.balnearioblancafort.com

Gran Hotel Guadalpin Banús [page 188]
Edgar Neville s/n
Nueva Andalucía
Marbella, Málaga
telephone: +34.952.899 700
facsimile: +34.952.899 701
email: reservas@guadalpin.com
website: www.granhotelguadalpin.com

Gran Hotel Guadalpin Marbella Spa
[page 190]
Blvd. Príncipe Alfonso de Hohenlohe
29600 Marbella, Málaga
telephone: +34.952.899 400
facsimile: +34.952.899 401
email: info@granhotelguadalpin.com
website: www.@granhotelguadalpin.com

Hotel Granados 83 [page 78]
Enric Granados 83, 08008 Barcelona
telephone: +34.93.492 9670
facsimile: +34.93.492 9690
email: granados83@derbyhotels.com
website: www.derbyhotels.com

Hacienda Benazuza [page 192]
41800 Sanlúcar la Mayor, Seville
telephone: +34.955.703 344
facsimile: +34.955.703 410
email: hbenazuza@elbullihotel.com
website: www.elbullihotel.com

Hacienda de San Rafael [page 194]
Apartado 28, Carretera N-IV
41730 Las Cabezas de San Juan, Seville
telephone: +34.95.587 2193
facsimile: +34.95.587 2201
email: info@haciendadesanrafael.com
website: www.haciendadesanrafael.com

HM Jaime III [page 240]
Paseo Mallorca 14B
07011 Palma, Mallorca
telephone: +34.971.725 943
facsimile: +34.971.725 946
email: recjaimeIII@hmhotels.net
website: www.hmhotels.net

Hospes Amérigo [page 158]
Rafael Altamira 7, 03002 Alicante
telephone: +34.965.146 570
facsimile: +34.965.146 571
email: amerigo@hospes.es
website: www.hospes.es

Hospes Las Casas del Rey de Baeza [page 196]
Santiago, Plaza Jesús de la Redención 2
41003 Seville
telephone: +34.954.561 496
facsimile: +34.954.561 441
email: reydebaeza@hospes.es
website: www.hospes.es

Hospes Maricel [page 236]
Carretera d'Andratx 11
07181 Calvià, Mallorca
telephone: +34.971.707 744
facsimile: +34.971.707 745
email: maricel@hospes.es
website: www.hospes.es

Hospes Palacio del Bailío [page 200]
Ramírez de las Casas Deza 10–12
14001 Córdoba
telephone: +34.957.498 993
facsimile: +34.957.498 994
email: palaciodelbailio@hospes.es
website: www.hospes.es

Hospes Palacio de los Patos [page 204]
Solarillo de Gràcia 1
18002 Granada
telephone: +34.958.536 516
facsimile: +34.958.536 517
email: palaciopatos@hospes.es
website: www.hospes.es

Hospes Palau de la Mar [page 162]
Navarro Reverter 14
46004 Valencia
telephone: +34.96.316 2884
facsimile: +34.96.316 2885
email: palaudelamar@hospes.es
website: www.hospes.es

Hotel La Malcontenta [page 80]
Paratge Torre Mirona, Platja Castell 12
17230 Palamós, Girona
telephone: +34.972.312 330
facsimile: +34.972.312 326
email: reservas@lamalcontentahotel.com
website: www.lamalcontentahotel.com

Hotel Maria Cristina [page 114]
Calle Oquendo 1, E-20004 San Sebastián
telephone: +34.943.437 600
facsimile: +34.943.437 676
email: hmc@westin.com
website: www.westin.com

Hotel Neptuno [page 166]
Paseo de Neptuno 2, 46011 Valencia
telephone: +34.963.567 777
facsimile: +34.963.560 430
email: reservas@hotelneptunovalencia.com
website: www.hotelneptunovalencia.com

Neri Hotel + Restaurante [page 84]
C/Sant Sever 5, 08002 Barcelona
telephone: +34.93.304 0655
facsimile: +34.93.304 0337
email: info@hotelneri.com
website: www.hotelneri.com

NM Suites [page 86]
Avinguda Onze de Setembre 70
17250 Platja d'Aro, Baix Empordà
telephone: +34.972.825 770
facsimile: +34.972.826 502
email: nm-suites@nm-suites.com
website: www.nm-suites.com

Hotel Omm [page 88]
Rosselló 265, 08008 Barcelona
telephone: +34.934.454 000
facsimile: +34.934.454 004
email: reservas@hotelomm.es
website: www.hotelomm.es

Pago del Vicario Hotel + Winery [page 146]
Carretera Ciudad Real, Porzuna km 16
13080 Ciudad Real
telephone: +34.926.666 027
facsimile: +34.926.666 029
email: reservas@pagodelvicario.com
website: www.pagodelvicario.com

Palacio Ca Sa Galesa [page 246]
Carrer de Miramar 8
07001 Palma, Mallorca
telephone: +34.971.715 400
facsimile: +34.971.721 579
email: reservas@palaciocasagalesa.com
website: www.palaciocasagalesa.com

Panticosa Resort [page 92]
Ctra. del Balneario km 10
22650 Panticosa, Huesca
telephone: +34.974.487 161
facsimile: +34.974.487 137
email: reservas@panticosa.com
website: www.panticosa.com

Pazo do Castro [page 130]
32318 O Barco de Valdeorras
Ourense, Galicia
telephone: +34.988.347 423
facsimile: +34.988.347 482
email: info@pazodocastro.com
website: www.pazodocastro.com

Pazo los Escudos Hotel + Resort [page 132]
Avda. Atlántida 106
36208 Vigo, Pontevedra
telephone: +34.986.820 820
facsimile: +34.986.820 801
email: reservas@pazolosescudos.com
website: www.pazolosescudos.com

La Pleta Hotel + Spa [page 82]
Ctra. de Baqueira a Beret, cota 1700
E25598 Baqueira-Lleida
telephone: +34.973.645 550
facsimile: +34.973.645 555
email: lapleta@rafaelhoteles.com
website: www.lapleta.com

Hotel Pulitzer [page 96]
Bergara 8, 08002 Barcelona
telephone: +34.93.481 6767
facsimile: +34.93.481 6464
email: info@hotelpulitzer.es
website: www.hotelpulitzer.es

Hotel RA Beach Thalasso-Spa [page 98]
Avinguda Sanatori 1
43880 El Vendrell, Tarragona
telephone: +34.977.694 200
facsimile: +34.977.694 302
email: hotelra@grupoamrey.com
website: www.hotelra.com

La Reserva Rotana [page 242]
Cami de s'Avall, km 3
07500 Manacor, Mallorca
telephone: +34.971.845 685
facsimile: +34.971.555 258
email: info@reservarotana.com
website: www.reservarotana.com

La Residencia [page 244]
Son Canals s/n
07179 Deià, Mallorca
telephone: +34.971.639 011
facsimile: +34.971.639 370
email: reservas@hotel-laresidencia.com
website: www.hotel-laresidencia.com

Hotel San Roque [page 262]
Esteban de Ponte 32
38450 Garachico, Isla Baja, Tenerife
telephone: +34.922.133 435
facsimile: +34.922.133 406
email: info@hotelsanroque.com
website: www.hotelsanroque.com

Seaside Grand Hotel Residencia [page 254]
Avenida del Oasis 32
35100 Maspalomas, Gran Canaria
telephone: +34.928.723 100
facsimile: +34.928.723 108
e-mail: info@grand-hotel-residencia.com
www.grand-hotel-residencia.com

Seaside Hotel Palm Beach [page 256]
Avenida del Oasis s/n
35100 Maspalomas, Gran Canaria
telephone: +34.928.721 032
facsimile: +34.928.141 808
email: info@hotel-palm-beach.com
website: www.hotel-palm-beach.com

Sheraton Bilbao [page 116]
Calle Lehendakari Leizaola 29
48001 Bilbao
telephone: +34.94.428 0000
facsimile: +34.94.428 0001
email: bilbao@sheraton.com
website: www.sheraton.com

Son Brull Hotel + Spa [page 248]
Carretera Palma-Pollença
PM 220 WM 49, 8
07460 Pollença, Mallorca
telephone: +34.971.535 353
facsimile: +34.971.531 068
email: info@sonbrull.com
website: www.sonbrull.com

Hotel Trias [page 100]
Passeig del Mar s/n
17230 Palamós, Girona
telephone: +34.972.601 800
facsimile: +34.972.601 819
email: infotrias@hoteltrias.com
website: www.hoteltrias.com

Hotel Urban [page 34]
Carrera de San Jerónimo 34
28014 Madrid
telephone +34.91.787 7770
facsimile: +34.91.787 7799
email: urban@derbyhotels.com
website: www.derbyhotels.com

Villa Jerez [page 210]
Avda de la Cruz Roja 7
11407 Jerez de la Frontera, Cádiz
telephone: +34.956.153 100
facsimile: +34.956.304 300
email: reservas@villajerez.com
website: www.villajerez.com

Hotel Villa Magna, a Park Hyatt [page 38]
Paseo de la Castellana 22
28046 Madrid
telephone: +34.91.587 1234
facsimile: +34.91.431 2286
email: villamagna@hyattintl.com
website: www.madrid.park.hyatt.com

Hotel Villa Real [page 40]
Plaza de las Cortes 10
28014 Madrid
telephone: +34.91.420 3767
facsimile: +34.91.420 2547
email: villareal@derbyhotels.com
website: www.derbyhotels.com